Tried and tested

What people across the UK are saying about the **Law Express** and **Law Express Question&Answer** series:

'Covers all the main areas in a clear and concise way, and provides some excellent advice on how to tackle exam problems and write essays.'
Gwilym Owen, Lecturer in Law, Bangor University

'Students should in this book find a useful and valuable revision guide. The Q&A format is an appropriate and effective means of enhancing students' preparation for law assessments and for improving academic performance. . .'
Dr George K. Ndi, PGR Leader, University of Huddersfield Law School

'A useful, practical and informative revision guide, which makes good use of various pedagogical features to enhance accessibility to students.'
Adam Pendlebury, Senior Lecturer in Law, Edge Hill University

'This series covers well the important techniques for identifying legal issues and applying case-law to factual scenarios.'
David Selfe, Director, School of Law, Liverpool John Moores University

'Revising with this series is like having a tutor there. . .'
Mariette Jones, Senior Lecturer in Law, Middlesex University

Question&Answer

CRIMINAL LAW

4th edition

Nicola Monaghan
Senior Lecturer in Law, Barrister, FHEA
University of Worcester

Pearson

Harlow, England • London • New York • Boston • San Francisco • Toronto • Sydney
Dubai • Singapore • Hong Kong • Tokyo • Seoul • Taipei • New Delhi
Cape Town • São Paulo • Mexico City • Madrid • Amsterdam • Munich • Paris • Milan

Pearson Education Limited
Kao Two
Kao Park
Harlow CM17 9NA
United Kingdom
Tel: +44 (0)1279 623623
Web: **www.pearson.com/uk**

First published 2012 (print and electronic)
Second edition published 2014 (print and electronic)
Third edition published 2016 (print and electronic)
Fourth edition published 2018 (print and electronic)

© Pearson Education Limited 2012, 2014, 2016, 2018 (print and electronic)

Contains public sector information licensed under the Open Government Licence (OGL) v3.0.
http://www.nationalarchives.gov.uk/doc/open-government-licence/version/3/

Contains Parliamentary information licensed under the Open Parliament Licence (OPL) v3.0.
http://www.parliament.uk/site-information/copyright/open-parliament-licence/

Pearson Education is not responsible for the content of third-party internet sites.

ISBN: 978-1-292-14897-7 (print)
        978-1-292-14913-4 (PDF)
        978-1-292-14921-9 (ePub)

British Library Cataloguing-in-Publication Data
A catalogue record for the print edition is available from the British Library

Library of Congress Cataloging-in-Publication Data
A catalog record for the print edition is available from the Library of Congress

10 9 8 7 6 5 4 3 2 1
22 21 20 19 18

Print edition typeset in 10/13 pt Helvetica Neue LT Pro by SPi Global
Printed by Ashford Colour Press Ltd, Gosport

NOTE THAT ANY PAGE CROSS REFERENCES REFER TO THE PRINT EDITION

Contents

Acknowledgements

I would like to thank the anonymous reviewers, both academics and students, who have provided feedback on the book during the writing process. This book is dedicated to my students, past and present.

Nicola Monaghan
University of Worcester

Guided tour

How to use features in the book 📖 and on the companion website 🖱

What to do for every question – Identify the key things you should look for and do in any question and answer on the subject, ensuring you give every one of your answers a great chance from the start.

How this topic may come up in exams – Understand how to tackle any question on this topic by using the handy tips and advice relevant to both essay and problem questions. In text, symbols clearly identify each question type as they occur.

Before you begin – Visual guides to help you confidently identify the main points covered in any question asked. You can also download them from the companion website to pin on your wall or add to your revision notes.

Answer plans and Diagram plans – A clear and concise plan is the key to a good answer and these answer plans and diagram plans support the structuring of your answers.

Answer with accompanying guidance – Make the most out of every question by using the guidance; recognise what makes a good answer and why. The length of the answers reflect what you could realistically achieve in an exam and show you how to gain marks quickly when under pressure.

Make your answer stand out – Impress your examiners with these sources of further thinking and debate.

Don't be tempted to – Spot common pitfalls and avoid losing marks.

Try it yourself – Compare your responses with that of the answer guidance on the companion website.

Visit **www.pearsoned.co.uk/lawexpressqa** for a wealth of
additional resources to support your revision, including:

All diagrams from the book to download and print. Pin
them to your wall or add them to your own revision notes.

Additional Essay and Problem questions with **Diagram
plans** give you more opportunity to help you to practise and
hone your exam skills.

You be the marker – Evaluate sample exam answers and
understand how and why an examiner awards marks.

Table of cases and statutes

■ Cases

■ Statutes

■ International Conventions

What you need to do for every question in Criminal Law

Books in the *Question and Answer* series focus on the *why* of a good answer alongside the *what,* thereby helping you to build your question answering skills and technique.

This guide should not be used as a substitute for learning the material thoroughly, your lecture notes or your textbook. It *will* help you to make the most out of what you have already learned when answering an exam or coursework question. Remember that the answers given here are not the *only* correct way of answering the question but serve to show you some good examples of how you *could* approach the question set.

Make sure that you refer regularly to your course syllabus, check which issues are covered (as well as to what extent they are covered) and whether they are usually examined with other topics. Remember that what is required in a good answer could change significantly with only a slight change in the wording of a question. Therefore, do not try to memorise the answers given here, instead use the answers and the other features to understand what goes into a good answer and why.

This book is intended to serve as a companion guide to supplement your study of Criminal Law. In addition to reading your main textbook, you should refer to this book for guidance on how to answer exam questions on Criminal Law. Both essay-style questions and problem scenarios on all the commonly assessed topics are covered in the book. As you read through the book, you should remember that each 'answer' given here is only one of a possible range of answers which could be given. These are by no means the 'right answer' but merely serve to demonstrate one possible approach to a question.

There are certain issues which should usually be addressed in every answer to a problem question on Criminal Law. First, you will need to identify the relevant offences which may have been committed in the scenario. Secondly, you will need to break down the offence into its actus reus and mens rea elements, and finally, you should apply the legal principles relating to these elements to the question. If a question involves identifying a defence, you should, similarly, break down and apply the elements of that defence to the question. You should adopt this logical structure for most answers to problem questions, and you will notice that this is the structure adopted throughout the book. Different skills are involved in answering essay questions on Criminal Law. You will need to identify the relevant issue that the question is addressing and provide a critical evaluation of the issue.

You will notice that the citations of cases have been included in the answers the first time the case is mentioned. In most institutions, you will not be expected to remember the citations of cases for the exam. However, you should check with your Criminal Law tutor to find out whether you are expected to know the dates of the cases.

Actus reus and mens rea

1

How this topic may come up in exams

Topics such as omissions and causation (actus reus) and intention and recklessness (mens rea) are popular with examiners. Omissions and causation could be examined separately in essay form or together in a problem question. Similarly, intention and recklessness could be examined separately by essays or with causation and/or omissions as a problem question on murder/manslaughter. Essay questions on omissions often ask you to consider the competing academic views. Essays on causation might ask for a critical appreciation of the rules of causation. Essays on intention and recklessness often focus more on a critical evaluation of the development of the law.

Before you begin

It's a good idea to consider the following key themes of actus reus and mens rea before tackling a question on this topic.

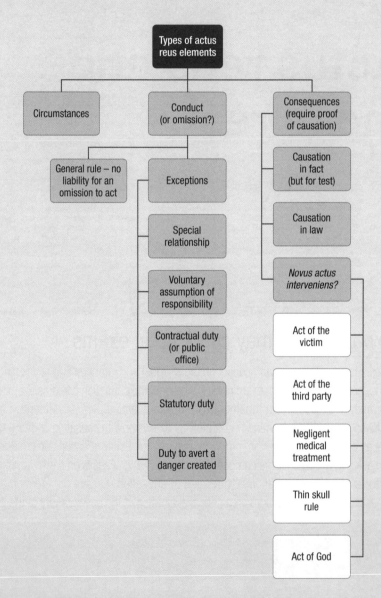

A printable version of this diagram is available from **www.pearsoned.co.uk/lawexpressqa**

🖎 Question 1

'The arguments for the conventional view may appear strong and practical, but they depend on a narrow, individualistic conception of human life which should be rejected as a basis for morality and . . . as a basis for criminal liability' (Ashworth, 'The Scope of Criminal Liability for Omissions' [1989] 105 LQR 424 at 430).

With reference to the above quote, critically evaluate the approach taken to omissions liability in English law.

Answer plan

➡️ Address the academic debate between Ashworth and Williams in your introduction.

➡️ Set out the general rule on liability for omissions.

➡️ Evaluate the exceptions to the general rule.

➡️ Consider the academic arguments put forward by Ashworth and the response by Williams.

Diagram plan

A printable version of this diagram plan is available from **www.pearsoned.co.uk/lawexpressqa**

Answer

[1] Begin by addressing the academic debate in the question directly. You could provide more detail on Ashworth's opinion here.

Professor Ashworth is a critic of what he calls 'the conventional view' of omissions liability. In the article from which this quote is taken, Ashworth advocates the social responsibility view which holds that A should be under a legal duty to assist B, because he argues that society recognises that we have a duty to support and help each other. The conventional view maximises individual autonomy and Ashworth argues that this view requires an 'individualistic conception of human life'.[1] However, Professor Williams argues that there is a clear moral distinction between an act and an omission. He states that we have 'stronger inhibitions against active wrongdoing than

[2] If you can remember key quotes from academic articles, these will increase your chances of earning a higher grade.

[3] Cite key academic articles and do not rely solely upon textbooks when revising.

against wrongfully omitting'[2] (Williams, B. (1991) Criminal omissions: the conventional view. LQR 86).[3]

In England and Wales, there is generally no liability for an omission to act, because such liability would restrict individual autonomy. This means that a person can only usually be held criminally liable where he/she has performed a positive act. However, there are six exceptions where the law imposes a duty to act upon a person and failure to so act can lead to criminal liability.

The first exception applies where there is a special relationship between the parties, such as a parent–child relationship (***Gibbins and Proctor*** (1918) 13 Cr App R 134) or a doctor–patient relationship (***Airedale NHS Trust v Bland*** [1993] AC 89). A special relationship will result in a duty being imposed upon the defendant to act to assist the other. However, there is uncertainty over how far this category extends to other relationships, such as siblings and spouses or civil partners.[4] ***Smith*** [1979] Crim LR 251 suggests that a married couple owe a duty to each other. However, this case was not relied upon in ***Hood*** [2004] 1 Cr App R (S) 73. A husband was deemed to owe a duty to his wife, but this decision appears to have been made on the basis of a voluntary assumption of responsibility (he was her carer).[5]

[4] Point out the uncertainty within the law as well as setting out the matters upon which the law is clear. This demonstrates that you have a fuller understanding of the topic.

[5] This sentence provides your interpretation of the case and shows that you have understood it fully.

A further exception to the general rule arises where the defendant voluntarily assumes responsibility for the victim (e.g. by acting as carer). In such circumstances, the law imposes a duty upon them to continue to do so (***Stone and Dobinson*** [1977] 2 All ER 341, ***Instan*** [1893] 1 QB 450 and ***Gibbins and Proctor***). A defendant may be under a contractual duty to act. Any failure to act in accordance with the terms of the contract may result in criminal liability (***Pittwood*** (1902) 19 TLR 37). Similarly, a person in public office, such as a police officer, will have a duty to act in accordance with their position (***Dytham*** [1979] QB 722). A statutory provision may impose a duty on a person to act, such as section 1 of the Children and Young Persons Act 1933, which makes it an offence for a person with responsibility for a child to wilfully neglect the child, and section 170 of the Road Traffic Act 1988, which makes it an offence for a person to fail to provide his details after an accident or to report it to the police.

There is a duty on a defendant to act in order to avert a danger which he/she has created. In *Miller* [1983] 2 AC 161, the defendant fell asleep smoking a cigarette and woke to find the mattress on fire. He then fell asleep in another room. He was convicted of arson. When the defendant noticed the fire, he was under a duty to take steps to avert the danger. He was convicted due to his failure to so act. The obligation imposed by the law upon the defendant here was not restrictive of his freedom, as only a minimal contribution from him was required (e.g. phoning the fire brigade).[6] This principle was applied in *DPP v Santana-Bermudez* [2003] EWHC 2908 (Admin) to impose a duty upon the defendant to warn a police officer that he had a hypodermic needle in his pocket. The duty arose after the defendant created a dangerous situation by telling the officer that he had no needles in his pockets prior to a search.

[6] Relate your answer back to the quote in the question. This sentence adds some commentary to your answer and avoids a wholly descriptive narrative.

The academic debate about omissions liability arose after Professor Ashworth published the article from which the quote in title is taken. Professor Williams published a response to Ashworth's article shortly after. While Ashworth subscribes to the social responsibility view and criticizes what he calls the conventional view, Williams comments that as a result of Ashworth's article, he finds himself to be a conventionalist.

Ashworth states that these two views are not polar opposites. Ashworth's 'social responsibility view' holds that A should be under a legal duty to assist B, because society recognises that we have a duty to support and help each other. Ashworth (1989) argues that this view '. . . grows out of a communitarian social philosophy which stresses the necessary interrelationship between individual behaviour and collective goods'. This approach relies on the argument that all of society will benefit from the duty to be helped when in extreme peril. However, it safeguards liability by insisting that the peril far outweighs cost or inconvenience to the person required to assist. Ashworth argues that liability should be limited to those who had particular opportunity to assist.

However, the conventional view is that A should not be compelled to serve B. According to this view, the law aims to maximise each individual's autonomy and liberty. Citizens should not be encouraged to interfere in the lives of strangers, nor should they be forced to help strangers; imposing such a duty upon citizens would be too onerous.

The conventional view holds that the criminal law should acknowledge an individual's choice, rather than compel an individual to act to protect a stranger. By compelling an individual to act, the law is 'allowing liability to be governed by chance' by thrusting the obligation to assist a person in peril upon 'a chance passer-by, who may well prefer not to become involved at all'. Ashworth states that 'stopping to help is part of the morality of aspiration, not the morality of duty'. Imposing a duty on individuals to act to help another in peril would also increase the possibility of mass liability and would be impractical. The conventional view holds that the criminal law should only impose liability for omissions in 'clear and serious cases' and should be confined to situations where the defendant has voluntarily assumed responsibility towards another or there exists a special relationship.

[7] This sentence demonstrates your knowledge of the comparative view.

European countries, such as France and Germany, impose a duty on citizens to assist in an 'easy rescue'.[7] However, in England and Wales, no matter how easy the rescue, no duty will be imposed upon a person to assist a person, unless an exception applies. However, 'the exceptions' are largely a construct of academics and the courts have not been quite so prescriptive when developing the law. This means that some cases might straddle two or more of the categories of exception. As the evaluation of the case law above shows, the boundaries of criminal liability for omissions would benefit from greater clarity.

✓ Make your answer stand out

- Use the famous example of A, who is able to save B from drowning by holding out his hand, but abstains from doing so in order that B might be drowned (see Stephen, J.F. (1887) *A Digest of the Criminal Law*. London: Macmillan).
- Refer to judicial comment, such as the judgments of Lord Coleridge CJ in *Instan* and Lord Lane CJ in *Stone and Dobinson*.
- Consider also more recent applications of the *Miller* principle, such as *DPP* v *Santana-Bermudez* [2003] EWHC 2908 (Admin) and *Evans* [2009] EWCA Crim 650.
- Refer to Professor Hogan's view that the law should not punish defendants like Dytham for the consequences which he might have prevented. He should only be punished for neglecting to perform the obligation of his office, and not for the harm he did not prevent but did not cause (see Hogan, B. (1987) Omissions and the duty myth, in P. Smith (ed.), *Criminal Law: Essays in Honour of JC Smith*. London: Butterworths).

! Don't be tempted to . . .

- Recite the facts of the cases on omissions at the expense of critical evaluation.
- Provide a purely descriptive narrative of the principles of law on omissions without referring also to the academic debate. The question requires more than a recitation of the law.

? Question 2

Margo, aged 7, attends the Brightside boarding school. One day, while at school, Margo starts to feel unwell. She tells her teacher, Sebastian, that she feels dizzy and sick. Sebastian thinks that Margo is exaggerating and he tells her to sit back in her seat. Unbeknown to Sebastian, Margo fell off the playground apparatus during the lunch break, and struck her head. An hour later, Sebastian notices that Margo is looking dazed and vacant. He takes her to the school nurse, Harriet. Harriet examines Margo, but thinks that she looks fine. She gives Margo a glass of water and lets her lie on the bed in the medical room. In fact, Margo was displaying symptoms of internal bleeding. Margo dies in the medical room from a brain haemorrhage. Medical evidence suggests that if she had received the appropriate treatment earlier, she would not have died.

Discuss the liability of Sebastian and Harriet for the death of Margo.

Answer plan

→ Consider whether Sebastian could be guilty of gross negligence manslaughter by his failure to seek immediate medical assistance for Margo.

→ Explore whether Sebastian's omission was a cause of Margo's death, including whether Harriet's conduct breaks the chain of causation.

→ Discuss whether Harriet might be guilty of gross negligence manslaughter in respect of Margo's death.

→ Consider whether Harriet is a cause of Margo's death.

Diagram plan

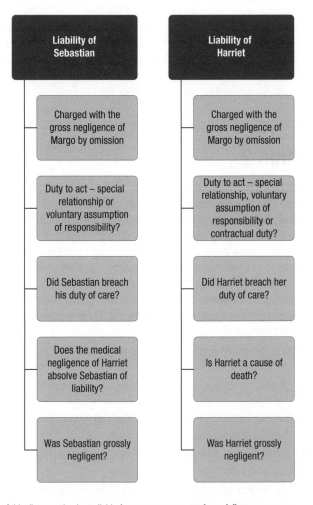

A printable version of this diagram plan is available from **www.pearsoned.co.uk/lawexpressqa**

Answer

[1] Identify the potential offences and the key issues at the very start to demonstrate that you have read and understood the question.

This question requires consideration of the criminal liability of Sebastian and Harriet for the death of Margo. Sebastian and Harriet could be charged with gross negligence manslaughter.[1]

2 The most logical structure for this question is to deal with the liability of each defendant in turn. Use headings to ensure that you maintain your structure and focus.

3 Set out the four elements of gross negligence manslaughter at the start and then apply the law relating to each one in turn.

4 Set out the general rule but explain that an exception might apply here.

Liability of Sebastian[2]

Sebastian could be charged with gross negligence manslaughter in respect of the death of Margo. There are four elements of gross negligence manslaughter: it must be shown that Sebastian owed Margo a duty of care, that he breached his duty of care, that his breach caused Margo's death, and that his conduct (or omission) was grossly negligent (see **Adomako** [1995] 1 AC 171).[3] A defendant may be liable for gross negligence manslaughter after committing an act or after failing to act when he/she has a duty to do so. While there is generally no liability for an omission to act, there are a number of exceptions.[4] If it can be shown that Sebastian owed Margo a duty of care, then he may be liable for his failure to seek medical help for her, in accordance with his duty to act. As Sebastian was Margo's school teacher at a boarding school, there could be said to be a special relationship which imposed a duty on Sebastian to seek medical assistance for his students. However, since there is no authority which supports this, a better argument would be that Sebastian has voluntarily assumed responsibility for Margo as she is a boarding student at the school. Thus, he can be said to have voluntarily assumed responsibility for Margo (**Stone and Dobinson** [1977] QB 354). It could be argued that he breaches that duty by falling below the standard to be expected of a reasonable person when he fails to seek medical assistance for Margo. However, since he was unaware of Margo's fall from the playground apparatus, it could be said that he had no reason to suspect that she was seriously hurt. Nevertheless, since she is a young student at a boarding school and she was feeling unwell in his care, he had a duty to seek some medical assistance for her. As such, he has not met the standard of care to be expected of a reasonable person, but he has fallen below that standard (**Adomako**), breaching his duty.

The next question requires consideration of the rules of causation. It must be proved that Sebastian was both the factual and legal cause of Margo's death. Causation in fact is established by applying the 'but for' test (**White** [1910] 2 KB 124). Applying this test, but for Sebastian's failure to seek medical assistance for Margo, would she have died? Medical evidence suggested that she would not have died had she received medical treatment sooner. Thus, but for Sebastian's failure to seek medical assistance for Margo, she might not have died.[5]

5 Ensure that you apply the test for factual causation.

As regards legal causation, the prosecution must prove that the omission by Sebastian was a more than minimal cause of Margo's death (*Cato* [1976] 1 WLR 110). In *Smith* [1959] 2 QB 35, it was held that a defendant would be the legal cause of the result if he/she was an 'operating and substantial' cause of the result. There is clearly more than one cause of death here: both Sebastian's failure to seek medical assistance for Margo and Harriet's negligent medical treatment are causes of her death. While Harriet might also be liable for the gross negligence of Margo, her liability will not absolve Sebastian of liability[6] because 'the accused's act need not be the sole cause, or even the main cause, of the victim's death, it being enough that his act contributed significantly to that result'[7] (per Goff LJ in *Pagett* (1983) 75 Cr App R 279). It can be said that Sebastian's failure to seek medical assistance contributed significantly towards Margo's death because medical evidence showed that she would have survived had she received the appropriate treatment sooner. There is nothing on the facts to suggest that the chain of causation is broken (no *novus actus interveniens* or intervening act). The only potential intervening act here is the negligent medical treatment provided by Harriet. However, for policy reasons, negligent medical treatment does not automatically break the chain of causation.[8] In order for Sebastian to escape liability, Harriet's conduct would have to be 'so independent' of Sebastian's omission and 'so potent in causing death' that it renders Sebastian's omission insignificant (per Beldam LJ in *Cheshire* [1991] 1 WLR 844). While Harriet may have been negligent, it does not render Sebastian's omission insignificant and thus does not absolve him of liability.

The final element the prosecution must prove is gross negligence. The jury must consider 'whether having regard to the risk of death involved, the conduct of the defendant was so bad in all the circumstances as to amount . . . to a criminal act or omission' (*Adomako*). The jury will consider the risk of death involved with Margo's complaint, and if they determine that Sebastian's conduct was grossly negligent, he will be convicted of gross negligence manslaughter.

Liability of Harriet

Harriet could be also charged with gross negligence manslaughter. The first issue to consider is whether Harriet owed Margo a duty of care. She could be considered to have a special relationship with her

[6] This sentence shows the examiner that you can distinguish between Harriet's potential liability and her treatment as a potential intervening event in respect of Sebastian's liability.

[7] If you can remember short key quotes from judgments, use them to support your argument.

[8] State the general rule at the start.

since she is a school medical attendant. This could be comparable to the doctor–patient relationship. Alternatively, it might be argued that Harriet has voluntarily assumed responsibility for Margo. She is the school medical attendant and is employed to care for those children who feel unwell.[9] Thus, she can be said to have voluntarily assumed responsibility for Margo (*Stone and Dobinson*). In light of her employment contract as a medical attendant at a school, Margo might also be under a contractual duty to act under *Pittwood* (1902) 19 TLR 37. It could be said that she breached that duty by falling below the standard to be expected of a reasonable person when she fails to identify the signs of a head injury. Harriet must have had some training as a medical attendant and thus should probably have noticed the signs.

Turning next to the rules of causation, Harriet is clearly the factual cause of Margo's death. Applying *White*, but for Harriet failing to recognise Margo's illness, she would not have died. Harriet is also clearly a legal cause of Margo's death because she was a more than minimal cause of death (*Cato*), and she was an 'operating and substantial' cause of her death (*Smith*). Finally, the prosecution must prove that Harriet was grossly negligent. The jury must again consider 'whether having regard to the risk of death involved, the conduct of the defendant was so bad in all the circumstances as to amount . . . to a criminal act or omission' (*Adomako*). There is a high risk of death involved in failing to properly diagnose a child's illness when they are unwell. It is likely that the jury would consider Harriet's conduct to be so bad in all the circumstances as to amount to a criminal omission and thus to be grossly negligent. Consequently, she is likely to be convicted of gross negligence manslaughter.

✓ Make your answer stand out

- Adopt a clear and logical structure, dealing with the liability of each defendant in turn.
- Use any short key quotes from judgments that you can remember. For instance, you could refer to the judgments of the courts in *Stone and Dobinson* and *Adomako* in this question.
- Ensure that you state the general approach of the courts to negligent medical treatment as an intervening event.
- You should correctly cite and apply the test in *Cheshire*.

! Don't be tempted to . . .

■ Confuse the liability of Harriet for gross negligence manslaughter and her negligent conduct as a potential intervening act in respect of Sebastian's potential liability; these are distinct issues.

■ There is no need to list all of the possible exemptions to the general rule that there is no liability for an omission. Just focus on those that are relevant to the particular question.

■ Similarly, there is no need to list all of the possible intervening events in respect of legal causation. Instead, you should apply the law that is directly relevant to the question.

◤◥ Question 3

'The reason for requiring that the defendant should be shown to have causal responsibility for the conduct, consequence or state of affairs lies in the principle of individual autonomy . . . Thus the approach of the criminal law is to affix causal responsibility to the last individual whose voluntary behaviour impinged on the situation' (Ashworth, A. (2009) *Principles of Criminal Law*, 6th edn. Oxford: Oxford University Press).

Critically evaluate the above statement in relation to causation.

Answer plan

→ Distinguish between factual and legal causation.

→ Discuss case law on intervening events.

→ Critically evaluate the law on causation.

→ Conclude by addressing the quote.

Diagram plan

Explain the tests for factual and legal causation → Consider when the chain of causation will be broken (*novus actus interveniens*) → Critically evaluate cases on causation using academic opinion → Conclude by addressing the quote

A printable version of this diagram plan is available from **www.pearsoned.co.uk/lawexpressqa**

Answer

This question requires a critical evaluation of the rules of causation and, in particular, the approach taken by the courts to *novus actus interveniens* (new intervening acts) which break the chain of causation. Ashworth states that the rules of causation are underpinned by the principle of individual autonomy which 'respects individuals as capable of choosing their acts and omissions' who can be regarded as responsible for the normal consequences of their conduct.[1] However, some events/acts will intervene to break the chain of causation and absolve a defendant of responsibility. The rules of causation are largely based upon voluntariness. A voluntary or foreseeable act of the victim or a third party will not break the chain of causation, whereas an involuntary (unforeseeable) act may.[2] However, causation is a complex area which lacks clarity, particularly in relation to the independence/potency test in respect of medical negligent treatment.[3]

The prosecution must prove that the defendant's act is both a factual and a legal cause of the prohibited consequence. Factual causation is satisfied by the application of the 'but for' test (**White** [1910] 2 KB 124). Legal causation is used to describe the requirement that the defendant's act must be sufficiently proximate to the consequence. It is often stated that the defendant's act must be a more than minimal cause of the consequence; this is the *de minimis test* (**Cato** [1976] 1 WLR 110). In **Pagett** (1983) 75 Cr App R 279, the 'significant contribution' test was applied in respect of legal causation and in **Smith** [1959] 2 QB 35 this was expressed as the 'operating and substantial cause' test. Even where factual causation has been established and the defendant is a more than minimal cause of the result, the defendant may be absolved of liability where there is an intervening event which breaks the chain of causation. However, the chain of causation will only be broken in certain circumstances.

Acts of a third party will only break the chain of causation if they are voluntary. This means they must be 'free, deliberate and informed': Goff LJ in **Pagett**. The defendant in **Pagett** was held responsible for the death of his girlfriend. He held her hostage and shot at a police officer who shot back, killing her. The defendant was convicted on the basis that the police officer was acting instinctively in self-defence and out of a public duty to arrest the defendant, thus his actions were not 'free, deliberate and informed'. The rationalisation of this decision can be criticised. Ashworth suggests that a better rationale would have been along the lines of a 'doctrine of alternative danger' (Ashworth, A. (2009) *Principles of Criminal Law*, 6th edn. Oxford: Oxford University Press).[4]

An act of the victim will break the chain of causation where it is 'daft' or so unexpected that 'no reasonable man could be expected to foresee it': *Roberts* (1971) 56 Cr App R 95. This approach was also adopted in *Williams and Davies* (1992) 95 Cr App R 1. In *Marjoram* [2000] Crim LR 372, the Court of Appeal confirmed that the subjective characteristics of the accused may be taken into account here.

However, a pre-existing condition of the defendant which renders the defendant particularly vulnerable to the injury inflicted or death will not serve to absolve the defendant of liability. This is known as the 'thin skull rule'. In *Blaue* [1975] 1 WLR 1411, the thin skull rule was extended to encompass religious beliefs. Lawton LJ stated that defendants 'must take their victims as they find them. This . . . means the whole man, not just the physical man'. Thus, a refusal of treatment based on religious beliefs will not break the chain of causation. How far this principle extends to other beliefs, however, is unclear.[5]

[5] This sentence demonstrates that you are thinking around the subject rather than simply stating everything you know about causation.

In respect of negligent medical treatment, the courts have been reluctant to allow the negligence of a doctor to absolve the defendant of liability for policy reasons. In *Smith*, it was held that only if medical negligence was 'so overwhelming as to make the original wound merely part of the history' would the chain of causation be broken (per Parker LJ).[6] Similarly, in *Cheshire* [1991] 1 WLR 844, the Court of Appeal held that medical negligence will not break the chain of causation unless the medical treatment was so independent of the defendant's acts and so potent in causing death that it renders the defendant's acts insignificant. This is the 'independence/potency' test and this test was also applied in *Gowans and Hillman* [2003] EWCA Crim 3935.

[6] Use quotes from judgments to show your wider knowledge of the subject.

However, a very different approach was taken in the earlier case of *Jordan* (1956) 40 Cr App R 152. In this case, it was held that medical negligence could break the chain of causation if it was 'palpably wrong'. However, this is an extreme authority, and although it has not been overruled, it has been limited to its own facts by Lawton LJ in *Blaue*.[7]

The independence/potency test may be criticised. As Ormerod states, 'It is difficult to know what "so independent" and "so potent" mean' (Ormerod, D. (2011) *Smith and Hogan Criminal Law*, 13th edn. Oxford: Oxford University Press). If one considers first the words 'so independent', in all of the cases on negligent medical treatment, the defendant's act causes the victim to undergo the treatment. Ormerod argues that if this in itself renders the act 'dependent', then the defendant has caused the death, irrespective of how 'outlandish' the treatment. Ormerod submits that this is not the intended meaning of 'so independent'. Similarly, the words 'so potent' are problematic. In criticising this term, Ormerod provides an example of a victim who is wounded by the defendant and hospitalised for that wound. If he then contracts MRSA in an unclean hospital as the wound has healed, and dies, did the court in *Cheshire* intend that the defendant is not a legal cause of death? Ormerod submits that this is unlikely. These criticisms demonstrate that the test in *Cheshire* is confusing and inaccessible and, as such, is of limited use.[8]

In criticising the 'independence/potency' test, Ormerod suggests that a better test would be one in which the chain of causation could be broken where the treatment was 'so extraordinary as to be unforeseeable'. Such a test based upon foreseeability would certainly bring negligent medical treatment into line with many of the other authorities relating to *novus actus interveniens*.[9]

In conclusion, it is clear that causation is generally based upon the principle of individual autonomy. A defendant will be absolved of liability where an unforeseeable or involuntary act of the victim or a third party intervenes to break the chain of causation. However, the approach taken in cases of negligent medical treatment seems somewhat out of line with the rest of the law relating to causation and this area of law could benefit from further clarification.

Make your answer stand out

- Refer to further academic critique on causation, such as Hart, H. and Honoré, A. (1985) *Causation in the Law*, 2nd edn. Oxford: Oxford University Press.
- You should refer to further cases on causation, such as *Hayward* (1908) 21 Cox CC 692 on the thin skull rule and *Holland* (1841) 2 Mood & R 351 and *Dear* [1996] Crim LR 595 on self-neglect by the victim.
- Consider the argument that the Court of Appeal in *Blaue* should have adopted the 'reasonable foresight' approach adopted in *Roberts*. You should also refer to the fact that this is the approach taken in the law of tort and the distinction drawn by Lawton LJ in *Blaue* between the functions of criminal law and that of tort. Consider whether this approach is justifiable and any academic commentary on this point (see Williams, G. (1976) Case commentary. CJL 15; and Allen, M.J. (2013) *Textbook on Criminal Law*, 12th edn. Oxford: Oxford University Press).
- You should refer to other academic commentary, such as Wilson, W. (2014) *Criminal Law*, 5th edn. London: Longman.

! **Don't be tempted to . . .**

- Simply set out everything you know about causation. A descriptive account will not provide you with the opportunity to attain the highest marks. You must address the question directly and include academic critique.
- Provide detailed accounts of the facts of every case. You should not really cite the facts of a case in an answer to an essay question unless they are particularly relevant to the point you are making. For an example, see the reference to *Pagett* in the essay above.

Question 4

'It might . . . be expected that the meaning of such a fundamental term [as intention] would have been settled long ago, but this is not so. The cases are inconsistent, judicial opinion has recently changed and there is still some measure of uncertainty' (Ormerod, D. (2011) *Smith and Hogan Criminal Law*, 13th edn. Oxford: Oxford University Press).

Critically evaluate the meaning of intention in criminal law. To what extent do you agree with the above statement?

Answer plan

➜ Define intention.

➜ Consider case law relating to the meaning of intention.

➜ Explore academic opinion.

➜ Conclude by addressing the quote.

Diagram plan

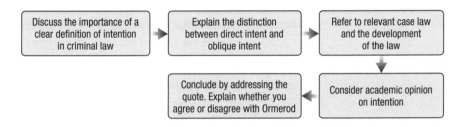

A printable version of this diagram plan is available from **www.pearsoned.co.uk/lawexpressqa**

Answer

[1] Address the quote in the question from the very start.

[2] Provide your opinion at the start to show that you have considered the question carefully.

This question requires consideration of the meaning of 'intention' in criminal law. Ormerod suggests that, despite the judicial attention given to intention, its meaning remains uncertain.[1] It is true that the decisions of the courts have been inconsistent and unclear over the years and Parliament has not intervened to clarify the law. However, the law has appeared more settled since the House of Lords decision in *Woollin* [1999] AC 82.[2] The importance of a clear definition of intention should not be underestimated. Intention is the mens rea requirement for some of the most serious offences in criminal law, including murder. Murder carries mandatory life imprisonment; such a serious threat to an individual's liberty upon conviction requires that the elements of the offence be precisely and clearly defined. As Lord Bingham states, '. . . the law must be accessible and so far as possible intelligible, clear and predictable' (Bingham, Lord (2007) The Rule of Law. CLJ 67). The law must be adequately clear and accessible so that an individual can find out what it is and be aware if his/her conduct will fall foul of it. The law must also be certain so that a trial judge is able to explain its meaning confidently to a jury.

[3] This paragraph shows the examiner that you recognise the importance of the question and this area of law and demonstrates wider thinking.

Nevertheless, the meaning of intention has been the subject of much uncertainty over the years.[3]

Although intention is now recognised as a subjective concept, it was given an objective meaning by the House of Lords in *DPP v Smith* [1961] AC 290. It was to be conclusively presumed that a person intends the natural and probable consequences of his acts. Such a presumption is not justifiable. Where the offence is of a serious nature, the mens rea required in order to establish criminal liability should depend upon the subjective state of mind of the actual defendant, rather than on any objective assessment. This case was criticised and it no longer represents the current law. Section 8 of the Criminal Justice Act 1967 confirms that intention is subjectively assessed.

In the majority of cases in which the issue of whether the defendant's intention is in issue, the jury are not given judicial direction as to the meaning of intention. This is because intention is an ordinary word used in everyday language, and the jury should use their common sense in determining its meaning. There are two types of intention: direct intent and oblique intent. Direct intent involves a defendant's aim or purpose. This form of intention is relatively straightforward, so the jury are not given any direction by the judge. Oblique intent may be present if, although the defendant did not desire the consequences, he did foresee that they were virtually certain to occur (*Woollin*). In the rare cases in which oblique intention arises, a judge should give the jury a direction as to the meaning of intention. Although one might have thought that intention should be easy to define, case law demonstrates that it has proved difficult to define the degree of foresight necessary for oblique intent.[4]

[4] This sentence indirectly refers to the quote and demonstrates that you are focused on the question.

According to the House of Lords in *Hyam* [1975] AC 55, intention could be established if the defendant foresaw death or GBH as a highly probable result. This test was criticised for being too close to recklessness. It is important to maintain a clear distinction between the meanings of intention and recklessness in order to adequately distinguish between the offences of murder and manslaughter. There is also a significant moral difference between wanting a result to occur and merely foreseeing it as highly probable.

[5] Compare the effect of the cases against one another.

In *Moloney* [1985] AC 905, the House of Lords retreated from *Hyam*.[5] Lord Bridge stated that the golden rule is that the judge should avoid any elaboration and leave it to the jury's good sense to decide whether the accused acted with the necessary intent, unless the judge is convinced that further explanation is necessary. His Lordship also stated that a jury should consider two questions: 'First, was death or really serious injury in a murder case . . . a natural consequence of the defendant's voluntary act? Secondly, did the defendant foresee that consequence as being a natural consequence of his act?'[6] If the answer is yes to both, the jury may infer that the defendant intended the consequence.

[6] It is worth learning the key quotes from leading judgments for the exam, along with the name of the judge.

In **Hancock & Shankland** [1986] AC 455, Lord Scarman held that '. . . the *Moloney* guidelines . . . are unsafe and misleading. They require a reference to probability. They also require an explanation that the greater the probability of a consequence the more likely it is that the consequence was foreseen and that if that consequence was foreseen the greater the probability is that that consequence was also intended'. The repeated references to 'probabilities' did little to clarify the position and to provide a certain distinction between intention and recklessness.

In **Nedrick** [1986] 1 WLR 1025, the Court of Appeal laid down a narrower test, which forms the basis of the current law. The court held that where a direction was necessary '. . . the jury should be directed that they are not entitled to infer the necessary intention, unless they feel sure that death or serious bodily harm was a virtual certainty . . . as a result of the defendant's actions and that the defendant appreciated [this]'. This is a much narrower test than that in **Hyam**, and it means that the distinction between recklessness and intention is clearer. This was approved by the House of Lords in **Woollin** (the word 'infer' was changed to 'find'). It was also held that foresight by the defendant that a result is a virtually certain consequence of his actions is merely evidence of intention. The trial judge in **Woollin** was criticised for directing the jury on intention using the phrase 'substantial risk'. The House held that the judge should not have departed from **Nedrick** and that 'substantial risk' was wider than 'virtual certainty'. Lord Steyn stated that 'By using the phrase "substantial risk" the judge blurred the line between intention and recklessness, and hence between murder and manslaughter. The misdirection enlarged the scope of the mental element required for murder'.

[7] Address the question in your conclusion.

In conclusion, although the meaning of intention has proved difficult to define, the law appears more settled now.[7] However, it should be

[8] This sentence demonstrates wider thinking and that you have read the *Nedrick/Woollin* direction properly.

[9] Include some academic opinion to demonstrate your wider reading.

acknowledged that most of the cases defining intention are murder cases. **Woollin** is limited specifically to murder, thus it remains unclear what approach the courts should take in respect of other offences.[8] Allen states 'it would be highly undesirable if courts were to adopt a different approach to the meaning of intention in other offences' (Allen, M.J. (2013)*Textbook on Criminal Law*, 12th edn. Oxford: Oxford University Press, p.74).[9] Thus, it is true that some degree of uncertainty as to the meaning of intention remains.

✓ Make your answer stand out

- As this area is very case law based, you should try to remember some of the key quotes from the main cases, along with the name of the relevant judge. This demonstrates to the examiner that you have a detailed understanding of the area.

- You could discuss the effect of the decision that foresight is evidence of intention, rather than intention as a matter of law and the case of *Matthews and Alleyne* [2003] 2 Cr App R 461.

- You could also discuss further the trend towards subjectivity in criminal law and the reasons why an objective approach to intention would not be appropriate. You should include discussion of the theoretical rationale behind different approaches to liability.

- Refer to academic opinion, such as Professor Smith's commentary on *Woollin* at [1998] Crim LR p. 890. Professor Smith welcomed the decision in *Woollin* because 'it draws a firm line between intention and recklessness' at p. 891.

- You might also refer to articles such as Norrie, A. (1999) After Woollin. Crim LR 532; and Williams, G. (1987) Oblique intention. CLJ 417 and (1989) The mens rea for murder: leave it alone. 105 LQR 387.

! Don't be tempted to . . .

- Misstate the direction from *Nedrick/Woollin*. There are two limbs to the direction, one objective one and one subjective one. It is not enough to simply refer to 'foresight of virtual certainty', you must set out the test in full.

- Recite the facts of *Hyam, Moloney, Woollin*, etc. Other than the fact that these cases all involved murder, the precise facts are not directly relevant to the question. You will waste time if you set out the facts when the question is asking for a critical appreciation of the judgments/opinions.

- Confuse the different tests from *Hyam, Moloney, Hancock* and *Shankland* and *Nedrick*.

Question 5

'[W]e are still some way from reaching a fair and coherent doctrine of recklessness in the English criminal law' (Halpin, A. (2004) *Definition in the Criminal Law*. Oxford: Hart Publishing, p. 120).

To what extent do you agree with the above statement?

Answer plan

➡ Refer to the current law on recklessness under *Cunningham* [1957] 2 QB 396 and *G* [2003] UKHL 50.

➡ Discuss the problems associated with the old law under *MPC* v *Caldwell* [1982] AC 341.

➡ Are there any criticisms of the current law?

➡ Include judicial and academic opinion on recklessness.

Diagram plan

A printable version of this diagram plan is available from **www.pearsoned.co.uk/lawexpressqa**

Answer

The law on recklessness has been subject to academic scrutiny for years. Prior to 2003, there were two legal tests of recklessness: one was a subjective meaning of recklessness from **Cunningham** [1957] 2 QB 396 and the other was an objective definition adopted by the House of Lords in **MPC v Caldwell** [1982] AC 341, which applied to criminal damage. In **G** [2003] UKHL 50, the House of Lords overruled **Caldwell**, confirming that a subjective test should apply in respect of criminal damage. Thus, since 2003 it would appear that the subjective approach to recklessness has prevailed and that the law is settled.

[1] Address the question in your introduction to ensure that you engage with the question asked.

[2] Set out the subjective test of recklessness to demonstrate your knowledge of the law.

[3] This sentence shows that you have fully understood the test.

[4] Set out the objective test of recklessness from *Caldwell*.

[5] If you do wish to mention the facts of a case in order to make a particular point, you should do so briefly.

However, academics have argued that the law is in fact still not settled following *G*.[1] Whether there is indeed a clear and settled definition of recklessness will be considered below.

The subjective test of recklessness from **Cunningham** requires that 'the accused has foreseen that the particular kind of harm might be done, and yet has gone on to take the risk of it' (per Byrne J). This test was further developed in later cases including **Stephenson** [1979] 1 QB 695, in which Lane LJ stated that recklessness involved conscious risk taking where the risk is an unreasonable one to take.[2] Thus, there is also an objective element to this test – a defendant will only be reckless where the risk is objectively unjustifiable.[3] This subjective (or advertent) test of recklessness was applied to offences until the decision in **Caldwell** in 1982, in which the House of Lords held that a second test of recklessness should apply in cases of criminal damage. This second test was expressed in more objective terms, Lord Diplock stating that recklessness requires the defendant to: (i) do an act which creates an obvious risk of damage; and (ii) give no thought to the possibility of there being any such risk, or recognising some risk he goes on to do the act anyway.[4] This was labelled as the objective test of recklessness due to the fact that a defendant who inadvertently took a risk which was obvious to the reasonable person would be deemed to be reckless. The **Caldwell** test was also applied to the offence of causing by reckless driving in **Lawrence** [1982] 1 AC 510. Thus, two tests of recklessness existed.

However, the **Caldwell** test was heavily criticised throughout its existence. One of the major problems with **Caldwell** was that this objective test could lead to harsh results when applied in respect of children or those with a lower capacity to appreciate risk: for example, see **Elliott v C** [1983] 1 WLR 939, in which the defendant was a child of low intelligence who did not appreciate the risk of criminal damage involved in her act due to her age, lack of understanding and exhausted state.[5] Such considerations were irrelevant under **Caldwell** and the High Court ordered the justices to convict the defendant. It was precisely this issue which eventually led to **Caldwell** being overruled in **G**. Lord Bingham stated that the decision in **Caldwell** led to 'obvious unfairness'.

Having two separate tests of recklessness was problematic as it over-complicated the law and was confusing for juries. Where a defendant was charged with both criminal damage and a non-fatal offence against the person, the jury would be directed to apply both tests of recklessness, a different test for each offence.[6] It was also illogical to have two separate tests and meanings of recklessness.

A further criticism was that the objective test of recklessness from **Caldwell** blurred the distinction between the concept of recklessness and that of negligence which is traditionally objectively assessed. It also contradicted the subjective trend within criminal law – intention is subjectively assessed. Lord Bingham stated that the mens rea of an offence should depend upon proof of a culpable state of mind and thus should be assessed subjectively. His Lordship took the view that mere stupidity should not expose a defendant to conviction of serious crime.[7]

[7] Referring to what a particular judge has said demonstrates that you have read and understood the judgment.

These criticisms led to the House of Lords overruling **Caldwell** in **G** and restoring a subjective test of recklessness in relation to criminal damage. Lord Bingham stated that the House of Lords in **Caldwell** has misinterpreted the meaning of 'recklessness' within section 1 of the Criminal Damage Act 1971. The House adopted the definition proposed by the Law Commission (1989): 'a person acts "recklessly" . . . with respect to: (i) circumstances when he is aware of a risk that it exists or will exist; (ii) a result when he is aware of a risk that it will occur; and it is, in the circumstances known to him, unreasonable to take the risk'.

However, despite this decision, academics argue that the law on recklessness is still not clear. One criticism of **G** is that the House restricted the decision to criminal damage. As **Caldwell** recklessness also applied to other offences, e.g. causing death by reckless driving and other statutory offences requiring proof of recklessness, the question which must now be asked is why these offences were not also dealt with or indeed whether **Caldwell** recklessness still applies to these.

Halpin (2004) expresses concern about Lord Bingham's understanding of mens rea. He criticises Lord Bingham for taking a 'strict subjectivist' approach, according to which culpability is associated with intention to bring about a result or awareness of a risk of that result. Halpin highlights serious offences which have required proof of objective recklessness or negligence; he comments: 'if we took Bingham's support of the strict subjectivist position seriously, it would follow that liability for the serious offences of causing death by reckless driving, manslaughter and rape has been established under English law without any requirement of mens rea, and without any need to find fault on the part of the defendant' (Halpin (2004), p. 104).

The question raised is to what degree inadvertence should be culpable. Some commentators support a test which provides a compromise between subjective and objective approaches[8] (Tadros, V. (2002) Recklessness and the duty to take care, in S. Shute and A. Simester (eds.), *Criminal Law Theory*. Oxford: Oxford University Press). Crosby recognises that 'a definition of recklessness that is too subjective can allow those who are blameworthy to avoid criminal liability. Alternatively, a test that is too objective can lead to injustice without being capacity based. It is submitted that a synthesis of the two approaches is required' (Crosby, C. (2008) Recklessness – the continuing search for a definition. 72 JCL 313). This is an issue requiring further consideration by the courts. Thus, although *G* appears to have simplified the law in certain respects, the decision of the House is open to academic criticism and there is a need for further judicial guidance.

✓ Make your answer stand out

- There is a wealth of academic literature on recklessness which you could refer to in your answer.

- You might wish to refer to some of the theory surrounding recklessness and culpability. A good starting point is Tadros, V. (2002) Recklessness and the duty to take care, in S. Shute and A. Simester (eds.), *Criminal Law Theory*. Oxford: Oxford University Press.

- You could also explore the judicial reasoning in cases such as *Caldwell, Lawrence, Elliott v C* in more detail and explore the case of *Reid* [1992] 3 All ER 673.

- You should include discussion of the theoretical rationale behind different approaches to liability, including the justifications for liability based on a subjectivist approach.

! Don't be tempted to . . .

- Set out the facts of *Cunningham, Caldwell* and *G* in detail – this will waste time in an exam. While you may wish to refer to specific facts, such as the fact that the defendants in *G* were children, you should be able to do this without regaling all of the facts of the cases.

- Merely provide a historical account of the development of the law from *Cunningham* to *Caldwell* and *G*. The question asks you to critically evaluate the development of the law and the current position.

✒ Question 6

To what extent does the imposition of criminal liability without proof of fault offend traditional notions of criminal responsibility?

Answer plan

➜ Refer to the presumption of mens rea and the situations in which the presumption may be displaced.

➜ Outline the arguments in favour of imposing strict liability on an individual.

➜ Outline the arguments against strict liability, considering also the extent to which strict liability offends traditional notions of criminal responsibility.

➜ Discuss any alternatives to strict liability.

Diagram plan

A printable version of this diagram plan is available from **www.pearsoned.co.uk/lawexpressqa**

Answer

This question requires a critical evaluation of strict liability and whether this violates fundamental traditional principles of criminal responsibility. Strict liability offences are offences which do not require proof of mens rea in respect of at least one of the actus reus elements.[1] They are largely statutory offences and usually regulatory offences which apply to matters such as pollution, food safety, road traffic, public health, etc. It is a fundamental principle of criminal law that liability requires proof of both actus reus and mens rea elements, commonly expressed as '*actus non facit reum nisi mens sit rea*' (an act does not make a man guilty of a crime, unless his mind be also guilty): Lord Hailsham in *Haughton v Smith* [1975] AC 476. It can be argued that imposing criminal liability upon an individual without proving a guilty mind

[1] Demonstrate that you understand what strict liability is by defining it at the outset.

violates traditional notions of criminal responsibility.[2] The arguments for and against the imposition of strict liability will be explored.

It is not necessarily apparent from reading a statutory provision whether an offence is one of strict liability or not. The courts have held that, where a statutory provision is silent as to mens rea, there is a presumption that mens rea elements are required: Lord Reid in **Sweet v Parsley** [1970] AC 132. However, this presumption may be displaced by the words of the statute or by the subject matter of the offence: **Sherras v De Rutzen** [1895] 1 QB 918.

[3] Set out the guidelines from a leading authority in order to demonstrate your understanding of the operation of the presumption and when it may be displaced.

In **Gammon (Hong Kong) Ltd v Attorney General of Hong Kong** [1985] AC 1, Lord Scarman laid down guidelines in order for determining whether an offence is one of strict liability. His Lordship held that the presumption of mens rea is particularly strong where the offence is 'truly criminal' in nature, rather than merely regulatory, and it can only be displaced by clear words or if it is by necessary implication the effect of the statute. The statute must involve an issue of social concern and the imposition of strict liability must promote the object of the statute by encouraging greater vigilance to prevent the prohibited act.[3]

[4] These sentences demonstrate a good understanding of the justification for strict liability offences.

[5] This quote shows that you have conducted effective research and read widely in your preparation for the examination.

The main argument for the imposition of strict liability is that it provides a degree of protection to the public through the promotion of care. Strict liability operates on a utilitarian approach.[4] Wilson comments that a welfarist paradigm of criminal responsibility, '. . . does not require proof of moral wrongdoing . . . In order to live a life of relative autonomy we require certain basic welfare needs to be ministered to . . . Only the criminal law can satisfactorily ensure that these collective needs can be properly catered for and this is only possible if the criminal law requires all citizens to satisfy standards of good rather than morally blameless citizenship. The essence of such crimes is to prevent harm rather than to punish a moral wrong' (Wilson, W. (2002) *Central Issues in Criminal Theory*. Oxford: Hart Publishing, p. 72).[5] Strict liability also has a deterrent element as it encourages people to comply with regulations in order to protect people from harm.

Another argument in favour of strict liability relates to the ease of proof. It is much easier for the prosecution to prove criminal liability where a state of mind does not have to be proved. Strict liability offences can be further justified by reference to the sanction they carry. As they only apply to regulatory (or quasi) crimes and not true offences, offences of strict liability usually carry only a small penalty as a sanction and do not pose any risk to the liberty of individuals.

However, consideration must also be given to the arguments against the imposition of strict liability. The main argument is that it violates the principle of coincidence of actus reus and mens rea, a traditional notion of criminal responsibility.[6] A defendant should not be held to be criminally liable for any offence unless a blameworthy state of mind is also proved. This was emphasised by Lord Bingham in *G* [2003] UKHL 50 '. . . it is a salutary principle that conviction of serious crime should depend on proof not simply that the defendant caused (by act or omission) an injurious result to another but that his state of mind when so acting was culpable. This, after all, is the meaning of *actus non facit reum nisi mens sit rea*'. Simester and Sullivan comment that 'Parliament normally does not, and indeed should not, intend to make criminals of those who are not blameworthy and do not warrant that label' (Simester, A. and Sullivan, R. (2007) *Criminal Law: Theory and Doctrine*. Oxford: Hart Publishing, p. 169).[7]

Another argument against strict liability is that it serves to punish reasonable behaviour where the defendant has taken all reasonable steps to prevent liability and has no guilty mind. Consider the case of *Smedleys Ltd* v *Breed* [1974] AC 839, in which a caterpillar was found in a tin of peas sold by the defendant.[8] The defendant manufacturer was convicted of a strict liability offence despite the fact that this occurred once during production of millions of tins. The steps that a defendant must take to avoid such an incident from occurring and to avoid liability are highly onerous and not practicable.

The House of Lords has affirmed that the presumption of mens rea applies to all statutory offences (see *B (a minor)* v *DPP* [2000] 1 AC 428 and *K* [2002] 1 AC 462). In both cases, the House held that serious offences are likely to require proof of mens rea. The more serious the offence, the more severe the sanction and stigma of conviction, the greater the presumption that mens rea must be proved. The stigma attached to conviction might affect a defendant's reputation and livelihood. However, Hyman Gross argues that there is no such stigma attached to conviction for a strict liability offence: 'Perhaps the most prominent feature of most strict liability offences is that conviction does not affect respectability. Neither his conduct nor the punishment he receives for it stigmatises the offender. These

[6] Address the question again midway through your answer in order to maintain focus and show that you are not simply writing everything you know about strict liability.

[7] Try to use a mixture of quotes from judgments and academic sources to support your arguments.

[8] If you do wish to state the facts of a case, do so briefly in a short sentence.

offences of low culpability are typically of the regulatory or public welfare variety, and so penal treatment is right viewed as simply an expedient way of encouraging or preventing certain consequences that flow from lawful activity, rather than as a public response to wrongdoing' (Hyman Gross, A. (1979) *A Theory of Criminal Justice*. Oxford: Oxford University Press, p. 344).

Alternatives to strict liability include offences containing a requirement of negligence or a no fault defence of due diligence. Although it may be true that the imposition of strict liability violates traditional principles of criminal responsibility, there are convincing justifications for the use of strict liability in respect of regulatory offences for the protection of the public.

✓ Make your answer stand out

- Consider the alternatives to strict liability in more detail.
- You could include a comparative view of approaches to strict liability in Canada, where the prosecution need not prove mens rea, but a defendant can prove a lack of fault to escape liability.
- Make reference to the distinction between absolute liability offences and strict liability offences. Consider whether absolute liability offences violate any further principles of criminal responsibility, such as voluntariness. See *Winzar* v *Chief Constable of Kent* (1983) *The Times*, 28 March and *Larsonneur* (1933) 24 Cr App R 74.
- Refer to further academic opinion, such as Simester, A. (2006) *Appraising Strict Liability*. Oxford: Oxford University Press and Horder, J. (2002) Strict liability, statutory construction, and the spirit of liberty. LQR 458.

! Don't be tempted to . . .

- Wrongly define strict liability and confuse absolute liability and strict liability.
- Set out all of the facts of every case on strict liability. This question asks you to critically evaluate the concept of strict liability and the facts of the cases are not directly relevant to this. The principles and justifications for strict liability or arguments against it are more important.

Question 7

Explain the meaning of the Latin maxim *actus non facit reum nisi mens sit rea* and critically analyse the way in which this principle is applied in criminal law.

Answer plan

→ Explain the meaning of the Latin maxim *actus non facit reum nisi mens sit rea*.

→ Explore the principle of coincidence.

→ Consider the major exception of offences of absolute liability and strict liability.

→ Examine other exceptions to this principle, such as the doctrine of transferred malice, the continuing act theory, the 'duty' principle and the 'single transaction' principle.

Diagram plan

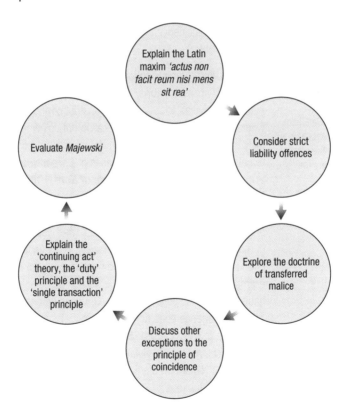

A printable version of this diagram plan is available from **www.pearsoned.co.uk/lawexpressqa**

Answer

[1] Begin your answer by explaining the fundamental principle of coincidence using the Latin maxim.

Liability for a criminal offence is governed by the Latin maxim *actus non facit reum nisi mens sit rea* which has been translated as 'an act does not make a man guilty of a crime, unless his mind be also guilty' (see Lord Hailsham in **Haughton v Smith** [1975] AC 476).[1] This means that both the actus reus (the 'guilty act') and the mens rea (the 'guilty mind') of an offence must be proved before a defendant may be convicted of a criminal offence. Thus, criminal liability usually requires proof of both actus reus and mens rea elements. This is often referred to as the principle of coincidence of actus reus and mens rea and this requires that the defendant form the requisite mens rea for the offence at some point during the actus reus. Generally speaking, if these two elements do not coincide, no offence will have been committed. However, there are a number of exceptions to this principle and situations in which the courts have circumvented the principle of coincidence in order to ensure that the defendant is held criminally liable.[2]

[2] You should address the question directly in your introduction by mentioning the fact that the courts have sought to avoid the principle.

The first important exception to the principle of coincidence is offences of absolute liability and strict liability. A defendant may be held criminally liable for an offence of strict or absolute liability even where the actus reus and mens rea do not coincide.[3] Absolute liability offences are offences which do not require proof of any mens rea at all. Examples include the cases of **Larsonneur** (1933) 97 JP 206 and **Winzar v Chief Constable of Kent** (1983) *The Times*, 28 March. Both of these cases involve 'state of affairs' offences, where the defendant is guilty of a criminal offence simply because a state of affairs is deemed to exist. In neither case was the state of mind of the defendant relevant to their liability. Strict liability offences are offences for which at least one element of mens rea is missing. One example of a strict liability offence is assault occasioning actual bodily harm, contrary to section 47 of the Offences Against the Person Act 1861; this offence does not require proof of mens rea in respect of the degree of harm caused: **Savage; Parmenter** [1992] 1 AC 699. Offences of strict liability violate the principle of coincidence because they do not require an element of mens rea to be proved for every element of actus reus.

[3] This is the obvious example of the courts avoiding coincidence. Provide a brief explanation of offences of strict liability and the way in which they violate the principle.

In addition to this exception to the principle of coincidence, the courts have sought to circumvent the principle in other situations.

The doctrine of transferred malice is one creative method used by the courts to circumvent the principle of coincidence. According to this doctrine, the defendant's intention in respect of one crime may be transferred to his/her performance of the actus reus in respect of another crime, provided that both offences are of the same type: *Latimer* (1886) 17 QBD 359. Thus, while the defendant may have the mens rea for murder in respect of A but he does not actually kill A (and thus has no actus reus in respect of A), if he accidentally kills B during his attempt to kill A, his mens rea in respect of A will be transferred to the killing of B. Thus, the actus reus and mens rea are said to coincide.[4] This, of course, is another creative way of circumventing the strict principle of coincidence.

[4] As the doctrine of transferred malice is difficult to explain, you could use an example to aid your explanation.

Another way of circumventing the principle of coincidence invented by the courts is the 'continuing act theory'. This was developed in the case of *Fagan* v *Metropolitan Police Commissioner* [1969] 1 QB 439. In this case, the defendant's act of driving on to the police officer's foot was deemed to be continuing until he later formed the mens rea when he realised and failed to drive off the officer's foot.[5] Thus, the court was 'willing to stretch the concept of an act in order to ensure that cases fall within the principle of coincidence' (Monaghan, N. (2016) *Criminal Law Directions*, 4th edn. Oxford: Oxford University Press, p. 76). This theory was also applied in the case of *Kaitamaki* [1985] AC 147 in respect of sexual intercourse in rape. This has since been incorporated into statute under section 79(2) of the Sexual Offences Act 2003.[6]

[5] If you wish to refer to the facts of the case, then you should do so as briefly as possible and by way of explanation of your point.

[6] Demonstrate your wider knowledge of the law by providing a further example of when the continuing act theory was applied in a later authority/statute.

The courts have also avoided the principle of coincidence by the creation and application of the 'duty' principle. This was first applied in *Miller* [1983] 2 AC 161, in which it was held that where a defendant inadvertently creates a dangerous situation by his actions, the law imposes a duty on him to act to avert that danger. The defendant will be liable when he fails to act to fulfil that duty, having realised that he has caused that danger and it is only at this stage that the mens rea is formed. This approach was more recently followed by the Divisional Court in *DPP* v *Santana-Bermudez* [2003] EWHC 2908 (Admin).

The courts have circumvented the application of the coincidence principle by inventing the 'single transaction' principle, by which the courts interpret a number of consecutive events as one single transaction. This was applied in the case of *Thabo Meli* v *R* [1954]

1 WLR 288, in which the defendants tried to kill the victim and then, believing him to be dead, they rolled his body off a cliff. The victim died later. While the defendants had the mens rea for murder when they first tried to kill the victim, they did not have the mens rea for murder when they actually caused the victim's death by rolling him off the cliff. Thus, there was no coincidence of actus reus and mens rea. Nevertheless, the court held that the series of acts constituted a single transaction and that the defendants would be guilty of murder provided they formed the mens rea at some stage during that transaction. This principle has since been applied in cases such as *Church* [1966] 1 QB 59, *Le Brun* [1991] 4 All ER 673 and *Attorney General's Reference (No. 4 of 1980)* [1981] 1 WLR 705.[7]

[7] If you have time, you could compare these cases as there are some significant differences between them, yet the courts have reached the same conclusion as to liability.

Finally, it has been argued that the rules on voluntary intoxication laid down in *DPP v Majewski* [1977] AC 443 also violate the principle of coincidence. Lord Elwyn-Jones held that a defendant who becomes intoxicated is reckless and thus he has the mens rea for any basic intent offence. The mens rea is formed before the actus reus of the offence is performed, while the defendant becomes intoxicated.[8] This rule, however, presumes that the defendant is reckless, despite a clear lack of subjective recklessness, and thus violates the principle of coincidence.

[8] Draw on your wider knowledge of the criminal law and examine the application of this defence as well. A well-voiced criticism of *Majewski* is that it violates the principle of coincidence.

In conclusion, while the principle of coincidence clearly has an important role to play in criminal law, the courts have used various inventive methods to circumvent the fundamental principle of coincidence in order to suit their desire to ensure criminal liability.

✓ **Make your answer stand out**

■ You could consider the rationale underlying the principle of coincidence.

■ You should include some discussion of the justifications for imposing criminal liability for offences of strict liability and provide some examples of cases.

■ You should expand upon some of the exceptions to the principle of coincidence as well as the rationale for the courts' creative approach in each case.

■ You could make reference to academic opinion on the principle of coincidence. For instance, see Sullivan, G.R. (1993) Cause and the contemporaneity of actus reus and mens rea. CLJ 487 and Marston, G. (1970) Contemporaneity of act and intention in crimes. 86 LQR 208.

Don't be tempted to . . .

- Simply provide the facts of the cases in which the courts have avoided the strict application of the principle of coincidence, such as *Fagan* v *MPC*. There are many cases you could mention in this answer and you will waste valuable time setting out the facts of all of these cases.
- Just set out the obvious exception of strict liability offences. This is not a question on strict liability, but it is one which requires you to think more widely about the criminal law and you should incorporate as many instances of circumventing the principle of coincidence as you can.

@ Try it yourself

Now take a look at the question below and attempt to answer it. You can check your response against the answer guidance available on the companion website (**www.pearsoned.co.uk/lawexpressqa**).

'. . . the State is justified in criminalising any conduct that causes harm to others or creates an unacceptable risk of harm to others' (Ashworth, *Principles of Criminal Law*, 6th edn, OUP, p.30).

Explain the use of the harm principle as a basis for criminalising conduct. To what extent is the law justified in going beyond merely criminalising harmful conduct?

www.pearsoned.co.uk/lawexpressqa

Go online to access more revision support including additional essay and problem questions with diagram plans, You be the marker questions, and download all diagrams from the book.

Murder

How this topic may come up in exams

Murder could be examined by way of an essay or a problem question. Problem scenarios might ask you to discuss murder only, or you might be required to identify and apply the partial defences to murder (see Chapter 3) or other general defences such as self-defence, intoxication or duress in a mixed problem question. Essay questions on murder might ask you to consider the proposed reforms to the definition of murder and the hierarchy of the homicide offences. Alternatively, you may be asked for a critical evaluation of an aspect of the law of murder, such as causation or intention (see Chapter 1).

Before you begin

It's a good idea to consider the following key themes of murder before tackling a question on this topic.

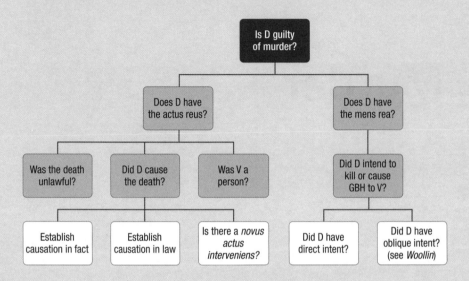

A printable version of this diagram is available from **www.pearsoned.co.uk/lawexpressqa**

❓ Question 1

Consider the liability of Bill and Janey for murder in the following scenarios:

(a) Bill goes to the cinema and sits in the front row of the screening of an action film. He sets off firecrackers during the film, causing the audience to panic. He then shouts, 'I have a bomb!' and waves a homemade bomb around for the audience to see. Toby, who is in the audience, opens a fire escape and jumps down the flight of stairs. He dies from the fall. Bill sets off the bomb. The bomb explodes and Cameron is wounded in the explosion. He is taken to hospital, but the doctor misdiagnoses the severity of his injury and he dies.

(b) Janey is a passenger in a helicopter which is being piloted by Steve. She holds a gun to Steve's head and tells him to divert the helicopter to a destination 50 miles away. Steve protests that there is not enough fuel to last the journey, but Janey does not believe him and threatens to shoot him unless he does what she says. After 40 miles, the helicopter runs out of fuel and crashes. Steve is killed, but Janey survives.

Answer plan

→ Discuss Coke's definition of murder.

→ Examine Bill's liability for murder in respect of the deaths of Toby and Cameron, including whether Bill caused those deaths and whether he had the requisite mens rea of murder.

→ Examine Janey's liability for murder in respect of Steve's death, including whether Janey caused Steve's death and whether she had the requisite mens rea of murder.

Diagram plan

Liability of Bill for Toby's death	• Are the AR elements of murder satisfied? • Are the rules of causation satisfied? Consider escape cases. • Does Bill have the MR for murder? Direct intent? Oblique intent?

Liability of Bill for Cameron's death	• Are the AR elements of murder satisfied? • Are the rules of causation satisfied? Consider negligent medical treatment cases. • Does Bill have the MR for murder? Direct intent? Oblique intent?

Liability of Janey for Steve's death	• AR of murder should be quite straightforward here. • Does Janey have the MR for murder? • What was her direct intent? • Apply *Nedrick/Woollin* on oblique intent.

A printable version of this diagram plan is available from **www.pearsoned.co.uk/lawexpressqa**

Answer

[1] As this question is about one offence, you should begin by defining the offence.

[2] This sentence shows that you have identified the actus reus elements within the definition.

[3] You should set out the mens rea in its more modern form rather than relying on the misleading phrase 'malice aforethought'.

This question requires consideration of the common law offence of murder. The classic definition of murder is provided by Coke:[1] 'Murder is when a man of sound memory, and of the age of discretion, unlawfully killeth within any county of the realm any reasonable creature *in rerum natura* under the King's peace, with malice aforethought . . .' (Coke, Sir E. 3 Inst. 47 *Institutes of the Lawes of England* 47). Thus, the actus reus of murder requires proof that the defendant unlawfully caused the death of the victim (a person in being) within the Queen's peace.[2] The mens rea is 'malice aforethought', which is more commonly expressed today as intention to kill or cause GBH (***Vickers*** [1957] 2 QB 664).[3]

Part (a) requires consideration of whether Bill could be convicted of murder in respect of the deaths of Toby and Cameron. Starting with Toby's death, the actus reus of murder is satisfied. Toby is a person in being and there is no evidence of self-defence, thus the killing is unlawful. The killing also occurs within the Queen's peace. Applying the tests of causation, factual causation is established because, but for Bill's actions, Toby would not have jumped down the fire escape and would not have died (**White** [1910] 2 KB 124). In relation to legal causation, Bill's actions do not need to be the sole cause of death, as long as they contributed significantly towards death (**Pagett** (1983) 75 Cr App R 279). Alternatively, it could be asked whether Bill's actions were a 'substantial and operative cause' of death (**Smith** [1959] 2 QB 35). It is clear that although his actions may not have been the only cause of death, they were a 'substantial' or 'significant' cause of death. Consideration must also be given to whether Toby's action of jumping down the fire escape breaks the chain of causation. The actions of a victim will not break the chain of causation where they are reasonably foreseeable and involuntary, but they will break the chain of causation where they are 'daft' (**Roberts** (1971) 56 Cr App R 95). Applying this, Toby's escape might be reasonably foreseeable in light of the fact that Bill was waving a bomb around having already set off firecrackers, but the question of why he didn't walk down the fire escape would also be pertinent.[4]

[4] You should never assume facts, but if your answer depends upon the existence of unknown facts you should state this.

It is also necessary to consider the mens rea of murder, which is intention to kill or cause GBH (**Vickers**). Considering direct intent first, it could be argued that Bill's aim or purpose in setting off the firecrackers was only to scare and not to kill or cause GBH. However, his aim in setting off the bomb may be different. It could be argued that Bill's aim or purpose here was to kill or cause GBH, but we might need to know more about the size of the bomb and why Bill says he made it and set it off. If direct intent cannot be established, oblique intent should be considered. Applying **Woollin**, it would need to be asked whether it was virtually certain that people would die or suffer GBH. Even if death or GBH was virtually certain, it would then need to be shown that Bill appreciated this. If oblique intention can be established, then the mens rea for murder will also be present and Bill will be guilty of Toby's murder. However, if there is no direct or oblique intent, he will not be guilty of murder here.

In relation to Cameron's death, the key issue with the actus reus for murder is causation. The other elements of the actus reus are present because Cameron is a person, the death is unlawful as there is no evidence of self-defence and it occurs within the Queen's peace. Applying the test for factual causation, but for Bill setting off the bomb, Cameron would not have been injured, misdiagnosed and would not have died (*White*). In relation to legal causation, although Bill's actions may not have been the only cause of death, his act of setting off the bomb was a 'substantial' cause of death (*Smith*).

The courts are reluctant to find that negligent medical treatment breaks the chain of causation so as to absolve a defendant of liability. In the exceptional case of *Jordan* [1956] 40 Cr App R 152, the chain of causation was deemed to be broken where the medical treatment was 'palpably wrong'. However, this is an extreme example and is limited to its own facts.[5] Applying the leading case of *Cheshire* [1991] 1 WLR 844, it must be asked whether the doctor's act of misdiagnosing Cameron's injuries was so independent of Bill's act and so potent in causing Cameron's death that it renders Bill's actions insignificant. In light of these authorities, it is very unlikely that the actions of the doctor will break the chain of causation, thus Bill was the legal cause of Cameron's death.[6] The mens rea must also be considered and will follow the same argument as above in respect of Toby's death.

Part (b) requires consideration of whether Janey may be guilty of the murder of Steve. Dealing first with the actus reus of murder, the victim is a person in being, there is no evidence of self-defence, thus the killing is unlawful, and the killing occurs within the Queen's peace. Applying the tests of causation, factual causation is established because, but for Janey's actions, Steve would not have died. In relation to legal causation, Janey's actions are the sole cause of death and it is clear that her actions did contribute significantly towards the death (*Pagett* (1983) 75 Cr App R 279). Thus, the actus reus of murder is established.

The main issue here relates to the mens rea. Did Janey have the necessary mens rea for murder? The question that must be asked is whether Janey intended to kill Steve or to cause him GBH (*Vickers*). In considering direct intention first, it is not entirely clear what Janey's aim or purpose was here. There is no clear evidence that her aim or purpose was to kill Steve or to cause him GBH. Thus, the virtual certainty test from *Woollin* [1999] AC 82 would then need to be applied in relation to oblique intention: was death or GBH virtually certain to occur and did Janey appreciate this?[7] The facts state that she doesn't believe Steve when he protests about a lack of fuel, suggesting that

[5] This sentence demonstrates that you understand the limited effect of this authority and the fact that it is unlikely to be applied.

[6] Ensure that you provide short conclusions at significant points throughout your answer, such as here, after dealing with the actus reus of murder.

[7] Ensure you state the test fully and accurately before you apply the law to the facts in the problem scenario.

Janey did not foresee Steve's death as virtually certain to occur. Thus, there is no evidence of indirect intent in respect of murder here. Consequently, the mens rea for murder might not be present and Janey might not be guilty of murder in respect of Steve's death.

 Make your answer stand out

- Ensure that you structure your answer in a logical way. Where there is more than one defendant, deal with each defendant's liability in full before moving on to the next defendant.
- In establishing a defendant's liability, you should ensure that you have defined murder (using Coke's definition) before applying the actus reus elements, and finally the mens rea.
- Ensure that you apply both limbs of the test for oblique intent, if relevant.
- You could also incorporate some academic critique into your answer.

! Don't be tempted to . . .

- Consider the liability of the doctor, as the question specifically asks you about the criminal liability of Bill. You must ensure that you read the instruction line carefully so that you address the issues that the examiners expect you to deal with.
- Consider the offence of involuntary manslaughter as the question specifically asks you about murder. You will gain no extra marks for discussing irrelevant material and you will only waste valuable time in your examination. If the question does not ask you about a specific offence, then you should consider other potential offences, such as manslaughter.

Question 2

Critically evaluate the Law Commission's recommendations for reforming the framework of homicide offences.

Answer plan

→ Consider the Law Commission proposals for reform.

→ Evaluate these, including using academic critique.

→ Refer to the current position of the law, including Coke's definition of murder, the scope of the homicide offences and the problems defining the mens rea of murder.

→ Evaluate the relationship between murder and manslaughter.

→ Consider any defences and partial defences to murder.

Diagram plan

A printable version of this diagram plan is available from **www.pearsoned.co.uk/lawexpressqa**

Answer

In 2005, the Law Commission recommended the creation of a new Homicide Act which would radically reform the law on homicide by providing a new framework of offences. These recommendations were made in Law Commission (2005) Consultation Paper, *A New Homicide Act for England and Wales?* (No. 177). The recommendations included new definitions of murder, manslaughter and the partial defences to murder within a grading structure of homicide offences which reflects different levels of culpability. While these recommendations have largely been applauded by academics, unfortunately they are yet to be adopted by Parliament. In light of the fact that the recommendations were published over a decade ago, it seems unlikely that they will be enacted.

Under the framework proposed by the Law Commission, the most serious offence of homicide would be first degree murder. This would be reserved for intentional killings and would carry a mandatory life sentence. The next serious offence would be second degree murder, which would cover killings with the intention of causing GBH, reckless killings with an indifference to risk, and killings where there is a partial defence to first degree murder. This offence would carry a discretionary life maximum sentence. Finally, the offence of manslaughter would cover killing through gross negligence and killing through an intentional act intended to cause injury or involving recklessness as to whether injury was caused or not. This offence would carry a maximum sentence of ten years' imprisonment.

These recommendations have been welcomed by academics who applaud the restriction of the scope of murder and manslaughter and the creation of a three-tier framework.[1] While first degree murder is reserved for intentional killings, other less culpable killings are more fairly labelled as second degree murder. Professor Dennis comments that the recommendations would also reduce the scope of manslaughter and 'result in a more coherent offence of manslaughter in terms of labelling' (Dennis, I. (2006) Reviewing the law of homicide. Crim LR 187). However, there are some criticisms of the recommendations. Rogers calls for cases where the victim has consented to being killed to be given further consideration (Rogers, J. (2006) The Law Commission's proposed restructuring of homicide. 70(3) JCL 223).[2] Under the recommendations, a mercy killing would fall under first degree murder because it is an intentional killing. Rogers argues that consent should be recognised as a partial defence to first degree murder, thus recognising the distinction between mercy killing and other types of intentional killing.

The current framework of homicide offences lacks a coherent structure and it prescribes for offences of murder and manslaughter which are too broad.[3] Murder and manslaughter are two of the most serious criminal offences and they carry heavy penalties: mandatory life and discretionary life imprisonment respectively. In light of their severity, it is vital that the scope of these offences and their relationship is clearly defined.[4]

Coke's classic definition of murder is still cited today: 'Murder is when a man of sound memory, and of the age of discretion, unlawfully killeth within any county of the realm any reasonable creature *in rerum natura* under the King's peace, with malice aforethought . . .' (Coke, Sir E. 3 Inst. 47 *Institutes of the Lawes of England* 47). The common law has sought to clarify the meaning of terms such as 'reasonable creature *in rerum natura*' and 'malice aforethought' and statutory provisions have made further amendments to the scope of murder, such as the Law Reform (Year and a Day Rule) Act 1996. While the Homicide Act 1957 dealt with the partial defences to murder, it failed

[1] An ability to summarise academic opinion before going on to explore the opinions of specific academics demonstrates your understanding of academic literature.

[2] These sentences provide an example of a criticism of the proposed reforms and shows that you appreciate both the positive and negative aspects of the recommendations.

[3] Identify the key problems with the law at the start.

[4] This shows that you understand why the structure and grading of homicide offences is important.

2 MURDER

[5] This sentence demonstrates your understanding of the development of the law and the failures of previous legislation.

to provide new definitions of murder or manslaughter or to deal with the wider issue of the grading of homicide offences.[5]

For many years, the scope of murder was uncertain and confused. This was largely due to the problem the courts had in defining 'intention' within the mens rea of murder. Murder requires proof of an intention to kill or cause GBH (**Vickers** [1957] 2 QB 664). At one stage, 'intention' was widely defined to include the defendant's foresight of the consequences as highly probable to occur (**Hyam** [1975] AC 55). This blurred the line between intention and recklessness, and thus between the offences of murder and manslaughter. Although the law on oblique intent is currently more settled (see **Nedrick** [1986] 1 WLR 1025 and **Woollin** [1999] AC 82), the offence of murder covers too broad a range of killings. Oblique intent is currently sufficient mens rea for murder, as is an intention to cause GBH.[6] This raises questions about the current scope of murder and the relationship between murder and manslaughter. A more appropriate grading system might be adopted in order to distinguish between these different degrees of culpability.

[6] Show that you know why the offence of murder is deemed to be very broad in its scope. The key to this lies in the mens rea of the offence which encompasses more than a mere intention to kill.

The law on voluntary manslaughter has also been plagued with problems. The defence of provocation has caused confusion in recent years; although it was recently abolished by the Coroners and Justice Act 2009, which created a new partial defence of loss of control. Similarly, diminished responsibility has been the subject of reform. These reforms, however necessary, still fail to deal with the overall structure of the law of homicide and merely add to the piecemeal developments which have taken place over the years.[7]

[7] This statement shows the examiner that your knowledge of the law is up to date.

Involuntary manslaughter is also a very wide offence. The mens rea of unlawful act manslaughter requires proof only that the reasonable man would foresee the risk of some harm, and not that the defendant himself foresaw the risk of death: **Church** [1966] 1 QB 59. This would cover a defendant such as the 'one-punch killer' (Mitchell, B. (2008) Minding the gap in unlawful and dangerous act manslaughter: a moral defence of one-punch killers. 72 JCL 537) as well as a defendant who foresaw a very real risk of death, such as one who set fire to a block of flats at night. According to Rogers (2006): 'The law of involuntary manslaughter is also too broad insofar as it currently equates cases which are not far short of murder, such as those defendants who firebomb houses in order to scare . . . with cases which (absent the misfortune of death) would ordinarily be nothing more than assaults'. Similarly, gross negligence manslaughter contains a broad and objectively assessed requirement that the defendant's conduct is 'so bad in all the circumstances as to amount . . . to a criminal act or omission' (*Adomako* [1995] 1 AC 171). These broad offences are also accompanied by a third head of subjectively reckless manslaughter. Although a subjectively reckless killing is arguably more culpable than killing by gross negligence, both are currently sufficient for manslaughter, demonstrating further incoherence in the present framework of offences.

Thus, it is evident that the law of homicide has been governed by a mixture of common law and statute, none of which has been coherent and systematic. The law has developed in a piecemeal way; one example is the development of the defence of provocation (now loss of control). The current broad homicide offences are in need of reform so that a more coherent framework of offences might be established. The Law Commission's recommendations for reform involve extending these two current offences into three offences, and they provide a sensible hierarchy of offences, which 'relates to the principles of fair and representative labelling' (see Rogers)[8]. However, while the recommendations of the Law Commission are favoured by academics, Parliament has yet to make any significant movement towards reform.

[8] This sentence identifies a key objective which the reforms aim to achieve.

✓ **Make your answer stand out**

- You could critically evaluate the Law Commission's recommendation that duress may amount to a partial defence to first degree murder.
- You could consider the practical implications on plea bargaining and the argument that the proposed structure would provide defendants with more incentive to maintain a not guilty plea to first degree murder and prosecutors with more incentive to accept a guilty plea to second degree murder.
- You should refer to further academic writing on the recommendations, such as Wilson, W. (2006) The structure of criminal homicide. Crim LR 471; and Ashworth, A. (2007) Principles, pragmatism and the Law Commission's recommendations on homicide law reform. Crim LR 333.
- You might offer a comparative view of the structure of homicide offences in other common law countries such as the USA, Australia, Canada, and New Zealand.

! Don't be tempted to . . .

- Simply set out the current law on murder and manslaughter – you are being asked specifically about the framework of homicide offences and reform.
- Use this question as an excuse to just 'rant' about the law of homicide. Instead, you must provide a structured critique of the structure of homicide offences and the proposed reforms.
- Focus on just one element of murder or manslaughter. This question is looking for a much wider appreciation of the scope of murder and manslaughter and their relationship.

@ Try it yourself

Now take a look at the question below and attempt to answer it. You can check your response against the answer guidance available on the companion website (**www.pearsoned.co.uk/lawexpressqa**).

To what extent, if at all, does the phrase 'malice aforethought' reflect the modern day expression of the mens rea of murder?

---

www.pearsoned.co.uk/lawexpressqa

 Go online to access more revision support including additional essay and problem questions with diagram plans, You be the marker questions, and download all diagrams from the book.

Voluntary manslaughter

3

How this topic may come up in exams

Voluntary manslaughter lends itself well to both essay and problem questions. As the law on loss of control and diminished responsibility continues to develop after the enactment of the Coroners and Justice Act 2009, this is a ripe area for an essay question requiring a critical evaluation of the defence of loss of control and a comparison with the common law defence of provocation. Similarly, an essay question might require consideration of the reforms of diminished responsibility, or even of partial defences more generally. Alternatively, examiners may favour a problem question which deals with one or both partial defences.

■ Before you begin

It's a good idea to consider the following key themes of voluntary manslaughter before tackling a question on this topic.

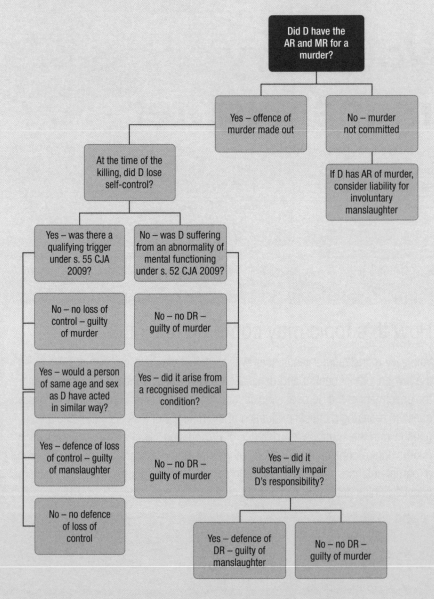

A printable version of this diagram is available from **www.pearsoned.co.uk/lawexpressqa**

❓ Question 1

Valerie has been suffering from dementia for the past 10 years. Her son, Damian, has been looking after her during this time and in recent years his role has become more one of carer. Valerie is bed bound and needs help to undertake all tasks of daily life, including washing, eating, and using the toilet. Seeing his mother in this state has been very upsetting for Damian and the emotional strain on him has been significant, as he has devoted more and more time to looking after his mother. He has recently been diagnosed with depression. He has also been drinking a lot more than usual and this is becoming a problem as he is finding it almost impossible to avoid drinking to get him through the day.

One evening, after Damian has had a stressful day at work, he goes round to his mother's house and discovers that she is having one of her bad days. She is very confused and doesn't recognise her son. She repeatedly asks Damian who he is over and over again. He finds that she is also being quite stubborn and she refuses to allow him to put her to bed. Damian becomes very frustrated with Valerie and loses his patience. He has a few drinks to calm himself down before he tries again to put her to bed. However, she resists and starts to shout at him. Eventually, Damian snaps and he strangles Valerie to death.

Damian is charged with murder. Discuss the likelihood of Damian's defence of loss of control being successful.

Answer plan

→ Outline the effect of a successful plea of loss of control.

→ Assess the legal and evidential burdens.

→ Discuss the elements of loss of control.

→ Did Damian suffer a loss of control?

→ Was there a qualifying trigger?

→ To what extent, if at all, can Damian's intoxication be taken into account?

→ Assess whether a person of Damian's sex and age, with a normal degree of tolerance and self-restraint and in the circumstances of Damian, might have reacted in the same or a similar way to Damian.

Diagram plan

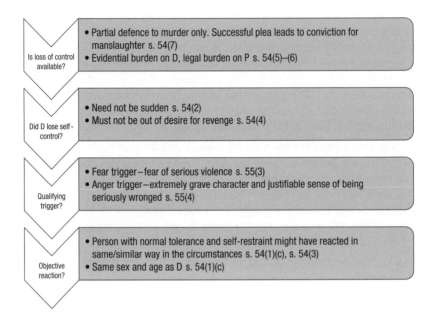

Is loss of control available?	• Partial defence to murder only. Successful plea leads to conviction for manslaughter s. 54(7) • Evidential burden on D, legal burden on P s. 54(5)–(6)
Did D lose self-control?	• Need not be sudden s. 54(2) • Must not be out of desire for revenge s. 54(4)
Qualifying trigger?	• Fear trigger – fear of serious violence s. 55(3) • Anger trigger – extremely grave character and justifiable sense of being seriously wronged s. 55(4)
Objective reaction?	• Person with normal tolerance and self-restraint might have reacted in same/similar way in the circumstances s. 54(1)(c), s. 54(3) • Same sex and age as D s. 54(1)(c)

A printable version of this diagram plan is available from **www.pearsoned.co.uk/lawexpressqa**

Answer

[1] This statement demonstrates that you have picked up on the fact that the focus of the question is the defence of loss of control and not the offence of murder.

[2] Show the examiner that you have a wider understanding of practical issues such as who bears the evidential burden and who bears the legal burden.

[3] Adopt a logical and clear structure. State that there are three elements and then deal with each one in turn.

Loss of control is a statutory defence which was created by section 54(1) of the Coroners and Justice Act 2009 (CJA 2009). It is a defence to murder only and it is a partial defence to murder, which, if successful, reduces liability to manslaughter (s. 54(7)). Since Damian is charged with murder, he may plead loss of control.[1] While the defendant bears the evidential burden to adduce evidence with respect to the defence (s. 54(6)), the legal burden of disproving the defence beyond reasonable doubt rests with the prosecution (s. 54(5)). It is for the trial judge to decide whether there is sufficient evidence to leave the defence to the jury: *Dawes; Hatter; Bowyer* [2013] EWCA Crim 322.[2]

Under section 54(1), there are three main elements of the defence of loss of control:[3] (a) at the time of the killing, Damian must have suffered a loss of self-control; (b) the loss of control must have had a qualifying trigger under section 55; and (c) someone of the same age and sex as Damian, with a normal degree of tolerance and self-restraint and in the circumstances of Damian, might have reacted in the same or a similar way to Damian.

The first element to consider is whether there was a loss of self-control. This is subjectively assessed – the key question is whether, in strangling Valerie, Damian lost self-control. It is clear on the facts that Damian finally snapped after becoming very frustrated with Valerie, and this is evidence that Damian did indeed lose self-control.[4] However, at some point between the initial triggering event that frustrates Damian and the attack, Damian had a few drinks. This raises the question of whether there was a delay between the trigger and the killing, and this may in turn depend upon what exactly constitutes the trigger. Whereas the old common law defence of provocation required that the loss of self-control be 'sudden and temporary' (**Duffy** [1949] 1 All ER 932),[5] under the CJA 2009, 'it does not matter whether or not the loss of control was sudden' (s. 54(2)). Thus, any delay would not be relevant. Under section 54(4), the defence will not be available if Damian 'acted in a considered desire for revenge'. This is consistent with the old common law which precluded the defence of provocation where the defendant had planned an attack out of revenge: **Ibrams** [1981] 74 Cr App R 154. The delay might be suggestive of planned revenge and if Damian is acting out of revenge, rather than as a result of a loss of self-control, the defence will not be available to him. However, in the circumstances he is likely to be able to counter the suggestion that he is acting in revenge. He will claim that he lost control after becoming frustrated at his mother's condition and conduct on that evening.

If there is sufficient evidence of a loss of self-control for the defence to be left to the jury (**Dawes; Hatter; Bowyer**), the next question to consider is whether there is a qualifying trigger under section 55. There are two types of qualifying trigger under the CJA 2009 and either one or a combination of both of them is sufficient for loss of control (s. 55(5)). The first is the 'fear trigger' under section 55(3), which applies where Damian's 'loss of self-control was attributable to his fear of serious violence' from Valerie against Damian.[6] This clearly does not apply in this case as there is no evidence on the facts that Damian feared violence from Valerie. This trigger will not apply here.

[4] Use the facts to apply the law to this specific problem scenario.

[5] This demonstrates an awareness of how the old defence of provocation and the new defence of loss of control differ.

[6] Deal with each type of qualifying trigger in turn, setting out the law and then applying it to the facts of the scenario.

[7] Use a new paragraph to deal with the second type of trigger in order to ensure your answer is easy to read.

The second trigger is the 'anger trigger',[7] which is 'attributable to a thing or things done or said (or both) which (a) constituted circumstances of an extremely grave character, and (b) caused [Damian] to have a justifiable sense of being seriously wronged' (s. 55(4)). If Damian relies on his mother's conduct caused by her condition as 'circumstances of an extremely grave character' which 'caused him to have a justifiable sense of being seriously wronged', he is unlikely to be successful in his plea of loss of control. The facts of this case are very similar to the case of **Zebedee** [2013] 1 Cr App R (S) 200, in the sense that this case also involved a defendant who killed his elderly father because of his frustration with his dementia. The jury in this case rejected the defendant's defence of loss of control, presumably on the basis that the circumstances were not 'extremely grave' in character. Thus, it is likely that a jury in Damian's case would reject the defence of loss of control on the same basis.[8]

[8] Ensure that you rely on recent authorities, especially where they are factually similar, but demonstrate your understanding that this case only offers guidance (and is not a binding authority) on the meaning of 'extremely grave'.

The third element of loss of control requires that someone of the same age and sex as Damian, with a normal degree of tolerance and self-restraint and in the same circumstances as Damian, might have reacted in the same or a similar way. This follows the approach taken in respect of the common law in **DPP v Camplin** [1978] 2 All ER 168 and **A-G for Jersey v Holley** [2005] UKPC 23 and is objectively assessed.[9] The age and sex of the defendant may be taken into account. Thus, the question is whether a man of Damian's age, with normal levels of tolerance and self-restraint but placed in the same circumstances as Damian, might have reacted in the same way or, at the very least, in a similar way.[10] According to section 54(3), the phrase 'all the circumstances' within section 54(1)(c) does not refer to circumstances which are relevant to the defendant's 'general capacity for tolerance and self-restraint'. Thus, characteristics which go to the gravity of the provocation are relevant, but characteristics which go to the level of control to be expected of the defendant are not to be taken into account. The Court of Appeal recently confirmed in **Asmelash** [2013] 1 Cr App R 449, that voluntary intoxication is not a characteristic which is relevant to the level of control to be expected of the defendant. Thus, Damian's intoxication may not be taken into account as a control characteristic, i.e. Damian's response must be measured against a sober person of normal tolerance and self-restraint.

[9] This sentence demonstrates that you understand how the CJA 2009 has developed from the old common law defence of provocation.

[10] Rephrase the law so as to show how it will be applied in this scenario.

In conclusion, Damian's defence of loss of control is unlikely to be successful since he is unlikely to satisfy the requirement of a qualifying trigger.

✓ Make your answer stand out

- You should demonstrate very good knowledge of the new statutory provisions under sections 54 and 55 of the CJA 2009 and the way in which these provisions are applied.
- You should also refer to relevant cases relating to the old common law defence of provocation as the courts may refer to these cases in interpreting the new legislation.
- You should refer to any new cases on loss of control that are relevant, such as *Gurpinar; Kojo-Smith* [2015] EWCA Crim 178 and *McDonald* [2016] EWCA Crim 1529.
- You could make reference to journal articles on the CJA 2009 and academic opinion on how the defence will work in practice or any problems that might arise, provided this is relevant to the particular facts in the question.
- You could also explain in further detail the meaning of the evidential burden being upon the defendant – see section 54(6), CJA 2009.

! Don't be tempted to . . .

- Waste time discussing whether the elements of murder are satisfied. The question tells you that Damian has been charged with murder and specifically asks you about the *defence* of loss of control, so you should focus on this. You must ensure that you read the instruction line carefully.
- Focus solely on explaining and applying the old law. You should refer to the old common law defence of provocation to demonstrate your knowledge of how the law has changed, and you must incorporate the legislation on loss of control.

? Question 2

Sid and Kavita have been living together for five years. Their relationship has always been a passionate but volatile one. Sid is a jealous man and he does not like Kavita having any male friends. Both Sid and Kavita are taking medication for depression. Kavita is frustrated by Sid's jealousy. She used to have a few male friends, but she has lost contact with most of them since being with Sid as he does not approve of her meeting up with them. Kavita confides in her one remaining male friend, Andrew.

After an argument with Kavita, Sid storms out of their house. Kavita calls Andrew and he comes round to comfort her. Sid goes to the pub. After several stiff drinks, Sid returns to the house and he finds Kavita in an embrace with Andrew. Sid grabs a poker from the fireplace and surges forward, striking Kavita round the head with the poker. The blow kills Kavita.

Consider Sid's criminal liability for the death of Kavita.

Answer plan

➡ Examine the elements of murder and whether Sid can be charged with this offence.

➡ Discuss the likelihood that Sid will successfully be able to plead loss of control under section 54, CJA 2009.

➡ Could Sid plead diminished responsibility under section 2(1), Homicide Act 1957?

Diagram plan

Elements of murder?	Defence of loss of control?	Defence of diminished responsibility?
• **Actus reus of murder:** Did Sid unlawfully cause Kavita's death? • **Mens rea of murder:** Did Sid have the intention to kill or cause GBH?	• Sufficiency of evidence? • Evidential burden on Sid • **Components of loss of control:** 1. Did Sid suffer a loss of self-control? 2. Was there a qualifying trigger? 3. Might someone of Sid's sex and age with a normal degree of tolerance and self-restraint and in the circumstances of Sid, have reacted in the same or a similar way?	• Burden of proof on Sid • **Components of diminished responsibility:** 1. Did Sid suffer an abnormality of mental functioning? 2. Was this caused by a recognised medical condition? 3. Did it substantially impair Sid's ability to understand the nature of his conduct, or form a rational judgement, or exercise self-control? 4. Does it provide an explanation for Sid's conduct in killing Kavita?

A printable version of this diagram plan is available from **www.pearsoned.co.uk/lawexpressqa**

Answer

[1] As the question does not specify an offence with which Sid has been charged but asks you to consider his liability, you should begin by identifying the offence he will likely be charged with.

As Sid has killed Kavita, he will most likely be charged with her murder.[1] Sid is both the factual and legal cause of Kavita's death. 'But for' his actions, she would not have died (*White* [1910] 2 KB 124) and his actions were an operating and substantial cause of her death

[2] This sentence applies the rules of causation succinctly and is all that you need bearing in mind the number of issues in the question and the fact that causation is not really controversial here.

[3] This sentence shows that you understand the implications of a successful plea of these defences.

(*Smith* [1959] 2 QB 35).[2] The mens rea for murder will be established by evidence of Sid's act of striking Kavita round the head with a poker. This demonstrates an intention to cause GBH, and possibly an intention to kill, thus it seems most likely that Sid would be charged with murder. However, he may plead the partial defences of loss of control or diminished responsibility. These are both statutory defences and they are defences to murder only. If Sid is successful in pleading either loss of control or diminished responsibility, he will be convicted of manslaughter instead of murder.[3]

Loss of control is a partial defence under section 54(1) of the Coroners and Justice Act 2009 (CJA 2009). There are three main elements of the defence of loss of control: (a) at the time of the killing, Sid must have suffered a loss of self-control; (b) the loss of control must have had a qualifying trigger under section 55; and (c) someone of the same age and sex as Sid, with a normal degree of tolerance and self-restraint and in the circumstances of Sid, might have reacted in the same or a similar way to Sid. Sid will bear the evidential burden to adduce evidence with respect to the defence. This means that he must adduce sufficient evidence 'to raise an issue with respect to the defence . . . which, in the opinion of the trial judge, a jury, properly directed, could reasonably conclude that the defence might apply' (s. 54(6)). After the evidence has been adduced, the trial judge will consider whether the evidential burden has been met: *Dawes; Hatter; Bowyer* [2013] EWCA Crim 322. The trial judge will consider each component of the defence separately and sequentially, and if there is insufficient evidence of one component, the defence will not be left to the jury: *Gurpinar; Kojo-Smith* [2015] EWCA Crim 178. The legal burden of disproving the defence beyond reasonable doubt rests with the prosecution (s. 54(5)).

The first element requires proof that Sid suffered a loss of self-control. This is subjectively assessed. There is certainly evidence of a loss of self-control. There is no delay between the trigger and Sid's act of striking her with the poker, and in fact under the CJA 2009, 'it does not matter whether or not the loss of control was sudden' (s. 54(2)). Sid's defence would be negated by any evidence that he 'acted in a considered desire for revenge' (s. 54(4)). While it could be argued that Sid might have been planning a revenge attack in the pub, there is unlikely to be such evidence here as Sid did not know that Andrew was with Kavita.

If there is a loss of control, it must also be shown that there is a qualifying trigger under section 55. Under section 55(5), CJA 2009 either the 'fear trigger' or the 'anger trigger' or both is sufficient for the defence of loss of control. The 'fear trigger' (s. 55(3)) applies if Sid's 'loss of self-control was attributable to [his] fear of serious violence'. There is no evidence of Sid fearing violence at all in this scenario, so the fear trigger will not apply.

The 'anger trigger' is one which is 'attributable to a thing or things done or said (or both) which (a) constituted circumstances of an extremely grave character, and (b) caused [Sid] to have a justifiable sense of being seriously wronged' (s. 55(4)). It is not clear what exactly constitutes things said and done of an extremely grave character, which cause a justifiable sense of being seriously wronged. If Kavita's act of embracing Andrew is of 'extremely grave character' and caused Sid a 'justifiable sense of being seriously wronged' could it be said that the 'anger trigger' applies? These terms have not been defined under the CJA 2009. On a subjective assessment, the embrace might be of extremely grave character to Andrew in light of his jealous nature. He probably also felt seriously wronged, but the trigger would only be satisfied if this was objectively justifiable. This is unlikely. The nature of the embrace is not clear on the facts. If it was a passionate embrace, it might be regarded as 'sexual infidelity' for the purposes of s. 55(6)(c) of the CJA 2009. However, this term is also not defined within the Act: **Clinton** [2012] EWCA Crim 2. If it is regarded as 'sexual infidelity', then it should be disregarded in determining whether there is a qualifying trigger. This is likely to leave Sid without a qualifying trigger.

In the event that a trigger can be established, the third element of loss of control requires that someone of the same age and sex as Sid, with a normal degree of tolerance and self-restraint and in the same circumstances as Sid, might have reacted in the same or a similar way. This element is objectively assessed and only the age and sex of the defendant may be taken into account, along with the circumstances of the defendant which do not bear on the defendant's 'general capacity for tolerance and self-restraint' (s. 54(3)).

[4] Ensure that you notice any characteristics that are mentioned within the question and explain whether these will be taken into account and why.

Thus, the fact that Sid suffers from depression will not be a relevant consideration, as he is expected to exercise the level of control of a person of his age and sex of normal tolerance and self-restraint.[4] The defence of loss of control is unlikely to be successful.

[5] Show the examiner that you understand that the CJA 2009 does not create a new defence but merely amends the existing defence under section 2(1), HA 1957.

However, there is another partial defence open to Sid, that of diminished responsibility under section 2(1) of the Homicide Act 1957 (HA 1957) (as amended by section 52 of the CJA 2009).[5] Unlike the defence of loss of control, the burden of proving diminished responsibility is on the defence (s. 2(2), HA 1957) and the elements of diminished responsibility must be proved on a balance of probabilities (*Dunbar* [1958] 1 QB 1). The defendant must prove that at the time of the killing: (i) he was suffering from an abnormality of mental functioning, (ii) which arose from a recognised medical condition (s. 2(1)(a)), (iii) substantially impairing the defendant's ability to understand the nature of his conduct, to form a rational judgement, or to exercise self-control (s. 2(1)(b) and s. 2(1A)), and (iv) which provides an explanation for the defendant's acts and omissions in the killing (s. 2(1)(c)). On the facts, Sid is suffering from depression, which does constitute an abnormality of mental functioning arising from a recognised medical condition (*Seers* (1984) 79 Cr App R 261).[6] Medical evidence is required to satisfy this element: *Bunch* [2013] EWCA Crim 2498. It is likely that the defence will be able to prove that this substantially impaired Sid's ability to form a rational judgement or to exercise self-control. According to *Brown* [2012] 2 Cr App R (S) 27, the impairment need only be more than minimal, and in *Ramchurn* [2010] 2 Cr App R 3, it was held that it need not extinguish the defendant's mental responsibility. However, in *Golds* [2016] UKSC 61, it was held that a judge should not explain the word 'substantial' to the jury, but if asked, the judge should convey to the jury that it is an ordinary English word and that they should use their collective good sense in applying it. Finally, under section 2(1B), this will provide an explanation for Sid's conduct in striking Kavita with the poker if it causes, or is a significant contributory factor in causing, him to carry out that conduct. On the facts, the defence of diminished responsibility is likely to be successful.

[6] Use existing case law to support your argument that depression amounts to an abnormality of mental functioning.

[7] Use the conclusion to briefly summarise the issues, but do not regurgitate your arguments all over again.

In conclusion,[7] Sid caused the death of Kavita and had the requisite mens rea for murder. He is more likely to be successful with a plea of diminished responsibility.

Make your answer stand out

■ Ensure that you adopt an appropriate and clear structure. You should deal with offences before looking at the elements of the possible defences.

■ If you are not permitted to take your statute book into the exam with you, you should learn the important parts of the statutory provisions so that you can quote from the relevant sections. If you are permitted a statute book in the exam, you should still ensure that you are familiar with the sections to save yourself time in the exam.

■ Ensure that you understand the effect of the new law under the CJA 2009 to both defences. While the CJA 2009 created the defence of loss of control (abolishing provocation), it merely amends the HA 1957 in respect of diminished responsibility.

■ Refer to case law where appropriate. In order to do this, you will need to be familiar with the various principles which have remained the same and those which have changed as a result of the 2009 Act.

! **Don't be tempted to . . .**

■ Spend too much time setting out the definition and elements of murder, and do not labour over the rules of causation as they are relatively uncontroversial here and there are many other more important issues to discuss.

■ Make the mistake of using this question as a forum for comparing the old and the new law, although you do need to show an awareness of the old law. This is a problem question and you are expected to explain how the current law will affect the defendant in this case.

Question 3

Critically evaluate the defence of loss of control. To what extent has the defence improved the law?

Answer plan

→ Consider the rationale behind the reforms and the abolition of the defence of provocation.

→ Discuss the subjective requirement of a loss of control which need not be sudden.

→ Refer to the new requirement of a qualifying trigger.

→ Examine the specific exclusion of sexual infidelity as a qualifying trigger and the case of *Clinton* [2012] EWCA Crim 2.

➡ Discuss the objective question which takes into account the age, sex and circumstances of the defendant.

➡ Evaluate academic opinion on the new defence.

Diagram plan

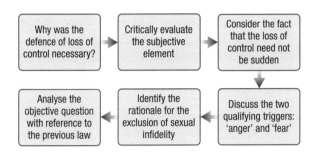

A printable version of this diagram plan is available from **www.pearsoned.co.uk/lawexpressqa**

Answer

The Coroners and Justice Act 2009 made fundamental changes to the partial defences to murder. Section 54(1) created a new partial defence of loss of control and section 56 abolished the old common law defence of provocation and repealed section 3 of the Homicide Act 1957. The defence of provocation has always been the subject of criticism. The subjective limb of the defence, which required proof that the defendant suffered a 'sudden and temporary' loss of self-control (**Duffy** [1949] 1 All ER 932), was criticised for failing to protect women in abusive relationships who lashed out as a result of a relatively minor incident of provoking conduct (the 'last straw').[1] There was no guarantee that women suffering from 'battered woman syndrome' would be able to successfully rely upon the defence where there was a delay between the provoking conduct and the killing, and such women would often be left with no choice but to plead diminished responsibility (**Ahluwalia** [1992] 4 All ER 889). The objective limb of the defence has caused the courts considerable confusion for over 60 years, although the situation intensified in recent years with conflicting House of Lords and Privy Council decisions in **Smith (Morgan James)** [2000] 4 All ER 289 and **A-G for Jersey v Holley**

[1] Having stated that the old law has been criticised, this sentence explains some of the problems with the subjective limb of the old law.

[2] This sentence demonstrates your awareness of some of the problems with the objective limb.

[3] You should show the examiner that you are aware of the reasons for the reforms.

[2005] UKPC 23.[2] Therefore, these reforms were intended to redress the gender imbalance and clarify the law,[3] hopefully putting an end to the criticism and confusion. However, in its short life to date, the new defence of loss of control has already been the subject of academic criticism.

According to section 54(1), the defence of loss of control contains three elements: (i) the defendant's acts or omissions in doing the killing resulted from the defendant's loss of self-control; (ii) the loss of self-control had a qualifying trigger; and (iii) a person of the defendant's sex and age, with a normal degree of tolerance and self-restraint and in the circumstances of the defendant, might have reacted in the same or a similar way.

[4] Include academic commentary to show that you have read more than just your textbook.

The first element contains the subjective question: whether the defendant actually lost self-control. Under the new law, there is no requirement that the loss of control was sudden (s. 54(2)). Leigh argues that[4] 'The implications of this are obscure . . . One can readily see how cumulative abuse might lead to a loss of self-control, but the notion of loss of self-control as such does rather suggest a sudden point of explosion'. (Leigh, L. (2010) Two new partial defences to murder. 174 JPN 53). The purpose of the removal of the requirement of suddenness was to protect those who have suffered cumulative abuse, who react after a minor incident (the 'last straw', as in **Humphreys** [1995] 4 All ER 889). This provision is a peculiar addition to a defence dealing with 'loss of control' because, as Leigh points out: 'It is . . . difficult to see how a killing that does not involve a sudden loss of control involves a loss of control at all'.

[5] This sentence shows you are able to compare both the old and new law and evaluate the new defence.

Section 54(4) stipulates that the defence does not apply if the defendant killed the victim 'in a considered desire for revenge'. This is similar to the case of **Ibrams** [1981] 74 Cr App R 154, which precluded the defence of provocation where the killing was a pre-planned revenge attack; however, one question which remains unanswered is the meaning of 'considered'.[5] Leigh questions 'what degree of deliberation is required in order to exclude [the defence]'. This will be a question for the jury to determine on a case-by-case basis.

The second requirement is that the loss of control has a qualifying trigger. Section 55 specifies two types of qualifying trigger which are based upon highly emotional states: the first is the 'fear trigger' under section 55(3), which applies where the 'loss of self-control

This demonstrates a wider knowledge of the comparative rules relating to general defences in criminal law.

was attributable to [the defendant's] fear of serious violence' from the victim against the defendant or another identified person. This trigger is similar to self-defence; however, unlike self-defence, it is not available if the defendant was the initial aggressor (s. 55(6)(a)).[6] The second trigger is the 'anger trigger', which is 'attributable to a thing or things done or said (or both) which (a) constituted circumstances of an extremely grave character, and (b) caused [the defendant] to have a justifiable sense of being seriously wronged' (s. 55(4)). Either of these qualifying triggers will be sufficient, or a combination of both of them. It is also notable that the key phrases within these provisions ('serious violence', 'extremely grave character' and 'justifiable sense of being seriously wronged') have not been further defined under the Act and will be left open to interpretation by the courts. In *Zebedee* [2013] 1 Cr App R (S) 200, the jury rejected the defence where the defendant killed his elderly father who suffered from dementia and incontinence. The defendant relied upon the anger trigger, arguing that the frustration of caring for his father caused him to lose his self-control. It must be presumed that the jury was not satisfied that this constituted 'circumstances of an extremely grave character'. Section 55 marks a significant departure from the old law which was much less restrictive in terms of the provoking words or conduct permitted. It seems rather odd that cases such as *Doughty* (1986) 83 Cr App R 319 will no longer be protected by the new defence.[7]

[7] Using an example is an effective way of demonstrating how these reforms will affect the law.

One highly controversial provision is section 55(6)(c), which states that, in determining whether there was a qualifying trigger, sexual infidelity is to be disregarded. The Court of Appeal has recently ruled that while sexual infidelity must be disregarded as a qualifying trigger, it may be considered as part of the contextual background to a case where there is another potential qualifying trigger (*Clinton* [2012] EWCA Crim 2). Section 55(6)(c) was introduced in order to preclude husbands who kill their unfaithful wives from relying upon the defence. This provision was strongly contested in the House of Commons and the government's arguments have been labelled as 'incoherent' (Leigh (2010)). It is difficult to see why sexual infidelity (something which is likely to incite a highly emotional reaction) may not constitute a qualifying trigger, while words spoken of a highly offensive or insulting nature may.[8] The government's objective in ensuring gender equality could be said to have swung too far the other way as a result of this provision.

[8] This sentence provides support for the opinion of the author which is expressed in the next sentence. Ensure that you express the reasons for your opinion.

The final element of loss of control is the objective question which calls for consideration of the reasonableness of the defendant's response. In line with **DPP v Camplin** [1978] 2 All ER 168, only two subjective characteristics can be taken into account: sex and age. However, as Norrie points out, 'it is unclear what role "sex" should play' (Norrie, A. (2010) The Coroners and Justice Act 2009 – partial defences to murder (1) Loss of control. Crim LR 275). Norrie observes that there is no explanation as to how exactly sex is thought to affect the capacity for self-control. Leigh (2010) states that 'The reference to sex . . . reflects anachronistic views' and argues that 'The relevant factors seem to lie in . . . the relative size and strength of the parties and the existence or not of a state of dependency . . .' Norrie also criticises the reference to age: 'Capacity for self-control is indeed an aspect of maturity, but age is not then the main issue, maturity is'.[9] Thus, problems are also evident with the 'objective' question. The courts have recently confirmed that voluntary intoxication is not a factor which may be taken into account in consideration of the objective question under section 54(1)(c): **Asmelash** [2013] 1 Cr App R 449. Although the CJA 2009 may have clarified the law in some respects, the new defence of loss of control is open to significant criticisms and has arguably shifted the 'gender balance' too far.[10]

[9] This paragraph contains several references to academic opinion. You will gain marks for crediting the relevant author with their academic opinion as this shows that you are widely read. You run the risk of falling foul of allegations of plagiarism if you do not reference properly.

[10] Ensure that you link your conclusion back to the title and briefly summarise your view.

✓ **Make your answer stand out**

- You should read the House of Commons debates in *Hansard* and incorporate the arguments put forward by Claire Ward MP for the government and Dominic Grieve QC MP in opposition into your answer.

- You could also incorporate references to recommendations made by the Law Commission in 2005 and consider the extent to which these reflect the current law.

- You should discuss the theoretical justifications behind the reforms. See Norrie, A. (2010) The Coroners and Justice Act 2009 – partial defences to murder (1) Loss of control. Crim LR 275 for a detailed discussion.

- You must discuss the old law on provocation as part of your answer as you need to be able to compare and contrast the old and new law.

- Discuss in more detail the ways in which the new law has improved the law, by creating clarity.

! Don't be tempted to . . .

- Spend a disproportionate amount of time discussing the old law and previous cases because you must also show the examiner that you are familiar with the new law.
- Merely set out the new and old law in a narrative fashion. You are required to critically evaluate the new law and this requires you to demonstrate that you are aware of the problems with the old law as well as improvements made by the new law and any problematic areas that you foresee might arise with the new law.

@ Try it yourself

Now take a look at the question below and attempt to answer it. You can check your response against the answer guidance available on the companion website (**www.pearsoned.co.uk/lawexpressqa**).

> Kate and Sandra, both aged 35, are best friends who have known each other since very young. They decide to go on a weekend break with a group of other friends. On the first evening of the weekend break, after a few drinks, Kate and Sandra begin to argue about a man that Kate has been seeing. Kate suffers from depression and paranoia and accuses Sandra of sleeping with him. Sandra responds, 'So what if I have?'. Two hours later that evening, Kate strikes Sandra over the head with a full champagne bottle, killing her.
>
> Discuss Kate's liability for Sandra's death.

www.pearsoned.co.uk/lawexpressqa

 Go online to access more revision support including additional essay and problem questions with diagram plans, You be the marker questions, and download all diagrams from the book.

Involuntary manslaughter

4

How this topic may come up in exams

Forms of involuntary manslaughter, such as unlawful act manslaughter, reckless manslaughter and gross negligence manslaughter, are popular with examiners and often appear in exam papers in problem scenarios. A problem question would expect you to identify the relevant offences and apply the elements of the offence to the facts in the question. An essay question could ask for a critical evaluation of any offence of involuntary manslaughter. Corporate manslaughter is a popular topic for essay questions.

■ Before you begin

It's a good idea to consider the following key themes of involuntary manslaughter before tackling a question on this topic.

A printable version of this diagram is available from **www.pearsoned.co.uk/lawexpressqa**

🔹 Question 1

Sam and Jack, both aged 12, are best friends. They spend a lot of time together at Sam's house playing the latest video games that Sam's older brother manages to get pre-release. One day, Sam invites Jack round to his house to play on 'Fist Fight 2', the long-awaited sequel to the best-selling 'Fist Fight'. Sam's older brother has given Sam a pre-release copy of the game and both Sam and Jack are very excited about trying it out. After an hour of playing the game, Sam and Jack get into an argument which eventually turns into a physical fight. Jack wrestles Sam to the floor and sits on top of him, shouting at him and punching him. At this moment, Sam's mother walks past and sees Sam and Jack fighting, but she ignores them. Sam manages to wriggle free and he punches Jack on the side of the head, knocking him unconscious.

Jack is taken to hospital and regains consciousness on arrival, but he complains about a headache and is dizzy and confused. The doctor treating Jack just gives him a paracetamol and sends him home. He doesn't perform any other tests and fails to diagnose that Jack is suffering from an internal bleed on the brain. A day later, Jack dies from a haemorrhage.

Discuss the criminal liability of the parties for the death of Jack.

Answer plan

➜ Consider Sam's liability for unlawful act manslaughter in respect of the punch to Jack's head and whether the doctor's conduct breaks the chain of causation.

➜ Consider the liability of Sam's mother for gross negligence manslaughter in respect of Jack's death and whether the doctor's conduct breaks the chain of causation.

➜ Examine the doctor's liability for gross negligence manslaughter in respect of Jack's death.

Diagram plan

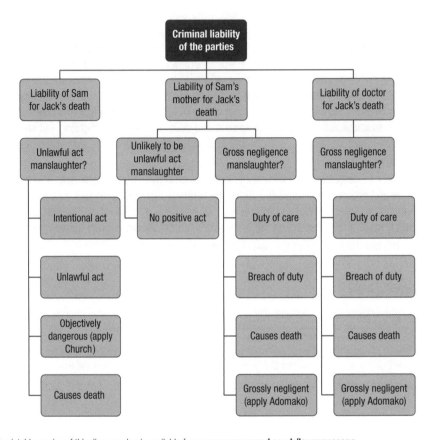

A printable version of this diagram plan is available from **www.pearsoned.co.uk/lawexpressqa**

[1] These sentences demonstrate that you understand the distinction between murder and involuntary manslaughter, and explain why you are ruling out murder here.

[2] As the question specifically asks you to consider the parties' liability for the death, there is no need to consider other offences (apart from those that constitute the unlawful act in unlawful act manslaughter).

Answer

Since Sam, Sam's mother and the doctor did not intend to kill or cause GBH to Jack, they will not be guilty of his murder (**Vickers** [1957] 2 QB 664).[1] When the mens rea of murder cannot be established, involuntary manslaughter[2] is charged.

Sam's liability re Jack's death

Sam might be guilty of unlawful act manslaughter. This offence was defined in **Larkin** [1944] 29 Cr App R 18: there must be an intentional act, which is unlawful, objectively dangerous and which

³ Set out the elements of the offence at the beginning of the paragraph and then deal with each element in turn.

causes death³ (Lord Salmon, **DPP v Newbury & Jones** [1977] AC 50). Thus, the first element that the prosecution must prove is that Sam intentionally did an act. This must be a positive act and not an omission: **Lowe** [1976] QB 702. Sam's act of punching Jack in the head is intentional.

Secondly, the act must be unlawful in the sense that it must constitute a criminal offence: **Franklin** [1883] 15 Cox CC 163. The criminal act here is a battery. Both the actus reus and mens rea elements of the unlawful act must be established: **Lamb** [1967] 2 QB 981. Battery is a common law offence, and the elements are satisfied. Sam commits a battery because he intentionally inflicts unlawful force on Jack by punching him in the head.⁴

⁴ This sentence is the application which shows that the unlawful act element is satisfied.

⁵ This is a key quote which you should learn.

The third element of unlawful act manslaughter is that the act must be objectively dangerous. The test comes from the case of **Church** [1966] 1 QB 59, in which it was stated that 'the unlawful act must be such as all sober and reasonable people would inevitably recognise must subject the other person to, at least, the risk of some harm . . . albeit not serious harm' (Edmund Davies J).⁵ Thus, the question is whether the reasonable person would recognise that punching someone in the head would subject a person to some harm. This is likely satisfied. It does not matter that Sam is not an adult – he is to be assessed against the standard of the reasonable adult.

⁶ Do not forget to apply the tests for causation and look out for a break in the chain of causation. Apply the relevant tests succinctly.

Finally, it must be proved that the battery caused death. The usual rules of causation apply. Applying the test for factual causation: but for Sam's act of punching Jack, he would not have died: **White** [1910] 2 KB 124. In terms of legal causation, Sam's act of battery was a more than minimal cause of Jack's death: **Cato** [1976] 1 WLR 110, but the issue of the doctor's negligence in failing to diagnose the severity of Jack's injuries must be explored. Negligent medical treatment will rarely constitute a *novus actus interveniens*; it will not break the chain of causation unless the doctor's negligence was so independent of Sam's acts and so potent in causing death that it renders Sam's acts insignificant: **Cheshire** [1991] 1 WLR 844.⁶ Thus, Sam is likely to be guilty of unlawful act manslaughter.

Liability of Sam's mother re Jack's death

Sam's mother may also be liable for manslaughter in respect of Jack's death because she sees the fight between the boys and chooses to ignore it. Since unlawful act manslaughter requires a positive act and is not satisfied by an omission (*Lowe*), she will probably not be guilty of unlawful act manslaughter because she doesn't perform a positive act in respect of Jack's death. However, she may be convicted of gross negligence manslaughter instead. In order to establish gross negligence manslaughter, the prosecution would need to prove that Sam's mother owed Jack a duty of care, that she breached this duty, that the breach caused Jack's death and that her act or omission was grossly negligent: *Adomako* [1995] 1 AC 171.

The question of whether Sam's mother owed Jack a duty of care is a question of law (*Willoughby* [2004] EWCA Crim 3365 and *Evans* [2009] EWCA Crim 650). The judge will direct the jury as to the law and explain that a duty will exist if the jury find certain facts. The ordinary principles of negligence apply to the meaning of 'duty of care' (Lord Mackay in *Adomako*). The court will consider the nature of the relationship between Jack and Sam's mother. There is no special relationship here because they do not have a parent–child relationship: *Gibbins and Proctor* (1918) 13 Cr App R 134, although she may have had a duty to act under this category in respect of Sam. Sam's mother may have voluntarily assumed responsibility for Jack when she allowed him to visit her home. A duty of care will arise where there is a voluntary assumption of responsibility: *Stone and Dobinson* [1977] 2 All ER 341. However, this category usually applies to situations where a person has taken on the role of carer. While Jack is a child, he is only visiting Sam's house temporarily and it may be difficult to prove that Sam's mother has assumed responsibility for him to this degree. Nevertheless, a duty to act may be imposed on Sam's mother by statute. Section 1, Children and Young Persons Act 1933 makes it an offence for a person with responsibility for a child to wilfully neglect the child. This provision might potentially be applied in order to establish that Sam's mother had a duty to act.

It must also be established whether Sam's mother breached her duty of care towards Jack. Breach requires that her conduct fell below that to be expected of a reasonable person. A reasonable person would act if they saw their own child sitting on top of another child, punching him. Thus, by failing to do so, she has breached her duty of care towards Jack. The usual rules of causation apply and would be satisfied here: but for Sam's mother's failure to intervene in the fight between the boys, Sam would not have punched Jack in the head, and Jack would not have died (*White*). Sam's mother's omission to intervene was a more than minimal cause of death (**Cato**). The argument that the negligence of the doctor breaks the chain of causation is unlikely to be successful: **Cheshire.**

[7] This is a key quote which you should learn.

Finally, it must be established that Sam's mother's omission was grossly negligent. This is a question of fact. The jury should consider 'whether having regard to the risk of death involved, the conduct of the defendant was so bad in all the circumstances as to amount in their judgment to a criminal act or omission'[7] (per Lord Mackay). A reasonably prudent person must have foreseen a serious risk of death: **Misra** [2004] EWCA Crim 2375. If the jury decides that Sam's mother's omission was grossly negligent, she will be convicted of gross negligence manslaughter.

Doctor's liability re Jack's death

Finally, the doctor who treated Jack at the hospital might also be guilty of gross negligence manslaughter. As a doctor treating a patient, he falls under the category of a special relationship (**Airedale NHS Trust v Bland** [1993] AC 89), thus he owed Jack a duty of care, which he breached by failing to diagnose the severity of Jack's injuries. It could be argued that but for his breach Jack would not have died (**White**) and that this was a more than minimal cause of death (**Cato**). The jury would have to consider whether the doctor's omission was grossly negligent. Applying **Adomako**, having regard to the high risk of death, the jury might find that his omission was so bad as to amount to a criminal omission. If so, he will be convicted of gross negligence manslaughter.

✓ Make your answer stand out

- Adopt a clear and logical structure. These offences each contain four elements which provide the structure of your answer for you. You simply need to define the offence and then apply each element in turn to the problem scenario.

- You should use headings to break up your answer and to ensure that you keep your focus and stick to your structure.

- You could draw upon academic opinion relating to involuntary manslaughter and/or comment upon the basis of criminal blameworthiness in respect of both unlawful act manslaughter and gross negligence manslaughter.

- Use key quotes from leading authorities where you can. It is suggested that in respect of unlawful act manslaughter, you learn the quote by Edmund Davies J in *Church* on the meaning of dangerousness.

> **❗ Don't be tempted to . . .**
>
> ■ Provide a lengthy narrative on the law of causation. Although the usual rules of causation apply, you only need to apply the principles and cases on causation which are directly relevant to the problem scenario.
>
> ■ Confuse the test for dangerousness with the thin skull rule (which relates to causation). Many students fail to deal with these tests separately. You should apply the test for dangerousness from *Church* before dealing with causation as a completely separate element of unlawful act manslaughter. It helps if you adopt a methodical approach to this offence, dealing with each element separately and in turn.

❓ Question 2

David and Jenny are both drug addicts. They ask Samantha, a drug dealer, to get them some heroin. Samantha hands over a quantity of heroin to both David and Jenny. They decide to sample the heroin in Samantha's presence in order to check the quality of the heroin. David prepares a syringe and asks Samantha to hold a tourniquet around his arm while he injects himself. Samantha does so and David takes the drugs. Jenny prepares a syringe and injects herself. Both David and Jenny fall unconscious. Samantha does not call for a doctor, but decides to leave them for a while in order that the effects of the drugs can wear off. Samantha goes to visit another client of hers, Ian. She prepares a syringe with a mixture of heroin and water for Ian and injects Ian with the substance. David, Jenny and Ian all die from the effects of the drugs.

Discuss Samantha's criminal liability for the deaths of David, Jenny and Ian.

Answer plan

→ Examine Samantha's liability for unlawful act manslaughter in respect of the death of David.

→ Consider Samantha's liability for unlawful act manslaughter or gross negligence manslaughter in respect of the death of Jenny.

→ Discuss Samantha's liability for unlawful act manslaughter in respect of the death of Ian.

Diagram plan

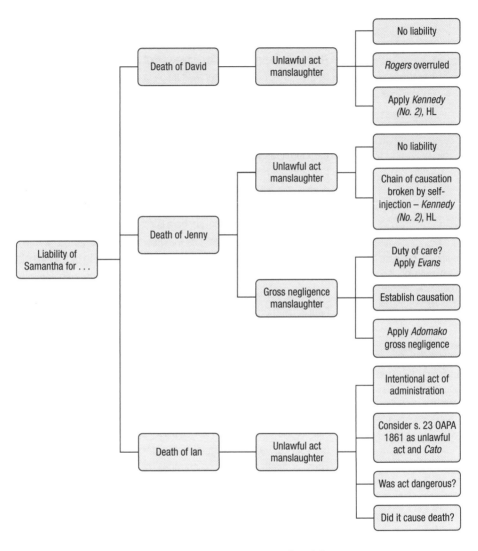

A printable version of this diagram plan is available from **www.pearsoned.co.uk/lawexpressqa**

Answer

It is unlikely that Samantha will be convicted of murder, because there is no evidence that she intended to kill or cause GBH to David, Jenny or Ian. Thus, she has no mens rea for murder. However, she might be charged with offences of involuntary manslaughter, namely unlawful act manslaughter and gross negligence manslaughter.

Samantha might be charged with unlawful act manslaughter in relation to David's death. Unlawful act manslaughter was defined in **Larkin** [1944] 29 Cr App R 18 and requires proof of four elements: there must be an intentional act, rather than an omission (**Lowe** [1976] QB 702), which is unlawful, objectively dangerous and which causes death (per Lord Salmon in **DPP v Newbury and Jones** [1977] AC 50).

However, although Samantha does an intentional act here by holding the tourniquet for David while he injects himself with the heroin, on the facts there are problems in establishing guilt here. The offence of unlawful act manslaughter requires that there is an unlawful act which is a criminal offence: **Franklin** [1883] 15 Cox CC 163. It could be argued that the criminal act here is assisting the malicious administration of a poison or noxious thing so as to endanger life or inflict GBH, and in **Rogers** [2003] EWCA Crim 945 the Court of Appeal held that a defendant could be guilty of unlawful act manslaughter where he held a tourniquet around the victim's arm while the victim injected himself with a drug because the defendant had played a part in the mechanics of the injection.[1] However, this was rejected by the House of Lords in **Kennedy (No. 2)** [2007] UKHL 38, in which Lord Bingham stated that 'the crucial question is not whether the defendant facilitated or contributed to administration of the noxious thing but whether he went further and administered it. What matters . . . is whether the injection itself was the result of a voluntary and informed decision by the person injecting himself'.[2] Lord Bingham concluded that the voluntary act of self-administration precluded a finding of guilt. Thus, Samantha will not be convicted of unlawful act manslaughter in respect of David's death.

Samantha is also unlikely to be convicted of unlawful act manslaughter in respect of Jenny's death because Jenny self-injects. Consequently, it is difficult to ascertain what the unlawful act would be that Samantha does which causes Jenny's death. If the act is the possession of drugs or the supply of drugs, proving causation is problematic. In fact, the House of Lords has now held that the free and voluntary self-administration of heroin by a fully informed and responsible adult would break the chain of causation: **Kennedy (No. 2)**.[3] Thus, provided that Jenny was acting freely and voluntarily in injecting herself

[1] Although this case has been overruled, it is worth mentioning because it is factually very similar to the problem scenario.

[2] It is worth learning a few key quotes from leading judgments for use in your examination. At the very least, you should be able to paraphrase key principles.

[3] As this is the leading authority on this point now, there is no need to trawl through the previous drugs cases.

4 This sentence is important
as it provides the application
of the law to the problem
scenario.

5 If it is clear that unlawful act
manslaughter does not apply,
rule it out and move on to a
more appropriate offence.

and that she was a fully informed and responsible adult, Samantha will not be guilty of unlawful act manslaughter here.[4]

Furthermore, Samantha cannot be convicted of unlawful act manslaughter for the failure to summon medical assistance as this offence requires a positive act: *Lowe.*[5]

However, Samantha may be convicted of gross negligence manslaughter on the basis that she left Jenny unconscious without summoning medical help. The offence of gross negligence manslaughter may be committed by either an act or an omission, so Samantha might be convicted on the basis that she failed to summon medical assistance or because she acted by walking off and leaving Jenny to die. The prosecution would need to prove that Samantha owed Jenny a duty of care, she breached this duty, the breach caused Jenny's death and that Samantha's omission was grossly negligent: *Adomako* [1995] 1 AC 171. The duty to act giving rise to criminal liability for omission is narrower than the civil duty of care.

Whether or not Samantha owed Jenny a duty of care is a question of law according to *Willoughby* [2004] EWCA Crim 3365 and *Evans* [2009] EWCA Crim 650. The judge will direct the jury as to the law in this regard. According to Lord Mackay in *Adomako*, the ordinary principles of negligence apply to the meaning of 'duty of care'. This scenario is factually similar to the case of *Evans*, in which the Court of Appeal held that the defendant did owe the victim a duty of care despite the fact that their relationship was not one upon which the law already imposed a familial duty. Lord Judge CJ stated that 'when a person has created or contributed to the creation of a state of affairs which he knows, or ought reasonably to know, has become life threatening, a consequent duty on him to act by taking reasonable steps to save the other's life will normally arise'.[6] Thus, applying this case, it is likely that a duty of care will be imposed upon Samantha to take reasonable steps to save Jenny's life when she realises (as she ought reasonably to) that Jenny is unconscious.

6 This quote supports the
argument that there is a duty
of care here and is a useful
application of the *Miller*
[1983] 2 AC 161 principle by
the Court of Appeal.

Next, it must be established whether Samantha breached this duty. Breach requires that Samantha's conduct fell below that to be expected of a reasonable person. This is likely to be the case here, as the reasonable person would have summoned medical assistance and not simply walked off and left Jenny.[7]

7 This sentence demonstrates
application to the problem
scenario.

The usual rules of causation apply. But for Samantha's act of supplying the heroin and then failing to summon medical assistance, leaving Jenny unconscious, Jenny would not have died: *White* [1910] 2 KB 124. Samantha's omission was also a more than minimal cause of death: *Cato* [1976] 1 WLR 110 and there was no intervening event.

Finally, it must be established that Samantha's conduct was grossly negligent. This is a question of fact and the jury should consider 'whether having regard to the risk of death involved, the conduct of the defendant was so bad in all the circumstances as to amount in their judgment to a criminal act or omission' (Lord Mackay in *Adomako*). A reasonably prudent person must have foreseen a serious risk of death: *Misra* [2004] EWCA Crim 2375. If Samantha's conduct was grossly negligent, she will be convicted of gross negligence manslaughter.

[8] Refer to factually similar authorities to demonstrate how liability will be established.

Samantha might be convicted of unlawful act manslaughter in relation to Ian's death. The intentional act here occurs when Samantha injects Ian with the heroin. This is a criminal offence (*Franklin*) under section 23 of the Offences Against the Person Act 1861, namely the malicious administration of a poison or noxious thing so as to endanger life or inflict GBH (see *Cato*).[8] The administration of the drug is an objectively dangerous act because it was such as 'all sober and reasonable people would inevitably recognise must subject the other person to, at least, the risk of some harm . . . albeit not serious harm' (Edmund Davies J in *Church* [1966] 1 QB 59). Finally, in order to establish Samantha's liability for unlawful act manslaughter in respect of Ian, it must be proved that Samantha's act of injecting Ian caused his death. The usual rules of causation apply. Applying the test for factual causation: but for Samantha's act of injecting Ian, he would not have died: *White*. Samantha's act was also a more than minimal cause of Ian's death (*Cato*) and there is no *novus actus interveniens* to break the chain of causation. Thus, Samantha is likely to be guilty of unlawful act manslaughter in respect of Ian's death.

✓ **Make your answer stand out**

■ Refer to specific statements made by judges in leading authorities. If you cannot remember quotes verbatim, you should be able to paraphrase the principles. In fact, the ability to accurately paraphrase a point made in a judgment demonstrates a better understanding of the specific issue. ▶

- Refer to academic opinion where appropriate. You might consider referring to Heaton, R. (2003) Dealing in death. Crim LR 497 (although be aware that this article was obviously written prior to the decision of the House of Lords in *Kennedy (No. 2)*, which was decided in 2007). You might also refer to Leigh, L. (2009) Duty of care and manslaughter. 173 JPN 296.

- You should be able to distinguish between all of the drugs cases, but you should demonstrate particularly good knowledge of the House of Lords' decision in *Kennedy (No. 2)*.

- Consider exploring further the extent to which criminal law relies upon definitions of civil law in defining the offence of gross negligence manslaughter and whether this is satisfactory in light of the severity of the offence.

! Don't be tempted to . . .

- Waste time going through all of the previous cases on the supply of drugs. In a problem question, you are expected to apply the current law and now that the law is settled as a result of *Kennedy (No. 2)*, this is the case you should apply. However, if the facts of a previous authority are directly relevant, you may make brief reference to it.

- Forget that some of the previous case law has been overruled by *Kennedy (No. 2)*. Make sure that you are aware which cases are still good law and which have been overruled so as to avoid applying incorrect law.

✒ Question 3

'For the objectivist, the consequences must be taken into account when assessing moral responsibility' (Ashworth (1993) 'Taking the Consequences' in Shute, Gardner and Horder (eds), *Action and Value in Criminal Law*, Oxford: Clarendon Press, p. 110).

With reference to the above quote, critically evaluate the offence of unlawful act manslaughter.

Answer plan

→ Address the question directly at the start of your answer.

→ Consider the elements of unlawful act manslaughter which reflect the moral responsibility of the defendant.

→ Discuss the extent to which the offence is consistent with general principles of criminal law.

→ Consider the example of the 'one-punch killer'.

Diagram plan

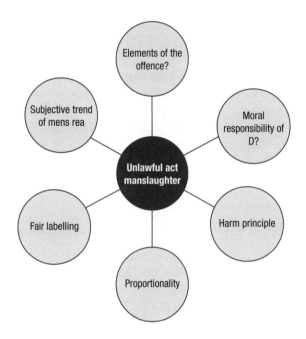

A printable version of this diagram plan is available from **www.pearsoned.co.uk/lawexpressqa**

Answer

Where a person performs an unlawful and dangerous act which causes the death of another human being, the law holds that an offence of manslaughter has been committed. The rationale for criminalising unlawful act manslaughter is based upon the harm principle. However, unlawful act manslaughter does not require proof of an intention to kill or cause GBH, and liability is constructed out of a lesser unlawful act (such as an assault) which causes the death of the victim even though that death is neither intended nor foreseen by the defendant. Thus, the defendant may be convicted in respect of unforeseen consequences which do not necessarily reflect his moral responsibility.[1] This offence was described as 'unjustifiable in principle' by the Law Commission (Law Commission (1996) Report, *Legislating the Criminal Code: Involuntary Manslaughter*, No. 237, Para. 5.15). This is a very serious offence which carries a potentially

[1] This sentence demonstrates that you have immediately identified the key issue and understand the problems associated with unlawful act manslaughter.

lengthy sentence of imprisonment, so it is important to ensure that there is a justifiable basis for criminalisation. While the objectivist would support liability based upon the consequences caused by the defendant, criminal law generally adopts a more subjectivist approach which requires a corresponding level of mens rea.[2]

The offence of unlawful act manslaughter requires proof of four elements: (i) an intentional act; (ii) which is unlawful; (iii) the act must be objectively dangerous; and (iv) it must cause death (*Larkin* [1944] 29 Cr App R 18 and *DPP v Newbury and Jones* [1977] AC 50). Although it is necessary to prove a causal link between the actions of the defendant and the death of the victim, there is no need to prove that the defendant intended or foresaw the risk of death or even harm. The dangerousness element is objectively assessed, such that it must

be questioned whether the act was 'such as all sober and reasonable people would inevitably recognise must subject the other person to, at least, the risk of some harm resulting therefrom, albeit not serious harm' (*Church* [1966] 1 QB 59).[3]

The offence has a very broad scope which has been criticised because it allows conviction for a serious criminal offence in respect of accidental and negligent deaths (as in *Meeking* [2012] EWCA Crim 641).[4] A defendant might be convicted of unlawful act manslaughter where a reasonable person would foresee the risk of some harm resulting from the defendant's actions, irrespective of whether the actual defendant foresaw any risk of harm. Even on the objective assessment, the reasonable person need not foresee the risk of death or serious harm. Thus, the mens rea element of unlawful act manslaughter is reduced to three requirements: (i) the defendant must intentionally do an act; (ii) the mens rea for the lesser unlawful act must be proved (the subjective elements); and (iii) the reasonable man would foresee the risk of some harm (the objective element).

While the harm principle provides a rationale for criminalising conduct that has caused harm to another, a further aim of criminal law is to ensure that culpable conduct is met with a proportionate response. This means that both the offence which the defendant is convicted of and the punishment imposed must be proportionate to the moral culpability of the defendant. The principle of fair labelling requires that offences 'should be categorised and labelled for symbolic reasons to capture the essence of the wrongdoing involved and to convey the level of rejection of the activity involved' (Clarkson, C. (2000) Context and culpability in involuntary manslaughter, in A. Ashworth (ed.), *Rethinking English Homicide Law*. Oxford: Oxford University Press, pp. 141–2). Clarkson argues that offences should be 'defined with sufficient specificity' to reflect the moral significance of the offence and 'structured to reflect a hierarchy of seriousness'. Clarkson suggests that the offence of unlawful act manslaughter 'fails both tests' (p. 142).

[5] This sentence (and the rest of this paragraph) sets out one side of the argument, criticising the current law.

Subjectivists would argue that a conviction for manslaughter should only be possible if the defendant foresaw a risk of harm at the very least,[5] and that the current offence of unlawful act manslaughter is 'contrary to principle' (Ashworth (1993) Taking the consequences, in Shute, Gardner and Horder (eds), *Action and Value in Criminal Law*. Oxford: Clarendon Press, p. 118). From a subjectivist standpoint, the culpability of the 'one-punch killer' who did not foresee a risk of harm, let alone death, is not so great as to warrant the label of 'manslaughter'. As far back as 1980 the Criminal Law Revision Committee recommended reform, criticising the current law because 'the offender's fault falls too far short of the unlucky result' (Criminal Law Revision Committee (1980) 14th Report, *Offences Against the Person*. London: The Stationery Office, Para. 120). Wilson points out

[6] This sentence demonstrates a wider understanding of criminal law by incorporating the approach taken by the courts in respect of the meaning of intention.

that, while the objective approach adopted in relation to the meaning of intention in murder was corrected, the objective approach in respect of the meaning of 'dangerous' in unlawful act manslaughter has not been corrected[6] (Wilson, W. (2011) *Criminal Law*, 5th edn. London: Longman, p. 397).

To highlight the absence of proportionality, Mitchell gives an example of the 'one-punch killer': 'in the course of a drunken fight, D punches V who falls over, hits his head on a hard surface causing a fractured skull from which V subsequently dies' (Mitchell, B. (2008) Minding the gap in unlawful and dangerous act manslaughter: a moral defence of one-punch killers. 72 JCL 537). The liability of the defendant is determined by the consequences of his actions, whether foreseen or not, and ultimately is based on luck. Professor Mitchell argues that the gap between what was foreseen or foreseeable and the death of the victim is 'too great'. Simester and Sullivan state that 'the connection between the unlawfulness of D's act and its dangerousness may be extremely tenuous' (Simester, A. and Sullivan, R. (2010) *Criminal Law: Theory and Doctrine*. Oxford: Hart, p. 378).

[7] This paragraph presents the opposing view – that supporting the current law.

Ashworth outlines the reasons objectivists would give to support the argument that the actions of the defendant should be labelled as manslaughter:[7] (i) the moral difference between the one-punch killer and a defendant who punches the victim without causing death. While the former feels 'morally burdened with the death', the latter does not; (ii) the one-punch killer 'cannot undo the results of his act'; and (iii) he 'should be censured for causing the death, since a law which convicted him merely of battery . . . would be suggesting that the death did not matter' (Ashworth (1993) p. 119).

[8] This final sentence ties your answer back to the question and sets out a recommendation for reform.

The offence of unlawful act manslaughter does not sit neatly within criminal law. It offends the subjectivist trend in criminal law through the existence of a gap between the moral responsibility of the defendant and the death.[8]

 Make your answer stand out

- Refer to a number of different academic sources and opinions to demonstrate your appreciation of the wide range of academic literature available.
- Present both sides of the argument. You should also consider the arguments in favour of having a low threshold for unlawful act manslaughter.
- If you have time, you might explore further the recommendations for reform made by the Law Commission.
- You might also consider where the offence of causing death by dangerous driving fits into the current framework of offences.

! Don't be tempted to . . .

- Simply set out the law on unlawful act manslaughter. The examiner is looking for an appreciation of the peculiarities of the mens rea of unlawful act manslaughter and the extent to which the offence reflects the moral culpability of the defendant.
- Just simply set out one side of the argument. You should explore both sides of the argument.

Question 4

'Despite a gestation period extending over thirteen years, the Corporate Manslaughter and Corporate Homicide Act 2007 is a disappointment. It is limited in its scope, restricted in its range of potential defendants and regressive to the extent that . . . it allows its focus to be deflected from systematic fault to individual fault' (Gobert, J. (2008) The Corporate Manslaughter and Corporate Homicide Act. 71(3) MLR 413–63).

Critically evaluate the above statement.

Answer plan

→ Discuss the background to the 2007 Act and gross negligence manslaughter.

→ Consider the scope of the offence of corporate manslaughter.

→ Address criticisms of the new legislation.

Diagram plan

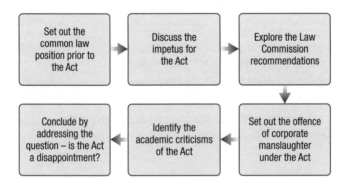

A printable version of this diagram plan is available from **www.pearsoned.co.uk/lawexpressqa**

Answer

The long overdue Corporate Manslaughter and Corporate Homicide Act 2007 (CMCHA 2007) came into force in April 2008, over a decade after corporate responsibility for causing deaths was initially considered by the Law Commission[1] (Law Commission (1994b) Consultation Paper, *Criminal Law: Involuntary Manslaughter*, No. 135). In 1996, the Law Commission recommended the creation of an offence of 'corporate killing' (Law Commission (1996) Report, *Legislating the Criminal*

[1] This sentence demonstrates your wider knowledge of the background to this piece of legislation.

2 Ensure that you address
the question directly in your
introduction.

Code: Involuntary Manslaughter, No. 237) and this led to a consultation paper in 2000 and the Act in 2007. However, despite over a decade of consultation and drafting, the CMCHA 2007 has attracted criticism from academics and been labelled a 'disappointment'.[2]

Prior to the Act, a corporation could be guilty of gross negligence manslaughter subject to the identification of an individual who represented the embodiment of the company and who could be said to be responsible for the acts and state of mind of the company (***Tesco Supermarkets Ltd v Nattrass*** [1972] AC 153). However, problems with the application of the identification doctrine led to unsuccessful attempts at prosecution.[3] Various sea and rail disasters from the late 1980s onwards and the failure to secure convictions for gross negligence manslaughter for the deaths of the victims led to public calls for a new offence of corporate killing. While it had been possible in some cases to bring successful prosecutions for health and safety offences, this was an unsatisfactory conclusion to such large-scale disasters as such convictions failed to adequately represent the severity of the offence which had in fact occurred. In the interests of fair labelling, the Law Commission recommended that a specific statutory offence of corporate manslaughter be created to increase the social stigma of conviction.[4]

Although the common law offence of gross negligence manslaughter still exists, section 20 of the CMCHA 2007 abolishes the application of the common law offence to corporations and any other body to which the 2007 Act now applies. Thus, the offence of gross negligence manslaughter now only applies to individuals. Section 1 of the CMCHA 2007 creates a new homicide offence which can only be committed by an organisation. Under section 1(1), an organisation is guilty of corporate manslaughter if the management or organisation of its activities by senior management causes the death of a person and amounts to a gross breach of a duty of care owed to the victim. Under section 1(3), an organisation is guilty only if the way in which its activities are managed or organised by its senior management is a substantial element in the breach. This is a complex offence which requires a number of elements to be proved before liability can be established: the body in question must constitute an organisation under the Act, there must be a relevant duty of care owed to the victim, there must be a gross breach of that duty, the management or organisation of the activities of the organisation must cause the

3 This shows the examiner
that you understand the
context within which the
legislation was created as
well as the problems with the
old law.

4 Explain why it was still
necessary to create an
offence of corporate
manslaughter even though
prosecutions for other
offences were possible.

death of the victim, the offence must be due to the way in which the activities of the organisation are managed or organised and senior management must contribute substantial elements in the breach.

Both the scope of the Act and that of the offence of corporate manslaughter require further consideration. While the Act has been criticised for its restrictive focus on just one offence (manslaughter) and its failure to deal with principles of corporate liability as a whole,[5] the specific offence under section 1 is broad in scope. The organisations it applies to are widely construed in section 1(2) and goes beyond the liability of a corporation. Thus, as Ormerod and Taylor state, 'Calling the offence "corporate manslaughter" is somewhat misleading' (Ormerod, D. and Taylor, R. (2008) The Corporate Manslaughter and Corporate Homicide Act 2007. Crim LR 589). The offence applies to police forces, partnerships, government departments and trade unions, and Ormerod and Taylor welcome the breadth of the definition of organisation. By contrast, Gobert comments that 'the extension of the Act to so diverse an array of organisations may be too broad' (Gobert, J. (2008) The Corporate Manslaughter and Corporate Homicide Act. 71(3) MLR 413).[6] The list of government departments in Schedule 1 to which the offence applies extends to the Ministry of Justice and Department of Health, thus a prison may be convicted in respect of the death of a prisoner in custody and hospital trusts may be convicted in respect of the death of a patient.[7] Gobert concedes that 'Criminal laws can and should be constructed to cover these types of situations', but he argues that 'a law of corporate manslaughter arguably is aimed at a more specific and quite different problem – that of companies which allow their pursuit of profit to blind them to concerns of safety' (Gobert, 2008).

Some elements requiring proof under the Act resemble elements required for the common law offence of gross negligence manslaughter, such as duty of care and gross breach. Both these elements have been questioned within the context of the common law: first, proof of a duty of care leads to concepts of civil law being adopted by criminal law despite the fact that each system has distinct and clearly defined aims. This requirement did not form part of the Law Commission recommendations in 1996 and Gobert questions whether it is in fact 'otiose' and 'simply provides defendants with another avenue for deflecting the trial from its main objective' (Gobert, 2008). Secondly, the test for 'gross breach' is ambiguous. Section 1(4)(b) refers to

[5] This enables you to provide a further criticism of the Act that it only deals with one aspect of corporate liability and does not develop general principles of corporate liability.

[6] These sentences show that you are able to compare and contrast differing academic opinions.

[7] Demonstrate to the examiner that you are familiar with the legislation and the extent of the impact that it may have.

[8] This sentence demonstrates that you are able to integrate criticisms of other areas of law into your argument where appropriate.

conduct which falls far below what can reasonably be expected of the organisation in the circumstances. The test for gross negligence from **Adomako** [1995] 1 AC 171 has endured criticism for its circularity and it appears similar criticism may be levelled at the meaning given to 'gross breach' under the Act.[8]

One of the reasons for the implementation of the 2007 Act was to avoid the evidential problems posed by the identification doctrine. However, the Act requires proof that individuals who amount to 'senior management' contribute a 'substantial element' to the breach. Gobert argues that this is not consistent with the recommendations made by the Law Commission which focused exclusively on 'systematic failure', rather than on 'individual failings'. Ormerod and Taylor comment that this is 'a further limiting factor to the offence and one which brings with it the potential for time consuming technical arguments' (Ormerod, D. and Taylor, R. (2008) The Corporate Manslaughter and Corporate Homicide Act 2007. Crim LR 589). Nevertheless, despite identifying individual failings, the Act does not permit individual liability, either as a principal or as an accessory to an offence committed by the organisation.

There are several criticisms that may be levelled at the 2007 Act, which is indeed disappointing in a piece of legislation that was over a decade in the making. Nevertheless, this was a long overdue piece of legislation and as Gobert suggests: 'The symbolic effects of the 2007 Act may in the long run overshadow [its] deficiencies' (Gobert, 2008).

✓ **Make your answer stand out**

- Cite academic opinion in your answer. You could refer to other academic literature on this topic, such as O'Doherty, S. (2008) The Corporate Manslaughter and Corporate Homicide Act 2007. 172 JPN 244.

- If you have time you could explore further the background to the legislation (see Wells, C. (1996) The Law Commission Report on Involuntary Manslaughter. Crim LR 545), or look more specifically at the impact of the Act (see Griffin, S. and Moran, J. (2010) Accountability for deaths attributable to the gross negligent act or omission of a police force: the impact of the Corporate Manslaughter and Corporate Homicide Act 2007. 74 JCL 358).

- You could consider further the common law prior to the 2007 Act and the reasons why the common law was unsatisfactory in dealing with corporate liability.

- You could explore the identification doctrine and academic opinion relating to this.

❗ Don't be tempted to . . .

- Simply set out the statutory provisions of the Act. This question asks you to explore the criticisms of the legislation rather than provide a narrative of the law.
- Spend too much time setting out the law relating to gross negligence manslaughter and the identification doctrine. Neither should your answer be solely a critique of the old law. You need to critically evaluate the new law (albeit with reference to the old law where appropriate).

@ Try it yourself

Now take a look at the question below and attempt to answer it. You can check your response against the answer guidance available on the companion website (**www.pearsoned.co.uk/lawexpressqa**).

> Stuart, a school teacher, takes a group of school children on a trip to the Welsh mountains. One afternoon, Stuart takes a group of 20 students on a hike through the mountains. Half an hour into the hike, one of the children, Ralph, falls and badly twists his ankle. Ralph is unable to walk on his ankle. Not wishing to ruin the hike for the other students, Stuart decides to leave Ralph on a rock close to a path and to continue on the hike. He plans to collect Ralph on the way back home. After the group has gone, Ralph gets hungry and tries to walk home himself. However, he falls on a cliff edge and plummets 50 feet down a cliff face. Later that afternoon, Stuart is unable to find Ralph, and calls a search and rescue team. However, the team do not find Ralph in time and he dies from hypothermia.
>
> Discuss Stuart's liability for Ralph's death.

www.pearsoned.co.uk/lawexpressqa

Go online to access more revision support including additional essay and problem questions with diagram plans, You be the marker questions, and download all diagrams from the book.

Non-fatal offences
against the person

How this topic may come up in exams

Non-fatal offences against the person could be examined by way of either a problem scenario or an essay question. A problem question would expect you to identify any of the five main non-fatal offences against the person and/or the sexual offences (covered in Chapter 6, with a mixed question in Chapter 13). You might also be expected to apply the law relating to consent and self-defence. An essay question could ask for a critical evaluation of the general area or it might focus on a specific issue, such as consent.

Before you begin

It's a good idea to consider the following key themes of non-fatal offences against the person before tackling a question on this topic.

A printable version of this diagram is available from **www.pearsoned.co.uk/lawexpressqa**

❓ Question 1

After they meet at a party, Claire becomes 'friends' with Abraham on Facebook. Over the next few weeks, they send each other flirtatious messages on Facebook. Encouraged by this, Abraham decides to ask Claire if she would go on a date with him. Claire rejects Abraham's offer of a date and tells him that she is not interested in him romantically. Confused by Claire's flirtatious behaviour and rejection, and angry at being used, Abraham starts sending Claire threatening messages on Facebook. After receiving several threatening and abusive messages from Abraham over the course of two weeks, Claire suffers an anxiety disorder.

Claire's friends decide to take her out to cheer her up. However, on the night out with her friends, Claire runs into Abraham in a nightclub. Abraham is delighted to see Claire and he starts dancing with her before touching her on the back. Claire is frightened at seeing Abraham and doesn't like him touching her, so she pushes him away from her. He stumbles backwards and falls to the floor, but is not injured.

The following day, Abraham meets up with his friends and they go out paintballing. As a joke, Abraham's friends decide to gang up against him and they all target him by shooting him with paintballs. One of his friends, Matthew, shoots paintballs at Abraham's back at close range, causing severe bruises.

Discuss the criminal liability of the parties.

Answer plan

→ Discuss the liability of Abraham for assault in respect of the Facebook messages.

→ Consider Abraham's liability for battery and implied consent.

→ Explore Claire's potential liability for battery and her use of self-defence.

→ Consider Abraham's consent to the paintballing, and thus to the infliction of ABH or GBH.

Diagram plan

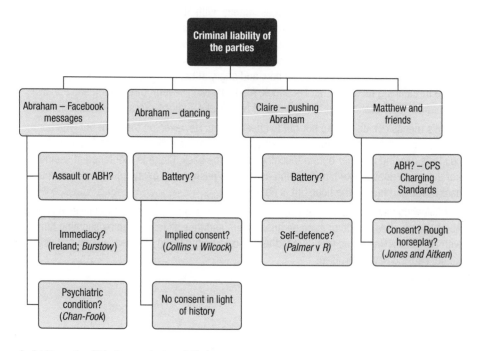

A printable version of this diagram plan is available from **www.pearsoned.co.uk/lawexpressqa**

Answer

This question requires consideration of the liabilities of the parties for non-fatal offences against the person and the issue of consent.

Facebook messages

Abraham may be charged with assault in respect of the threatening Facebook messages he sent to Claire. Assault is charged contrary to section 39 of the Criminal Justice Act 1988 (CJA) and involves intentionally or recklessly causing a person to apprehend immediate and unlawful personal violence: **Fagan v MPC** [1969] 1 QB 439.[1] An assault may be committed by words alone: **Ireland; Burstow** [1998] AC 147. It must also be proved that the Facebook messages caused Claire to apprehend immediate and unlawful personal violence. This is likely to be satisfied since the messages were threatening and they

[1] There is no need to set out the facts of the case here. The legal principle is more important and you will waste time going through the facts of cases.

caused Claire to suffer anxiety. This is evidence that she was worried about the threats being carried out, although it is less clear whether the apprehension was of immediate personal violence since the messages were sent through a social networking website and there is no evidence that Abraham was anywhere near Claire at the time. However, 'immediacy' has been widely construed. In *Constanza* [1997] 2 Cr App R 492, it was held that immediacy meant any time 'not excluding the immediate future'. In *Ireland; Burstow*, Lord Steyn held that silent telephone calls could be sufficient to satisfy the requirement of immediacy. In light of these authorities, messages sent via Facebook could potentially be sufficiently immediate.[2]

[2] Use the facts of a key case and the principle derived from that case to reach a sensible conclusion on slightly different facts.

The mens rea of assault is also present because Abraham intends to cause such apprehension. He is likely to be subjectively reckless because he must have recognised the risk that sending threatening Facebook messages might cause such apprehension, and he went ahead and took that risk (*Cunningham* [1957] 2 QB 396).[3]

[3] Try to set out the principle of law and apply it in one sentence as this demonstrates a more sophisticated style of writing as well as saving you time in the exam.

Finally, Abraham might be guilty of assault occasioning ABH (s. 47, Offences Against the Person Act (OAPA) 1861). A clinically recognised psychiatric injury may amount to ABH, but this does not include mere emotions: *Chan-Fook* [1994] 1 WLR 689. The effect of the Facebook messages was to cause Claire to suffer an anxiety disorder. Provided the anxiety disorder is deemed to be a clinically recognised psychiatric condition, this will be sufficient to constitute ABH.

Abraham dancing and touching Claire

Abraham could be charged with assault and battery. The assault might be based upon Abraham's act of dancing near Claire. Taking into account their history and the Facebook messages, Claire may have apprehended immediate and unlawful personal violence, and Abraham is likely to have been reckless as to such apprehension at the very least. In respect of Abraham touching Claire's back, there may be a battery. Battery is charged contrary to section 39 of the CJA. It is defined under common law as intentionally or recklessly inflicting unlawful force on a person without consent: *Collins v Wilcock* [1984] 1 WLR 1172.[4] 'Force' merely requires 'the least touching of another': *Cole v Turner* (1705) 6 Mod Rep 149, thus when Abraham touches Claire on the back, this is sufficient. The mens rea of battery is also present because it is clear that Abraham intends to apply force to

[4] Where it is less obvious, ensure that you set out the definition of the key offence at the start and cite appropriate authorities.

[5] Do not forget to state and apply the mens rea of the offence.

[6] Use the facts to reach a sensible conclusion.

(or touch) Claire.[5] It could be argued that the touching was not unlawful because Claire had impliedly consented to it. According to Robert Goff LJ in **Collins v Wilcock**, most of the physical contacts of everyday life are impliedly consented to. While this defence applies to accidental contact, such as bumping into someone, it is not clear that it would apply to this type of touching, especially in light of the history between them.[6] It is unlikely that Claire will be deemed to have consented to this touching as she has previously rejected Abraham's advances.

Claire pushing Abraham

[7] Where it is obvious that no offence has been committed, get to the point and explain why at the start.

When Claire pushes Abraham away, this might also amount to a battery and the main issue here is one of self-defence. Claire is unlikely to attract any liability for battery when she pushes Abraham away, as she is clearly acting in defence of herself here.[7] She honestly believes that the use of force is necessary to defend herself from being touched by Abraham and she only uses reasonable force in pushing him away: **Palmer v R** [1971] AC 814 and s. 76, Criminal Justice and Immigration Act 2008.

Paintballing

[8] This is a good quote to remember. Try to remember key quotes from judgments which define the crucial elements of the offences.

[9] Refer to relevant parts of the CPS Charging Standards in questions on non-fatal offences against the person in order to show that you are familiar with them.

Matthew (and Abraham's other friends) might be guilty of assault occasioning actual bodily harm (s. 47, Offences Against the Person Act 1861). This offence requires proof of either an assault or a battery, which causes actual bodily harm. There may be an assault here as Abraham does apprehend that he will be struck with paintballs and the friends and Matthew are, at the very least, reckless as to causing such apprehension. There is also a battery because striking Abraham with the paintballs involves intentionally or recklessly inflicting unlawful force. There need only be the least touching to constitute 'force' and this is evident here. 'Actual bodily harm' is defined under **Miller** [1954] 2 WLR 138 as 'any hurt or injury calculated to interfere with health or comfort'.[8] According to the most recent CPS Charging Standards (http://www.cps.gov.uk/legal/l_to_o/offences_against_the_person/\#a24), the injuries must be 'serious' to constitute ABH and 'relevant factors may include, for example, the fact that there has been significant medical intervention and/or permanent effects have resulted'.[9] There is no evidence on the facts that Abraham has had to receive any medical treatment in relation to the bruising, nor is there any evidence of permanent scarring. Nevertheless, these

¹⁰ Ensure you explain why/ how the principle could be extended to apply to the specific problem scenario you are dealing with.

¹¹ Correctly state the mens rea for this offence. Students often make the mistake of thinking that additional mens rea is required.

factors serve only as examples and since the bruises are stated to be severe, it might be that this is enough to constitute ABH.¹⁰

The mens rea required is the mens rea for the assault or battery. No additional mens rea in respect of the degree of harm caused need be proved according to **Roberts** (1971) 56 Cr App R 95 and **Savage; Parmenter** [1992] 1 AC 699.¹¹ Here, the mens rea of the battery must be proved, and it is clear that Matthew and the other friends intended to inflict force on Abraham.

As the injuries were sustained during a game of paintballing, Matthew and the other friends might try to argue that Abraham consented to the injury by relying on 'rough horseplay'. The general rule is that a person may not consent to the infliction of actual bodily harm or grievous bodily harm: **Donovan** [1934] All ER 207. However, such injuries inflicted during 'rough horseplay' are consented to. However, this exception applies to injuries sustained during horseplay which were not intentionally inflicted: **Jones** (1986) 83 Cr App R 375; **Aitken** [1992] 1 WLR 1006. It could be argued that the injuries here were inflicted intentionally, thus the defence of consent is unlikely to be available here and Matthew and the other friends may be guilty of assault occasioning ABH.

✓ Make your answer stand out

- Each time you set out a relevant legal principle, you should cite an authority which supports that principle and then apply it to the facts in the problem scenario.

- In your revision, you should choose some key quotes and names of judges who gave leading judgments in key cases to refer to (only where appropriate) in the exam.

- You could discuss any potential liability under the Protection from Harassment Act 1997 in respect of the Facebook messages.

- You should develop your discussion of the issue of self-defence in respect of the push and provide further detail about this defence.

- You could provide reference to some academic opinion on issues such as consent or immediacy to make your answer stand out. For instance, read Ormerod, D. (2011) *Smith and Hogan Criminal Law*, 13th edn. Oxford: Oxford University Press. You could also make reference to the Law Commission (1994) Consultation Paper, *Consent and Offences Against the Person* (No. 134).

> **! Don't be tempted to . . .**
>
> ■ Forget to apply the principles of law relating to the mens rea. If you merely establish the actus reus you have only really dealt with half of the question. In order to establish liability, both the actus reus and mens rea must be satisfied.
>
> ■ Make the mistake of writing everything you know about any offence that you have identified without referring to the problem scenario. The examiner does not want to read two pages of description before you refer to the facts of the problem scenario. You must refer to the facts in the problem scenario from the very start of your answer and combine statements of law with application to the facts.

? Question 2

After having unprotected sexual intercourse with a string of different partners, Mitchell discovers that he is HIV positive. He is distraught by this and resolves to try to spread the virus to as many new partners as possible. One evening, Mitchell meets Bernard in a nightclub. Bernard reveals to Mitchell that he is married to a woman, but that he has only recently told her that he is gay. He confides in Mitchell that he has never slept with a man. Mitchell goes home with Bernard and has unprotected sexual intercourse with him, hoping that he will transmit the virus to Bernard. Bernard is unaware that Mitchell is HIV positive. Bernard later tests positive for HIV. The following week, Mitchell signs up to an online dating website. He meets Gavin and they date for several months. One morning, while they are in bed together, Mitchell declares his undying love for Gavin and asks Gavin if he will carve Gavin's initials into Mitchell's buttocks. Gavin reluctantly agrees and uses a hot knife to do so. Unfortunately, the area that had been branded becomes infected and Mitchell has to seek medical advice.

Discuss the criminal liability of the parties.

Answer plan

→ Consider Mitchell's liability for maliciously wounding or inflicting GBH under section 20, OAPA 1861 in respect of the transmission of HIV to Bernard.

→ Explore the issue of consent and the cases of *Dica* [2004] QB 1257 and *Konzani* [2005] EWCA Crim 706.

→ Discuss Gavin's potential liability for assault occasioning ABH under section 47, OAPA 1861 in respect of the injuries caused to Mitchell's buttocks.

→ Consider whether the elements of maliciously wounding or inflicting GBH under section 20, OAPA 1861 are satisfied.

→ Consider whether consent applies and the cases of *Brown* [1994] 1 AC 212 and *Wilson* [1997] 1 QB 47.

Diagram plan

A printable version of this diagram plan is available from **www.pearsoned.co.uk/lawexpressqa**

Answer

On the facts, Mitchell and Gavin might be liable for various non-fatal offences against the person. In particular, Mitchell might be criminally liable for the transmission of HIV to Bernard and Gavin might be criminally liable for the injuries to Mitchell's buttocks. Both cases also require consideration of the issue of consent.[1]

[1] Use your introduction to briefly set out the key issues that you will be addressing.

Liability of Mitchell

The first offence which requires consideration is that of maliciously wounding or inflicting GBH under section 20, OAPA 1861. Mitchell might be convicted under section 20 in respect of the transmission of HIV to Bernard. In *Dica*, the Court of Appeal held that the reckless transmission of HIV could amount to an offence under section 20. The actus reus of this offence is satisfied because Mitchell inflicts GBH on Bernard by transmitting HIV to him. The infliction of GBH does not require proof of an assault (*Wilson (Clarence)* [1984] AC 242) and GBH means 'really serious harm' (*DPP v Smith* [1961] AC 290). The offence under section 20 also requires proof that Mitchell intended or was reckless as to whether some harm was caused: *Savage; Parmenter* [1992] 1 AC 699. This is the mens rea of the offence. Since Mitchell hopes to transmit HIV to Bernard, it can be argued that he intended to cause some harm to Bernard. However, even if this is not proved, Mitchell recognises the risk of causing some harm to him when he has unprotected sexual intercourse with him, and he takes that risk, thus he is likely to be subjectively reckless as to whether some harm would be caused: *Cunningham* [1957] 2 QB 396. If Mitchell intends to cause Bernard GBH, he may be guilty of causing GBH under section 18, OAPA 1861.

Mitchell might argue that he has a defence to a charge of section 20 or section 18 on the basis that Bernard consented to unprotected sexual intercourse with Mitchell. However, this is no defence. Bernard was not aware that Mitchell was HIV positive and the case of *Dica* provides that by consenting to sexual intercourse Bernard is not to be taken to be consenting to the risk of the transmission of HIV. This is supported by the case of *Konzani*, in which Lord Judge CJ reiterated the fact that the defence of consent would only be available where the victim knew about the risk of HIV and gave his/her informed consent to running the risk of transmission.[2] Since Bernard was not aware that Mitchell had tested HIV positive, he did not provide any informed consent to run such a risk. Thus, the defence of consent will not be available to Mitchell and, at the very least, he will be guilty of maliciously inflicting GBH under section 20, OAPA 1861.

[2] Cite supporting authorities without repeating yourself, by referring to a specific point made by a judge.

Liability of Gavin

[3] Begin by clearly identifying the most relevant offence which might apply.

Gavin could be charged with assault occasioning actual bodily harm under section 47, OAPA 1861 in respect of the injuries to Mitchell's buttocks.[3] This offence requires proof of an assault or battery which causes ABH. Battery is defined as intentionally or recklessly inflicting unlawful force on a person without consent (*Collins v Wilcock* [1984] 1 WLR 1172) and 'force' merely requires 'the least touching of another' (*Cole v Turner* (1705) 6 Mod Rep 149). There is clearly a battery here when Gavin brands his initials into Mitchell's buttocks. The mens rea of battery is also present because it is clear that Gavin intends to apply force to Mitchell. 'Actual bodily harm' is defined under *Miller* [1954] 2 WLR 138 as 'any hurt or injury calculated to interfere

⁴ Be aware of the CPS Charging Standards, as these are used to determine the charge and this demonstrates some knowledge of legal practice.

with health or comfort'. The Crown Prosecution Service Charging Standards suggest that the injuries must be 'serious' to constitute ABH and 'relevant factors may include, for example, the fact that there has been significant medical intervention and/or permanent effects have resulted'. Since Mitchell's injuries required medical treatment, it is clear that Mitchell's injuries constitute ABH under the Charging Standards.[4] The mens rea required for the offence under section 47 is simply the mens rea for the assault or battery. According to **Roberts** (1971) 56 Cr App R 95 and **Savage; Parmenter**, no additional mens rea in respect of the degree of harm caused need be proved. Thus, it must be proved that Gavin had the mens rea of battery, and it is clear here that Gavin intended to inflict force on Mitchell.

⁵ Once you have dealt with the offence that is most likely to apply, you should consider other relevant offences.

Gavin might be charged with maliciously wounding or inflicting grievous bodily harm under section 20, OAPA 1861 if the injuries to Mitchell are more serious.[5] This offence requires proof that Gavin wounded or inflicted GBH to Mitchell. A wound is a break in the continuity of the skin: **Moriarty v Brookes** (1834) 6 C & P 684. We are not told whether Mitchell has sustained a wound for the purposes of section 20. Depending upon the severity of the injuries, this could constitute 'really serious harm': **DPP v Smith**. The mens rea of this offence is intention or recklessness as to whether some harm was caused: **Savage; Parmenter**.[6] If there is no evidence that Gavin intended to cause some harm to Mitchell, he is likely to be subjectively reckless as to whether some harm would be caused. This is because it is likely that he recognises the risk of causing some harm to Mitchell when he brands him with a hot knife, and he goes ahead and takes that risk: **Cunningham**. If Gavin intends to cause Mitchell GBH, he will in fact be guilty of the more serious offence of wounding or causing GBH under section 18, OAPA 1861.

⁶ Ensure that you correctly state the mens rea of section≈20. Many students misstate this crucial element.

Gavin might argue that he should have a defence in light of Mitchell's consent to the branding. Generally speaking, consent is only a defence to assault and battery, and it will provide no defence to ABH or GBH: see **Donovan** [1934] All ER 207 and **Attorney General's Reference (No. 6 of 1980)** [1981] 2 All ER 1057. However, there are a number of exceptions to this rule. Gavin would seek to rely on the case of **Wilson** in order to support his argument that consent absolves him of liability. The facts of **Wilson** are quite similar to the facts in the scenario. The Court of Appeal in **Wilson** compared the

[7] Set out the arguments that would be put forward in Gavin's defence along with supporting authorities.

act of branding to tattooing, which is rendered lawful by consent. The court held that consensual activity between husband and wife in the privacy of the matrimonial home should not be prosecuted.[7] Although they are not married, this case should also be applied to Mitchell and Gavin.

There is no suggestion on the facts that the branding was carried out for sexual gratification. Rather, the facts suggest that it was conducted out of a sense of commitment to each other. Thus, the prosecution would find it difficult to distinguish **Wilson** and to align this case with the sado-masochistic conduct in **Brown**, in which the House of Lords refused to allow the defence of consent for reasons of public policy, namely the protection of the public against 'a cult of violence'.[8] Lord Templeman stated that sex was no excuse for violence and he was 'not prepared to invent a defence of consent for sado-masochist encounters which breed and glorify cruelty'.[9] Similarly, in **Emmett** (1999) *The Times*, 15 October, consent was no defence where the injuries sustained were more serious than those inflicted in **Wilson**. The court would be likely to follow **Wilson** in respect of Gavin's potential liability since the facts are similar, although this may depend upon whether the injuries sustained by Mitchell were of comparable severity.

[8] Make reference to the rationale for the decision to demonstrate your understanding of the decision of the court and the wider factors which were considered.

[9] Try to remember key quotes from leading authorities to demonstrate detailed knowledge.

✓ Make your answer stand out

- Where there are a number of offences which might apply, you should deal with the most appropriate offence first before also exploring the alternative potential offences.

- Ensure that you fully define the offences setting out both the actus reus and mens rea elements.

- Make reference to the CPS Charging Standards when choosing the most appropriate charge as this demonstrates your knowledge of the way in which the offences will be charged in practice.

- You should also make reference to specific points made by judges or quotes from judgments in order to demonstrate a wide and detailed knowledge of the area.

- Refer to academic opinion if you can, particularly in relation to issues of consent. Consider Ryan, S. (2006) Reckless transmission of HIV: knowledge and culpability. Crim LR 981.

! Don't be tempted to . . .

- Misstate the mens rea for maliciously wounding or inflicting GBH under section 20, OAPA 1861. This is a mistake made by many students in criminal law exams every year.
- Provide a recitation of the facts of key cases simply because the case is relevant. For instance, in this question, repeating in detail the facts of *Brown* or *Dica* adds nothing of substance to your answer and wastes valuable time in the exam. You should instead focus on applying the relevant legal principles to the facts of the problem scenario.

🖎 Question 3

'The 1861 Act has been in force for over 150 years. It has been frequently amended. Despite a long history of criticism of many aspects of the 1861 Act and repeated efforts at reform, it remains in heavy use . . . Frequent changes to the law have left it in an incoherent and confusing state, with more provisions repealed than currently in force' (Law Commission, *Reform of Offences Against the Person* (Law Com. No. 361, 2015) at para. 1.4).

Critically explore whether the Law Commission is right to suggest that there is a need for reform of the non-fatal offences against the person.

Answer plan

→ Address the question regarding reforms and the Law Commission proposals directly at the start of your answer.

→ Consider the extent to which the current statutory framework is logical and coherent.

→ Critically evaluate the Offences Against the Person Act 1861 and relevant case law.

→ Incorporate academic opinion into your answer.

Diagram plan

A printable version of this diagram plan is available from **www.pearsoned.co.uk/lawexpressqa**

Answer

In November 2015, the Law Commission published a Scoping Report containing recommendations to the government on reforming the law relating to the non-fatal offences against the person (Law Commission, *Reform of Offences Against the Person* (Law Com. No. 361, 2015)). The Law Commission was critical of the current legal framework which is largely based on common law and legislation which is over 150 years old, namely the Offences Against the Person Act 1861. It is agreed that the current law lacks coherence and is confused, and that the area is in need of reform.[1]

[1] Refer directly to the quote in your introduction to show your engagement with the question and that you are not about to set out everything you know about the offences.

The Offences Against the Person Act 1861 (OAPA) 'is much disparaged by today's criminal lawyers' (Gardner, J. (1994) Rationality and the rule of law in offences against the person. 53 CLJ 502).[2] When it was initially drafted, the Act was a consolidatory Act. The OAPA did not create new offences but consolidated those that already existed in various other pieces of legislation into one Act. Consequently, the statutory framework fails to provide a clear legislative hierarchy of offences: not only are the five offences spread over two different Acts (both the Offences Against the Person Act 1861 and the Criminal Justice Act 1988), but also the section numbers themselves are not set out in any logical sequence.[3] The most serious of the five offences is maliciously wounding or causing GBH with intent under section 18, OAPA; the next offence decreasing in severity is maliciously wounding or inflicting GBH under section 20, OAPA; the next offence is assault occasioning ABH under section 47, OAPA; and the least serious offences are battery and then assault under section 39, CJA. It is abundantly clear that the OAPA is not logically drafted and there is no clear hierarchy.

[2] Make reference to excellent academic sources where you can to provide evidence of your wider reading.

[3] This sentence sets out a key criticism of the OAPA 1861 and provides reasoning for the critique.

It was acknowledged by the draftsman of the Offences Against the Person Act that '[n]one of [the sections were] rewritten; on the contrary, each contains enactments taken from different Acts passed at different times and with different views, and frequently varying from each other in phraseology' (Greaves, C. (1862) *The Criminal Law Consolidation and Amendment Acts*, 2nd edn. London: Stevens, Sons and Haynes, Sweet and Maxwell).[4] Gardner argues that, while 'the Act as a whole is often found guilty by association, these serious

[4] This demonstrates your understanding of the background to the OAPA 1861 and the reasons why the law has developed in the way that it has.

accusations are being levelled, for the most part, at just a few of its provisions', namely the offences under section 47, section 20 and section 18.

While the above statutory provisions provide for the main offences, they fail to actually provide definitions for the offences adequately. It is not clear from simply reading the relevant statutory provisions what the elements of the offences are; thus, the law is inaccessible and uncertain. Sections 47 and 20, OAPA do not clearly set out what the mens rea of these offences are. The mens rea elements have instead been established by case law: *Savage; Parmenter* [1992] 1 AC 699. Further, section 47, which necessarily requires proof of an assault, does not specify the elements of this lesser, inherent offence. Section 39, CJA makes no reference to any of the elements of assault and battery. Thus, the definition of the elements of these offences is left to the courts to develop. As the provisions of the OAPA and CJA fail to provide adequate detail regarding the elements of these offences, there is necessarily a large base of common law which explains the terms used in the Acts. Thus, the non-fatal offences against the person have been moulded and created by the judiciary through the development of the common law.

The two offences of GBH are distinguishable by their mens rea. However, the actus reus elements are also expressed in different terms. While section 20 requires the 'infliction' of GBH, section 18 requires that GBH is 'caused'. This lack of consistency is explained by the manner in which the Act was drafted. As a consolidating piece of legislation, it cannot be argued that there was any intended distinction between the different terms used: Lord Steyn states, '[t]he difference in language is . . . not a significant factor' (*Ireland; Burstow* [1998] AC 147).[5]

[5] Try to remember some key parts of important cases. This is a House of Lords authority and clearly an important case in this area of law.

The use and meaning of the word 'maliciously' in sections 20 and 18, OAPA have caused problems in application and required clarification from the courts. In respect of section 20, 'maliciously' means 'intentionally or recklessly' (*Savage; Parmenter*). However, recklessness is not sufficient for an offence under section 18 (*Belfon* [1976] 1 WLR 714), thus the word 'maliciously' is rendered redundant where the charge is maliciously wounding or causing GBH with intent to cause GBH. However, 'maliciously' does have practical application

[6] This demonstrates a nuanced understanding of the elements of the section 18 offence and the mens rea requirements.

[7] Demonstrate your awareness of the practical application of the offences by referring to the CPS Charging Standards.

[8] Explain why the maximum sentences for these offences are illogical.

where the charge involves an intention to resist or prevent arrest under section 18, although academics' opinions differ on the degree of harm which must be foreseen.[6]

There is further difficulty in the practicality of charging these offences because the theoretical interpretation of the law is not easily reconcilable with the CPS Charging Standards.[7] A 'wound' is a break in the continuity of the skin (***Moriarty v Brookes*** (1834) 6 C & P 684), thus stabbing someone with a pin and drawing blood technically constitutes a wound and could be charged under section 20. Yet, causing a victim to lose consciousness would only attract a charge under section 47. In practice, stabbing a person with a pin would never be charged under section 20 and would be more likely to be a battery.

A further, related criticism is that there is no logical distinction between the maximum sentences available for each offence. While the most serious offence under section 18 carries a discretionary life sentence of imprisonment, the offences under sections 20 and 47 both carry a maximum sentence of five years' imprisonment. This is so despite a clear distinction in severity between the actus reus elements:[8] section 47 requires actual bodily harm, while section 20 requires proof of a higher degree of harm, grievous bodily harm (or 'really serious harm': ***DPP v Smith*** [1961] AC 290). Assault and battery also both carry the same maximum sentence of six months' imprisonment; although perhaps this is more justifiable as neither offence requires proof of any harm being caused.

In conclusion, the offences are in need of reform in order to create consistency and certainty in the law. The Law Commission has suggested adopting a modified version of the Home Office's 1998 Draft Bill that contains a logical hierarchy of offences which use clear language to describe the offences. The proposed hierarchy is intentionally causing serious injury (clause 1), recklessly causing serious injury (clause 2), intentionally or recklessly causing injury (clause 3), aggravated assault (a proposed addition to the Draft Bill), and physical and threatened assault (clause 4). The clauses in the Draft Bill are quite broadly drafted and leave phrases such as 'serious injury' and 'injury' undefined. Nevertheless, adopting the Draft Bill would be a significant improvement on the current antiquated and confusing legislative and common law framework.

✓ **Make your answer stand out**

■ Explore and critique the Law Commission's proposals in more detail and offer some academic critique on the recommendations.

■ Add further reference to judicial comment to your answer. For instance, you could refer to the fact that Lord Diplock states that the word maliciously 'adds nothing' to section 18 (see *Mowatt* [1967] 3 WLR 1192).

■ You could also refer to the academic opinion on the degree of harm which must be foreseen for a conviction under section 18 where the charge involves an intention to resist or prevent arrest. Ormerod states that there must be proof that the defendant foresaw the specified result (Ormerod, D. (2011) *Smith and Hogan Criminal Law*, 13th edn Oxford: Oxford University Press).

■ Where possible, you should contrast differing academic opinion on this point. In contrast with Ormerod's approach, Jefferson states that the defendant must merely foresee some harm (Jefferson, M. (2011) *Criminal Law*. London: Pearson Longman).

■ Provide your opinion to demonstrate to the examiner that you are capable of independent thought and to make your answer stand out from other answers which merely regurgitate the law.

! **Don't be tempted to . . .**

■ Set out everything you know about the non-fatal offences against the person. This question is very specific and does not ask you for a recitation of the elements of each of the offences. Instead, you must demonstrate a critical appreciation of the law and select some of the key problem areas.

■ Recite the facts of the cases. There is a lot that could be discussed in this answer and you will waste time by regaling the facts of cases which are not relevant to the question.

📝 Question 4

To what extent do policy considerations influence the use of consent as a defence to non-fatal offences against the person?

Answer plan

➜ Briefly outline the general rule that consent is a defence to assault and battery only.

➜ Explain the exceptions to this and the rationale for these exceptions.

➡ Consider problematic areas, such as consent and sexual gratification and the conflict between *Brown, Wilson* and *Emmett*.

➡ Explore whether consent plays a part in the transmission of HIV through consensual sex and *Dica* and *Konzani*.

➡ Discuss the role of policy considerations and the public interest.

Diagram plan

A printable version of this diagram plan is available from **www.pearsoned.co.uk/lawexpressqa**

Answer

[1] This sentence shows that you have identified the competing interests at the very start.

Public policy considerations play a significant role in the law on consent and non-fatal offences against the person. There are two conflicting principles: the protection of the public from harmful conduct and respect for individual bodily autonomy.[1] The law faces the precarious task of finding a suitable balance between allowing dangerous consensual activity and restricting individual autonomy. The courts are not willing to permit one person to lawfully cause actual or grievous bodily harm to another unless it is in the public interest

[2] Address the question directly in your introduction.

that such harm be caused. Thus, policy considerations are taken into account in deciding whether in certain circumstances an individual should be permitted to consent to activity which causes harm and would otherwise be a criminal offence.[2]

[3] This sentence demonstrates that you understand the rationale for the general rule.

The general rule is that consent is only a defence to assault or battery: **Donovan** [1934] All ER 207 and **Attorney General's Reference (No. 6 of 1980)** [1981] 2 All ER 1057. These are both offences which require no proof of any harm being caused to the victim.[3] However, the courts are stricter when a degree of harm is actually caused; thus, consent is no defence to charges of assault occasioning actual bodily harm (s. 47, OAPA 1861), maliciously wounding or inflicting grievous bodily harm (s. 20) and wounding or causing GBH with intent (s. 18). The law also dictates that we impliedly consent to physical contact of everyday life: *Collins* v *Wilcock* [1984] 1 WLR 1172.

However, the law would be incredibly restrictive on our daily lives if it did not permit some deviations from this general rule. Thus, there are certain socially acceptable exceptions when the law allows such harm in the public interest. These exceptions were outlined by Lord Lane CJ in *Attorney General's Reference (No. 6 of 1980)* and each is justifiable on grounds of public policy. For instance, reasonable surgical intervention must be permissible for the protection of the health of individuals and to protect the sanctity of life. This exception also includes cosmetic surgery, but the justifications for permitting cosmetic surgery are different and must concern the protection of individual bodily autonomy.[4] Similarly, forms of body adornment, such as tattooing and body piercing are permissible to protect individual autonomy. Since cutting a substantial amount of hair off a person's head was deemed to constitute ABH in *DPP* v *Smith* [2006] 1 WLR 1571, hairdressing must also fall under these exceptions.

Injuries caused during properly regulated sports are not subject to criminal sanction because the promotion of exercise is in the greater public interest and sport is a socially acceptable form of entertainment. The Court of Appeal has held that prosecutions for injuries sustained during properly regulated sports should be reserved for grave conduct which is sufficiently serious to be criminal: see *Barnes* [2004] EWCA Crim 3246. While injuries caused unintentionally as an incidental by-product of sports such as rugby and football are easy to justify, it is much harder to justify the use of consent to render lawful injuries intentionally inflicted during sports such as boxing.[5]

Unintentional injuries sustained during 'rough horseplay' are deemed to be consented to: see *Jones* (1986) 83 Cr App R 375 and *Aitken* [1992] 1 WLR 1006. The rationale for this lies in the often used phrase 'boys will be boys'. The law would be too restrictive if criminal liability was imposed on individuals for unintentionally causing harm during rough horseplay among willing participants. Other exceptions include: lawful chastisement, dangerous exhibitions, ritual circumcision and religious flagellation, which was deemed necessary to avoid a conflict with Article 9 of the European Convention on Human Rights (see Lord Mustill in *Brown* [1994] 1 AC 212).

[4] Show the examiner that you are able to distinguish between the different justifications for the different exceptions to the general rule.

[5] Including this reference to boxing shows that you appreciate that the legality of boxing is not necessarily justified using policy considerations.

One problematic area is that involving injuries inflicted during sexual activity. The House of Lords has ruled that consent is no defence to harm deliberately inflicted for sexual gratification: **Brown**. This case involved sado-masochistic conduct between a group of consenting men. The men sustained wounds and injuries which had deliberately been inflicted, and their conduct was videoed and videos were circulated among members. The defendants' convictions for offences under section 47 and section 20, OAPA 1861 were upheld in the Court of Appeal and House of Lords. The rationale for imposing criminal liability upon a defendant in such circumstances was expressed by Lord Templeman as the need to protect society against a 'cult of violence' which would 'breed and glorify cruelty'.[6] His Lordship was also concerned by the risk of transmission of HIV and other STDs and the corrupting effect that such behaviour could have on younger members of society.[7] However, this decision of the House of Lords may be criticised for casting moralistic judgments on the defendants in question.[8] The protection of the public was the overriding consideration in this case, and this outweighed respect for individual autonomy. By contrast, later cases involving heterosexual couples have confused the issue by taking the opposite approach.

In **Slingsby** [1995] Crim LR 570, consent was a valid defence where the victim accidentally sustained an internal wound caused by vigorous consensual sexual activity and which ultimately led to her death. Similarly, in **Wilson** [1997] 1 QB 47, **Brown** was distinguished on the basis that branding with a hot knife constituted body adornment. This act was committed with full consent but was not done for purposes of sexual gratification, and thus can be distinguished on this basis. The Court of Appeal was keen to emphasise the fact that consensual sexual activity between husband and wife which takes place in private is not a matter for criminal investigation; thus, placing great weight on personal autonomy and privacy. However, this approach was not followed in **Emmett** (1999) *The Times*, 15 October, a case involving sado-masochistic activity between an engaged couple. The Court of Appeal held that the severity of the injuries meant that intervention by the law was in the public interest.

It must be asked whether the law should be able to restrict the behaviour of consenting adults, thus overriding individual autonomy and the freedom to be able to consent to injury or the risk thereof. According to Ashworth, consent 'embodies a recognition that the autonomy of the other person is involved, and that if that person agrees to the conduct

[6] Try to remember short key quotes from relevant judgments.

[7] This shows that you have read the opinion and understood the reasoning provided by the judge.

[8] This sentence demonstrates your ability to question (rather than merely accept) the decision of the judge.

there should be no offence' (Ashworth, A. (2009) *Principles of Criminal Law*, 6th edn. Oxford: Oxford University Press, p. 318). This freedom appears to have been respected in both **Dica** [2004] QB 1257 and **Konzani** [2005] EWCA Crim 706 in respect of the risk of transmission of HIV. In both cases, the Court of Appeal held that an informed consent to the risks of having unprotected sexual intercourse with a partner infected with HIV would be a valid defence to a charge under section 20, OAPA 1861 in the event of the virus being transmitted.

In conclusion, policy considerations clearly influence the use of consent as a defence. The courts face the difficult task of finding a suitable and consistent balance between the competing principles of the protection of the public and respect for individual autonomy.

 ## Make your answer stand out

- You should explore in more detail the reasoning of the judges in the House of Lords in *Brown*.
- You should compare the opinions of the majority in *Brown* with the dissenting opinion of Lord Mustill. You should refer to Malcolm, T. (2012) How far is too far? The extent to which consent is a defence to non-fatal offences against the person, in N. Geach and C. Monaghan, *Dissenting Judgments in the Law*. London: Wildy, Simmonds and Hill, p. 317, for academic commentary on Lord Mustill's dissenting opinion.
- You could elaborate on the issue of to what extent morality should influence the decisions of judges and include reference to the Hart–Devlin debate.
- You should refer to academic opinion, such as Weait, M. (2005) Knowledge, autonomy and consent: *R* v *Konzani*. Crim LR 763; Bamforth, N. (1994) Sado-masochism and consent. Crim LR 661; and Gunn, M. and Ormerod, D. (1995) The legality of boxing. 15 *Legal Studies* 181.

! Don't be tempted to . . .

- Provide factual accounts of all of the cases as you will not have time to do this and address the issue of policy in the exam.
- Set out the elements of the offences. This question asks you specifically about consent and you will waste time by setting out the actus reus and mens rea elements of the non-fatal offences against the person.
- Forget to address the question directly throughout your answer, as well as in your introduction and conclusion.

Try it yourself

Now take a look at the question below and attempt to answer it. You can check your response against the answer guidance available on the companion website (**www.pearsoned.co.uk/lawexpressqa**).

> 'I would. . . reject the proposition that an assault can never be committed by words. That brings me to the critical question whether a silent caller may be guilty of an assault. The answer to this question seems to me to be "yes, depending on the facts".' (*per* Lord Steyn in *R* v *Ireland; R* v *Burstow* [1998] AC 147 at 162).
>
> Critically evaluate the above statement.

www.pearsoned.co.uk/lawexpressqa

 Go online to access more revision support including additional essay and problem questions with diagram plans, You be the marker questions, and download all diagrams from the book.

Sexual offences

How this topic may come up in exams

Sexual offences could be examined by way of an essay or a problem question. Essay questions might require you to compare the old law with that under the Sexual Offences Act 2003, or to critically evaluate the meaning of consent. Problem questions will require you to have good knowledge of all elements of the offences and of the law on consent. You should check your syllabus so that you know whether you could be examined on the four main sexual offences, whether your syllabus includes child sex offences, or whether you will only be examined on the offence of rape.

Before you begin

It's a good idea to consider the following key themes of sexual offences before tackling a question on this topic.

A printable version of this diagram is available from **www.pearsoned.co.uk/lawexpressqa**

🔯 Question 1

Prior to the Sexual Offences Act 2003, the law on sexual offences was 'archaic, incoherent and discriminatory' and failed to 'reflect the changes in society and social attitudes' (Home Office (2002) Protecting the Public, Cm 5668, p. 9).

Critically evaluate the law on rape and the extent to which the law has been improved.

Answer plan

→ Outline the offence of rape under the SOA 2003.

→ Analyse the changes to the elements of rape.

→ Explore the meaning of consent.

→ Discuss whether the SOA 2003 has improved the law.

→ Consider whether the law is coherent and reflects changes in society.

Diagram plan

A printable version of this diagram plan is available from **www.pearsoned.co.uk/lawexpressqa**

Answer

This question requires a critical evaluation of the Sexual Offences Act 2003 (SOA 2003). The law on rape underwent radical reform in 2004, when the SOA 2003 came into force. The Act intended to modernise the law and add coherence and clarity to an area which had developed in a piecemeal fashion.[1] Rape is defined under section 1(1). The actus reus requires the penile penetration of the vagina, anus or mouth, without consent. The mens rea requires intentional penetration, where the defendant had no reasonable belief in consent.

[1] State the aims of the SOA 2003 to demonstrate wider knowledge beyond the elements of the offence.

In 2004, the actus reus of rape was extended to cover non-consensual oral sex (previously indecent assault), which was deemed to be serious enough to amount to rape because it is just 'as abhorrent, demeaning and traumatising' as vaginal and anal rape and 'equally, if not more, psychologically harmful' (Home Office (2003) Government Reply to the Fifth Report from the Home Affairs Committee Session 2002–2003).[2] The Act dispensed with the phrase 'sexual intercourse', which was used to define rape under the SOA 1956. This phrase was incredibly vague as to when intercourse begins. The SOA 2003 is clear in only requiring slight penetration (s. 79(9)). The Act also places the authority of *Kaitamaki* [1985] AC 147 on a statutory footing by stating that penetration is a continuing act (s. 79(2)).

[2] Use key quotes from government publications where appropriate to show awareness of the lead up to enactment.

Another notable change was the use of gender neutral terminology. The SOA 2003 dispensed with gender-specific words, to ensure that the offence of rape can apply to those who have undergone gender reassignment surgery. The old law was discriminatory in this respect and failed to reflect changes in society and social attitudes. The reforms to the actus reus of rape were a welcome improvement to the outdated and vague definition of rape which existed previously.[3]

[3] Provide your opinion at a midway point of your answer to maintain focus.

The SOA 2003 also defined consent for the first time (s. 74) and provided for evidential and conclusive presumptions relating to consent (ss. 75 and 76). Sections 75 and 76 placed the common law onto a statutory footing. The conclusive presumptions under section 76(1) that the complainant did not consent and that the defendant did not believe that she consented are relevant where: (a) A intentionally deceived B as to the nature or purpose of the act; or (b) A intentionally induced B to have sex by impersonating a person known personally to B. This section placed cases such as *Flattery* [1877] 2 QBD 410, *Williams* [1923] 1 KB 340 and *Linekar* [1995] QB 250 onto a statutory footing, while incorporating the approach adopted in *Tabassum* [2000] 2 Cr App R 328 in relation to fraud as to the purpose of the act. In relation to fraud as to the identity of the defendant, the case of *Elbekkay* [1995] Crim LR 163 was placed on a statutory footing but it also extended the law beyond the impersonation of a spouse or partner.[4]

[4] Compare and contrast the law to show that you are aware of the effects of the SOA 2003.

Section 75(1) sets out evidential presumptions that the complainant did not consent and that the defendant did not reasonably believe that she consented, which are relevant where one of the circumstances in section 75(2) applies and A knew this. The presumptions are rebuttable, so where A adduces some evidence to rebut the presumptions, it will be for the prosecution to prove beyond reasonable doubt that there was no consent and that A did not reasonably believe B was consenting. Only an evidential burden is placed on the defendant and the legal burden rests with the prosecution (*Ciccarelli* [2011] EWCA Crim 2665). Section 75 placed cases such as *Larter* [1995] Crim LR 75 on a statutory footing.

The SOA 2003 codified much existing case law, but it could be argued that the presumptions are not easy to explain to a jury. It is difficult to explain why deception qualifies as a conclusive presumption, but the use of violence only an evidential presumption. This difficulty is especially evident when one considers the approach taken by the House of Lords towards sexual gratification by violence in *Brown* [1994] 1 AC 212.[5] One might also question whether the use of conclusive presumptions is a satisfactory method of securing convictions.

[5] This sentence demonstrates your ability to think critically and to link this topic to other topics in criminal law.

One problem which was not addressed by the Act is that of intoxication and consent. Although the Act deals with cases where the complainant is unconscious or asleep and 'date rape' situations through the use of evidential presumptions under section 75, situations in which the defendant has sex with an intoxicated complainant were not directly addressed (*Bree* [2008] QB 131).[6] As such, the issue of consent is left to the jury and recourse must be had to the definition of consent. Consent has been defined under section 74 as agreeing by choice, having the capacity and freedom to make that choice. Consent is a question for the jury who will receive no detailed direction on consent from the trial judge. Another problem concerns submission and consent. Whether submitting to sexual intercourse as a result of non-violent threats constitutes consent is not addressed by the Act (*Olugboja* [1982] QB 32). Although the Act is to be commended for codifying existing legal principles which evolved under the common law, it left many situations unexplored which consequently have had to be dealt with by broad definition of consent under section 74 and the interpretation given by the jury. Recently, the common law seems to have developed in such a way as to create a form of conditional consent. Where X agrees to sexual intercourse on condition that her partner does not ejaculate inside her, but he deliberately decides to do so and then does so, X is deprived of choice and her consent is negated (*R (F) v DPP* [2013] EWHC 945 (Admin)). The Divisional

[6] This paragraph demonstrates your awareness of topical problems as well as up-to-date case law.

Court held that 'choice' is crucial to consent (see also **Assange v Swedish Prosecution Authority** [2011] EWHC 2849 (Admin)).

Since there was no definition of consent under the common law, the 'parameters [of rape were] unclear' (Temkin, J. (2002) *Rape and the Legal Process.* Oxford: Oxford University Press). However, the definition under section 74 is very broad and leaves much to the interpretation of the jury. It has been criticised for being 'vague in its terms' and for leaving 'too much uncertainty in the application of the law to a whole range of familiar situations' (Temkin, J. and Ashworth, A. (2004) Rape, sexual assaults and the problem of consent. Crim LR 328).[7] This is certainly true in respect of intoxication and consent and cases of submission. The extent to which the Act has achieved its aim of clarifying the law by explaining what behaviour is and is not acceptable must be questioned.

[7] Cite academic opinion where appropriate to show that you have read widely.

Another significant amendment to the definition of rape concerned the mens rea. The SOA 2003 contains no mention of the concept of recklessness, but rape requires a reasonable belief that the complainant was consenting. It dispensed with the subjective test under **DPP v Morgan** [1976] AC 182 in relation to a mistaken belief in consent. The old law requiring an honest belief in consent was replaced by an objective requirement that the belief is reasonable.

In conclusion, although certain aspects of the SOA 2003 are welcomed, such as the extension of the actus reus of rape, the Act was disappointing in other respects. The law on consent is confusing and the long-awaited definition is too broad and leaves much to the interpretation of the jury. Thus, the SOA 2003 has not provided the clarity craved by the law on rape.[8]

[8] Link your conclusion back to the question.

✓ Make your answer stand out

■ Develop the discussion about intoxication and consent and *Bree.* You could also discuss cases such as *Jheeta* [2007] EWCA Crim 1699 and *Zhang* [2007] EWCA Crim 2018 on consent.

■ Expand upon the issue of submission and consent and refer to the article by Gardner, S. (1996) Appreciating *Olugboja.* 16 *Legal Studies* 275.   ▶

- Expand upon the discussion of consent and fraud, discussing cases such as *Tabassum*, *B* [2013] 2 Cr App R 29 and the difference between fraud as to the 'quality' of the act and fraud as to the 'purpose' of the act. Also consider *McNally* [2013] EWCA Crim 1051.

- Discuss the question raised by Temkin and Ashworth (Temkin, J. and Ashworth, A. (2004) Rape, sexual assaults and the problem of consent. Crim LR 328) as to whether the categories of presumptions are 'intended to reflect some kind of moral hierarchy' or simply organised to ensure 'clarity and certainty' or a mixture of the two 'with an added element of common law history'.

- Elaborate upon the change to the test applied to mistaken belief in consent. Consider whether the introduction of an objective approach is in line with the subjectivist nature of criminal law. Read Wells, C. (1982) Swatting the subjectivist bug. Crim LR 209.

- Consider whether the actus reus of rape should have been extended to cover non-consensual oral sex or whether this should have been categorised as assault by penetration.

! Don't be tempted to . . .

- Discuss other offences such as assault by penetration, sexual assault and causing a person to engage in sexual activity without consent. The question is limited to the offence of rape, so do not waste valuable time.

- Write out large swathes of statute. It is better to ensure that you understand the meaning of the relevant sections, and to learn short extracts of the sections by heart. This question requires a critical appreciation of the law rather than a mere recital of the law.

? Question 2

Rachel and Steve are married, although they separated a year ago and have been living apart. One evening, they unexpectedly meet at a mutual friend's party and speak to each other for the first time in a year. They are surprised to find that they get on really well. They enjoy spending the evening talking and they share a few glasses of wine together. Unbeknown to both Rachel and Steve, the wine has been spiked with vodka. After a lovely evening, Steve walks Rachel back to her flat. Rachel invites Steve in for a coffee, and since it is late she suggests that he stays over and offers him the sofa to sleep on. They talk late into the night until Steve suggests that he sleeps in Rachel's bed. Rachel is reluctant at first, but Steve assures her that he simply wants a good night's sleep and nothing more. Eventually, Rachel agrees to allow Steve to stay in her bed. During the night, after Rachel has fallen asleep, Steve wakes Rachel up and asks her if he can have sexual intercourse with her. In a half-asleep state, Rachel says 'no', but after Steve pleads with her, she eventually gives in to Steve's demands on the condition that he does not ejaculate inside her vagina. They have sexual intercourse and Steve does ejaculate inside Rachel's vagina.

Consider whether Steve is criminally liable for any offence.

Answer plan

→ Consider Steve's liability for the offence of rape. You will need to address the issues of marital rape and consent.

→ In particular, you will need to consider whether the evidential presumptions under section 75(1) are triggered here by section 75(2)(f), SOA 2003 in respect of the wine being spiked and whether the fact that this act was carried out by another person and unbeknown to Steve has any bearing on his potential liability here.

→ You will need to discuss whether the evidential presumptions under section 75(1) are triggered here by section 75(2)(d), SOA 2003 in light of the fact that Rachel is half-asleep during sexual intercourse.

→ You will also need to explore the definition of consent under section 74 and the issue of consent and submission. Make reference to the cases of *Olugboja* [1982] QB 32 and *McAllister* [1997] Crim LR 233.

→ You should consider the recent Divisional Court cases on conditional consent, such as *R (F) v DPP* [2013] EWHC 945 (Admin) and *Assange* v *Swedish Prosecution Authority* [2011] EWHC 2849 (Admin).

Diagram plan

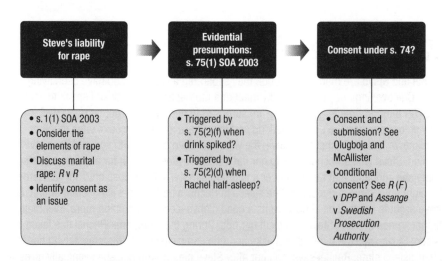

A printable version of this diagram plan is available from **www.pearsoned.co.uk/lawexpressqa**

Answer

This question requires consideration of the liability of Steve for the offence of rape. Rape is defined under section 1(1) of the Sexual Offences Act 2003 (SOA 2003). The actus reus requires the penetration of the vagina, anus or mouth, with the defendant's penis, where the complainant does not consent. The mens rea is intentional penetration, where the defendant had no reasonable belief in consent.[1]

[1] Set out the definition of rape at the start so that you do not need to do this throughout the answer.

Steve may be guilty of the rape of Rachel. It is clear from the question that vaginal sexual intercourse took place. It is also clear that the penetration is intentional.[2] Steve and Rachel are married, albeit estranged; the law is clear that marital rape is recognised as rape (*R* v *R* [1991] 3 WLR 767). The issue in this question is really one of consent. The prosecution must establish that Rachel was not consenting and that Steve did not reasonably believe that she was consenting.[3] Consideration must be given to the evidential and conclusive presumptions under section 75(1) and section 76(1), SOA 2003.

[2] Although you do not need to define rape again here, you must apply the elements to the facts.

[3] Identify the key issues at the beginning of your answer.

There is no evidence to suggest that the presumptions under section 76(1) apply since none of the circumstances under section 76(2) apply.[4] However, the evidential presumptions under section 75(1) need further discussion. Section 75(1) sets out two evidential presumptions: that the complainant did not consent and that D did not reasonably believe that she consented. These are relevant where one of the circumstances under section 75(2) is applicable and D knew this. These presumptions may apply due to the fact that Rachel's drink was spiked (s. 75(2)(f)) or because she was half-asleep when Steve begins to have intercourse with her (s. 75(2)(d)).[5] Section 75(2)(f) applies where a person administers or causes to be taken by the complainant a substance capable of causing or enabling the complainant to be stupefied or overpowered at the time of sexual intercourse. Here, Rachel's drink has been spiked with vodka, which is a substance that is capable (in sufficient quantities) of causing Rachel to be stupefied or overpowered. The person administering the substance need not be the defendant, but the defendant must be aware that Rachel's drink was spiked. Since Steve was not aware that Rachel's drink had been spiked, section 75(2)(f) does not apply. Section 75(2)(d) applies where the complainant is asleep or unconscious and the defendant knows that. Here, Rachel is only half-asleep so it is not entirely clear whether

[4] If the conclusive presumptions do not apply, rule them out at the start.

[5] There is no need to list all of the circumstances under section 75(2). Choose the most appropriate circumstance on the facts.

[6] Use the facts in the problem scenario to substantiate the conclusions you draw.

the evidential presumptions under section 75(1) are triggered. Since Rachel responds verbally to Steve, he may argue that she was not asleep and that if she was, he was unaware that she was asleep.[6] Thus, the presumptions under section 75(1) will not apply. This will mean that it will not be presumed that Rachel was not consenting and it will not be presumed that Steve did not reasonably believe that she was consenting.

If the presumptions under sections 75(1) and 76(1) do not apply, the definition under section 74 will need to be applied in order to establish whether or not Rachel was consenting. Steve may adduce evidence to the effect that Rachel eventually gave in to his request. He would argue that this was evidence of her consent; however, Rachel will argue that her submission did not constitute consent. Section 74 defines consent as agreeing by choice, with the capacity and freedom to make that choice. The facts here raise the issue of whether submission amounts to consent or not. The law is not very clear in relation to submission to sexual intercourse when non-violent demands are made. In *Olugboja*, the Court of Appeal held that it was up to the jury to decide whether there was consent on a case-by-case basis. In *McAllister*, it was held that the judge was not required to direct

[7] This demonstrates your awareness that the pre-SOA 2003 cases may apply here and why.

the jury that reluctant acquiescence amounted to consent. Although these were cases decided before the enactment of the SOA 2003, they follow the approach adopted today.[7] Consent is a question for the jury and they will receive no detailed direction on consent from the trial judge. Before deciding whether Rachel in this scenario agreed

[8] These few sentences justify your conclusion on this point.

by choice, the proportionality between the demands and the act of sex must be explored. The gravity of the demands must also be considered. It could be argued that the demands issued here were not sufficiently grave to warrant Rachel acceding to them.[8] It may be necessary to know a little more about the circumstances of their relationship. However, on the facts it is likely that the jury will consider consent to be present, and thus there will be no conviction for rape.

If it is established that Rachel did not consent to sexual intercourse, it must also be established that Steve did not reasonably believe that she was consenting. Whether a belief is reasonable is to be determined having regard to all the circumstances, including any steps Steve has taken to ascertain whether she is consenting (s. 1(2)), such as asking her for sexual intercourse, as Steve did here. While the facts show that Rachel clearly said 'no' after his initial request for sexual intercourse, she eventually gives in to his demands. Thus, even if she was not in fact consenting to sexual intercourse, Steve may argue that he reasonably believed that she was because she gave in to his requests for sex.

Finally, the issue of conditional consent must be considered. When Rachel eventually gives in to Steve's demands for sex, she does so on the condition that he does not ejaculate inside her vagina. Recent jurisprudence from the Divisional Court suggests that where a complainant gives conditional consent and the defendant's actions go beyond the conditions of that consent, the complainant is deemed not to have consented. *R (F) v DPP*, was a case about a woman who consented to sexual intercourse with her partner on the basis that he would not ejaculate inside her vagina. The Divisional Court held that the woman's consent was negated where her partner ejaculated inside her vagina. The court examined the history of the relationship between the parties, noting that the woman's partner was abusively dominating. The court stated that 'choice' is crucial consent. Thus, it might be argued that Rachel's consent was negated by the fact that Steve did in fact ejaculate inside Rachel's vagina. While this case is only a Divisional Court authority (and thus is not binding), the principle of conditional consent is supported by the earlier Divisional Court decision in *Assange v Swedish Prosecution Authority*[9] in which it was stated that the prosecution could rely on section 74 to prove that a complainant had not consented to unprotected sexual intercourse where she consented to sexual intercourse with a condom. Thus, Steve could be convicted of the rape of Rachel on the basis that he went beyond the condition of the consent that Rachel gave.

[9] This sentence shows that you are aware of the hierarchy of the courts and the fact that this case is not binding, but that the emerging body of case law is persuasive.

✓ Make your answer stand out

- Although the law on rape is now contained within the SOA 2003, you should apply any pre-2003 cases which might be relevant, particularly in relation to consent and submission.
- Demonstrate a clear understanding of how the presumptions work in practice and the distinction between the evidential and the conclusive presumptions under sections 75(1) and 76(1) respectively. ▶

- You could incorporate some academic opinion into your answer, particularly relating to contentious issues that arise on the facts of the problem question. For instance, in this question, you could also consider academic opinion on submission, such as Gardner, S. (1996) Appreciating *Olugboja*. 16 *Legal Studies* 275.

- Although the main issues in this question require a discussion of the provisions relating to consent, you must also apply the other elements of rape in order to provide a complete answer and to demonstrate a rounded knowledge of the SOA 2003.

! Don't be tempted to . . .

- Forget that the presumptions under section 75(1) require not only the existence of a circumstance under section 75(2), but also require the defendant to be aware of the existence of that circumstance.

- Confuse an evidential burden and a legal burden. The evidential presumptions may be rebutted. This requires the defendant to discharge an evidential burden (raise some evidence to rebut the presumptions). This is not a burden of proof. The legal burden still rests with the prosecution to prove (beyond reasonable doubt) that there was no consent and that the defendant had no reasonable belief in consent.

- Set out the circumstances under sections 75(2) and 76(2) which do not apply to the particular problem scenario you are dealing with. You will gain no extra marks for providing irrelevant information and you will merely highlight your inability to distinguish between relevant and irrelevant information.

? Question 3

Answer **ALL** parts.

Consider the criminal liability of the parties for any sexual offences in **ALL** of the following scenarios:

(a) Harold has a foot fetish. He tells Kelly that he will punch her unless she lets him remove her shoes and stroke her feet. Kelly lets Harold touch her feet.

(b) Lionel offers to give Sandra a lift home in his car. However, instead of driving her home, he takes her to a remote field and locks the car doors. He refuses to let Sandra out of the car unless she performs oral sex on him. She does so.

(c) Jenny asks Daryl to take a bath while she watches him. She tells him to masturbate in front of her. When he refuses to do so, she strikes him over the head with a gun. Daryl does what Jenny tells him to do.

Answer plan

➜ Explore the liability of Harold for sexual assault under section 3, SOA 2003 in respect of Kelly. In particular, you will need to address the meaning of 'sexual' under section 78. The issue of consent and the evidential presumptions under section 75(1) triggered by section 75(2)(a) will also be important here.

➜ Discuss the liability of Lionel for the offence of the rape under section 1, SOA 2003. You will need to consider here the issue of consent and the possibility of the evidential presumptions under section 75(1) being triggered by section 75(2)(c).

➜ Consider the liability of Jenny for causing a person to engage in sexual activity without consent under section 4, SOA 2003. You should refer here to the meaning of 'sexual' under section 78 and the evidential presumptions under section 75(1) as triggered by section 75(2)(a).

Diagram plan

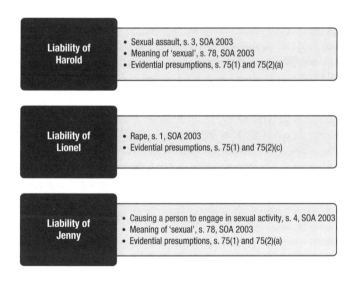

| **Liability of Harold** | • Sexual assault, s. 3, SOA 2003
• Meaning of 'sexual', s. 78, SOA 2003
• Evidential presumptions, s. 75(1) and 75(2)(a) |

| **Liability of Lionel** | • Rape, s. 1, SOA 2003
• Evidential presumptions, s. 75(1) and 75(2)(c) |

| **Liability of Jenny** | • Causing a person to engage in sexual activity, s. 4, SOA 2003
• Meaning of 'sexual', s. 78, SOA 2003
• Evidential presumptions, s. 75(1) and 75(2)(a) |

A printable version of this diagram plan is available from **www.pearsoned.co.uk/lawexpressqa**

[1] List the offences that you will be discussing at the very start to demonstrate that you have identified the key offences.

[2] This question provides your structure for you. Ensure you divide your answer into parts (a) to (c).

Answer

This question involves consideration of the offences of sexual assault, rape and causing a person to engage in sexual activity under sections 3, 1 and 4, SOA 2003 respectively.[1] The liability of Harold, Lionel and Jenny will be explored.[2]

(a) Harold

Harold could be guilty of sexual assault under s. 3(1), Sexual Offences Act 2003. This offence requires proof that Harold intentionally touched Kelly without her consent and that the touching was sexual. It must also be proved that Harold did not reasonably believe that Kelly consented. Harold does intentionally touch Kelly as he asks her if he can remove her shoes and touch her feet before then doing so. According to the case of *Thomas* (1985) 81 Cr App R 331, touching the hem of a girl's skirt is sufficient for battery and under section 79(8), 'touching' includes touching with any part of the body and through anything.[3] Thus, the fact that Harold touches Kelly's shoes is sufficient to constitute an assault, but in any event he also touches her feet directly, so we have an assault here.[4] It is necessary to consider whether the touching was 'sexual' under section 78. Section 78 defines the word 'sexual' and the Court of Appeal examined its meaning in *H* [2005] 1 WLR 2005.[5] The jury must consider whether the act was sexual. Under s. 78(a), an act is sexual if a reasonable person would consider that because of its nature, it is sexual, irrespective of its circumstances or any person's purpose in relation to the act. Touching a person's shoes or feet is not inherently sexual, so section 78(a) will not apply here. However, s. 78(b) provides that an act is sexual if a reasonable person would consider that because of its nature it may be sexual and because of its circumstances or the purpose of any person in relation to it, it is sexual. Here, we know that Harold has a foot fetish, so the touching will be deemed to be sexual if a reasonable person would consider that touching a person's shoes and feet might be sexual, and that Harold's purpose here was indeed sexual.

A further issue to be considered here is that of consent. Consent is defined under section 74 as agreeing by choice, having the freedom and capacity to make that choice. On the facts, it is clear that Kelly does not agree by choice to the touching, she only agrees because of the threat of violence. It would be appropriate to explore the evidential presumptions under section 75(1) here as they are likely to apply. The circumstances under section 75(2)(a) exist because Harold has threatened Kelly with violence when he threatens to punch her. Since Harold was aware of the threat that he made, the rebuttable presumptions under section 75(1) are triggered. So, it is presumed that Kelly did not consent and that Harold did not reasonably believe that Kelly was consenting. Thus, Harold will be guilty of sexual assault unless he can

[3] Cite any relevant definition sections to demonstrate your wider knowledge of the statute.

[4] Ensure that you apply the law using the specific facts in the problem scenario.

[5] This sentence and the following paragraph incorporate both the relevant statutory provision and case law to demonstrate wider knowledge.

rebut these presumptions. He only bears the evidential burden here, so he need only raise some evidence in rebuttal. However, there is no evidence to rebut these presumptions on the facts.

(b) Lionel

Lionel could be charged with raping Sandra. The offence of rape is provided for under s. 1(1), Sexual Offences Act 2003. The actus reus requires the penetration of the vagina, anus or mouth, with the defendant's penis, where the complainant does not consent. The mens rea is intentional penetration, where the defendant had no reasonable belief in consent. Intentional penile penetration of the mouth has occurred here.[6]

[6] Do not labour over these elements if they are quite clearly satisfied.

Thus, the main issue with respect to Lionel's liability is one of consent. The evidential presumptions under section 75(1) could apply because Sandra has been unlawfully detained by Lionel who locks her in the car and Lionel is not himself detained (s. 75(2)(c)). It is also clear that Lionel knew that Sandra was unlawfully detained because he is the one who locked the car doors after driving her to a secluded location.[7] Consequently, under section 75(1) it is presumed that Sandra did not consent to the penetration, and that Lionel did not reasonably believe that she was consenting. Thus, Lionel will be guilty of rape unless he can rebut these presumptions. There appears to be no such evidence on the facts.

[7] This demonstrates that you have fully understood that both the circumstances under section 75(2)(c) must be present and the defendant must have known about the existence of those circumstances.

(c) Jenny

Jenny could be guilty of causing a person to engage in sexual activity (s. 4(1)). This offence requires proof that Jenny intentionally caused Daryl to engage in a sexual activity without his consent and that she did not reasonably believe that Daryl was consenting. It is clear that Jenny intentionally caused Daryl to engage in a sexual activity. Applying the meaning of 'sexual' under s. 78, watching somebody take a bath is not inherently sexual under s. 78(a). It is not immediately clear from the facts whether Jenny derives some sexual pleasure from watching him. If the reasonable person would consider that because of its nature, watching somebody take a bath might be sexual, and that Jenny's purpose is sexual, then Jenny watching Daryl taking a bath could be 'sexual' under s. 78(b). In any event, masturbation is inherently sexual under section 78(a), so proving this element will not cause the prosecution any difficulty.

A further issue here is that of consent. The evidential presumptions under section 75(1) are likely to apply here. The circumstances under section 75(2)(a) exist because Jenny actually uses violence against Daryl and the fact that she is holding a gun may also constitute a threat of violence. Since Jenny was clearly aware of the existence of these circumstances, the rebuttable presumptions under section 75(1) are triggered. So, it is presumed that Daryl did not consent and that Jenny did not reasonably believe that Daryl was consenting. Jenny will be guilty of causing a person to engage in sexual activity unless she can rebut these presumptions. There is no evidence to rebut these on the facts.

✓ Make your answer stand out

- Demonstrate a clear understanding of the distinction between the four different offences under the SOA 2003. Many of the elements for each offence are different and examiners will be looking to see if you are aware of the elements of each offence.
- Ensure that you cite key case law, such as *H* in respect of the meaning of 'sexual'. You must explain why you are mentioning the case.
- Ensure that you apply the law to the facts of the problem scenario throughout your answer. This question addresses all four main offences and is quite technical in some respects, but you must apply all elements rather than simply deal with the contentious ones.
- You could incorporate some academic opinion into your answer, such as Bantekas, I. (2008) Can touching always be sexual when there is no sexual intent? 73 *Journal of Criminal Law* 251 on the meaning of 'sexual' for the purposes of section 78, SOA 2003.

! Don't be tempted to . . .

- Gloss over the meaning of 'sexual', which is defined under section 78.
- Write out the relevant statutory provisions verbatim. You will gain no extra marks for remembering the precise wording of the statute and you will waste valuable time writing it out. Instead you should ensure that you know all of the required elements for each offence and the meaning of the key terms. The examiner is looking for evidence of your understanding and application of the law, not a fantastic memory.

Try it yourself

Now take a look at the question below and attempt to answer it. You can check your response against the answer guidance available on the companion website (**www.pearsoned.co.uk/lawexpressqa**).

Consider whether the parties will be liable for any sexual offences in the following scenarios. You should assume that all parties are aged 18 or over.

1. In a lingerie store, a shop assistant, Geraldine, persuades Helen, a customer, to let her touch her breasts by pretending that she is measuring Helen for a bra. In fact, Geraldine is not trained as a fitting assistant and she derives pleasure from touching Helen's breasts.

AND

2. James and Karen are engaged and decide not to engage in any sexual activity until after they are married. However, James threatens to break off the engagement unless Karen agrees to some sexual contact between them. Reluctantly, Karen agrees to let James insert his fingers into her vagina.

AND

3. One evening, Linda goes on a night out with her friend Michelle. As they have both had a few drinks, Michelle tells Linda that she can stay over at Michelle's house. Linda is very pleased because she had always fancied Michelle's husband, Nav. When Michelle falls asleep on the sofa, Linda sneaks into bed with Nav and persuades him to have sexual intercourse with her by pretending that she is Michelle. When Nav realises that he has had sex with Linda, he is horrified.

www.pearsoned.co.uk/lawexpressqa

 Go online to access more revision support including additional essay and problem questions with diagram plans, You be the marker questions, and download all diagrams from the book.

Theft

How this topic may come up in exams

Theft is one of the main offences against property and is a popular topic with examiners and students. Theft may be examined by way of a problem question which requires students to identify any relevant areas of law and apply the law to the factual scenario. Alternatively, it may be examined by way of an essay question which requires a critical appreciation of the topic and might focus in more detail on particular elements of theft, such as appropriation or dishonesty. You should pay particular attention to the structure of answers to both problem questions and essay questions on theft.

Before you begin

It's a good idea to consider the following key themes of theft before tackling a question on this topic.

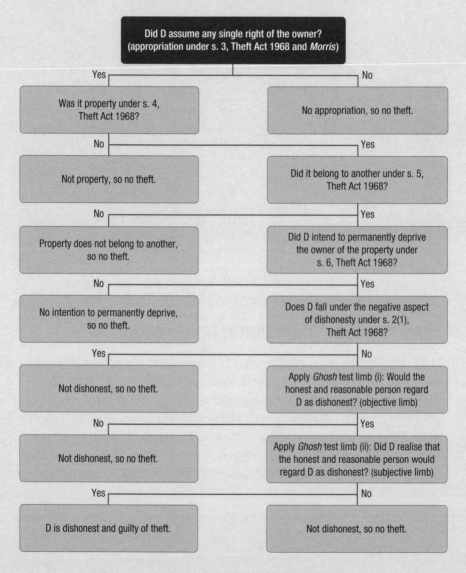

A printable version of this diagram is available from **www.pearsoned.co.uk/lawexpressqa**

Question 1

'The concept of "appropriation" was intended to broaden the notion of "taking" so as to be able to encompass a wider range of situations and objects. But the statutory definition in terms of "any assumption . . . of the rights of an owner", including later assumptions of rights after an initially non-theftous acquisition (although excluding the purchaser in good faith), threatens to take on such a wide meaning as effectively to undermine its status as a genuine requirement of or restriction on the definition of theft' (Lacey, Wells and Quick, (2003) *Reconstructing Criminal Law Text and Materials*, 3rd edn., Cambridge: Cambridge University Press, p. 367).

Critically evaluate the above quote.

Diagram plan

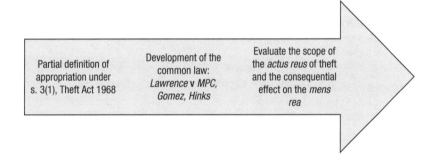

A printable version of this diagram plan is available from **www.pearsoned.co.uk/lawexpressqa**

Answer plan

➡ Consider the meaning of appropriation under section 3(1), Theft Act 1968 and how the courts have developed the partial definition under the statute.

➡ Explore the key cases of *Lawrence* v *MPC*, *Gomez* and *Hinks* on appropriation.

➡ Evaluate the scope of the element of appropriation and its neutrality.

➡ Consider the consequential importance of the *mens rea* of theft.

Answer

[1] Ensure that you address the question directly in your introduction in order to demonstrate that you are able to engage with the question.

The meaning of 'appropriation' has been the subject of much consideration by both the courts and academics. In the quote above, Lacey, Wells and Quick argue that 'appropriation' within the Theft Act 1968 has taken on such a wide meaning that it threatens to render the element redundant within the definition of theft.[1] This question requires consideration of the scope of the actus reus of theft, with particular reference to the element of appropriation. It is true that the actus reus elements of theft have been very widely interpreted by the courts. This has important consequences for the determination of liability for theft as it means that liability hinges upon the mens rea elements. This in turn requires attention to be given to the law relating to the mens rea elements; in particular, the *Ghosh* [1982] 2 All ER 689 test applied in respect of dishonesty must be scrutinised, although the Court of Appeal recently confirmed that *Ghosh* is good law in *Cornelius* [2012] EWCA Crim 500.[2]

[2] These two sentences draw further on the consequences of the observation made in the quote in the question. The explanation put forward here demonstrates a very good degree of knowledge and appreciation of the subject and will gain you higher marks.

[3] This paragraph provides a brief overview of the elements of the offence and where it comes from.

Theft is defined in section 1(1), Theft Act 1968 as the dishonest appropriation of property belonging to another with the intention to permanently deprive the other of it.[3] The prosecution must prove all five elements in order to secure a conviction: *Lawrence v MPC* [1971] 2 All ER 1253. The actus reus elements of 'appropriation', 'property' and 'belonging to another' have all been widely interpreted.

Section 3(1) of the Theft Act 1968 provides a partial definition of appropriation. It involves any assumption of the rights of the owner over the property. This means that the defendant appropriates property by doing something with the property that the owner has the right to do. Many different forms of conduct may constitute appropriation, such as using the property, keeping it, lending it to someone else, selling it, destroying it, etc. The law does not restrict liability by requiring a defendant to assume all of the rights of the owner, but takes a broader approach by requiring the assumption of any single right: *Morris* [1983] 3 All ER 288.[4] Under section 3(1), a later appropriation is also sufficient; thus, where the defendant comes by the property innocently but later does something with it by which he assumes the rights of the owner, he appropriates it.

[4] This paragraph focuses specifically on the element of appropriation, the scope of which has been the subject of much debate. This part of the answer provides some evidence of the wide interpretation of appropriation.

The courts have provided further jurisprudence on the meaning of appropriation, particularly in relation to the relationship between appropriation and consent. This issue has been the subject of much debate. There are a number of cases which relate to the question of whether an authorised assumption of the owner's rights could amount to appropriation. In **Lawrence**, the House of Lords held that an authorised assumption of the rights of the owner could amount to appropriation. The House held that the defendant had appropriated money from a student's wallet, despite the fact that the student had consented to him taking money from his wallet. Viscount Dilhorne[5] stated that the absence of any words in section 3(1) of the Theft Act 1968 requiring the appropriation to take place without consent meant that Parliament had relieved the prosecution of having to prove that the appropriation took place without the owner's consent. Thus, consent was unequivocally deemed to be irrelevant to appropriation.

[5] Use the name of the relevant judge where possible in order to demonstrate the detail of your knowledge to the examiner.

This issue was reconsidered by the House of Lords in **Morris**, but the House reached a different conclusion in this case. Lord Roskill stated *obiter* that 'an act expressly or impliedly authorised by the owner' did not constitute appropriation, but appropriation did involve 'an act by way of adverse interference with or usurpation of [the owner's] rights'. According to Lord Roskill in **Morris**, an authorised act could not amount to appropriation, thus picking up goods to buy in a super-market would not constitute appropriation, neither would the act in **Lawrence**. After **Morris**, there existed a clear conflict on the issue of consent in appropriation between two House of Lords' authorities. However, it should be noted that **Morris** was only persuasive on this point as Lord Roskill's statement was an **obiter dictum**, whereas **Lawrence** laid down a binding **ratio decidendi**.[6]

[6] Ensure you acknowledge the fact that Lord Roskill's comment in *Morris* was only an *obiter* statement in order to demonstrate to the examiner that you understand that the statement was only persuasive. By contrast, the fact that *Lawrence* provided a binding *ratio* is also highlighted.

This issue was again revisited by the House of Lords in **Gomez** [1993] 1 All ER 1 and the House sought to use this opportunity to clarify the confusion which arose from **Lawrence** and **Morris**. The House of Lords held that **Lawrence** and **Morris** could not be reconciled, so one approach had to be chosen. The House followed **Lawrence** and held that consent was irrelevant to appropriation, thus appropriation did not require an unauthorised assumption of the rights of the owner. Lord Browne-Wilkinson considered the word 'appropriation' in isolation as 'an objective description of the act done' irrespective of the mental state of the defendant. In his commentary to **Gomez** in the Criminal Law Review, Professor Smith [1993] Crim LR 304 stated that 'anyone doing anything whatever to property . . . with or without the

[7] This key quote from a highly esteemed academic is worth remembering.

[8] The final sentence here refers back to the question in order to ensure that the focus of the essay is the quote in the title.

[9] Examine the gift cases after considering the cases on consent and appropriation. This chronological approach provides the ideal structure for this question.

[10] The last lines of this paragraph go further than simply agreeing or disagreeing with the quote. They acknowledge the consequences of such a wide interpretation of the actus reus of theft. However, as the criticisms of *Ghosh* are not within the scope of this essay (and in fact provide a whole essay themselves), you are unlikely to have time to discuss them here.

authority or consent of the owner, appropriates it'.[7] Consequently, the element of appropriation has been widely construed.[8]

This broad approach was later extended to apply to situations where the defendant receives a gift from a suggestible or vulnerable donor.[9] In *Mazo* (1997) 2 Cr App R 518, the Court of Appeal held that property given to the defendant with consent could be appropriated if the consent was obtained by fraud. However, this narrow interpretation of *Gomez* meant that there could be no appropriation where a valid gift was given *inter vivos*. In *Hopkins and Kendrick* [1997] 2 Cr App R 524, the Court of Appeal criticised *Mazo*. The position was finally considered by the House of Lords in *Hinks* [2001] 2 AC 241. The House extended the approach taken in *Gomez* and held that a valid gift could be appropriated. This decision has been criticised for extending the scope of appropriation too far and creating a conflict between criminal and civil law.

As 'appropriation' is so widely defined, the actus reus of theft is easily proved by the prosecution. Consequently, the mens rea elements of theft are particularly important in determining the liability of a defendant. As liability will hinge upon proof of dishonesty and the intention to permanently deprive, it is important that the law relating to these elements is beyond criticism. However, the suitability of the *Ghosh* test for dishonesty sparks another debate. The importance placed upon the mens rea of theft means that the jury's application of *Ghosh* and its interpretation of 'honesty' dictate the fate of the defendant.[10]

✓ Make your answer stand out

- Refer to opinions of specific judges in cases such as *Lawrence*, *Morris* and *Gomez*.
- Refer to academic opinion. In particular, note Professor J.C. Smith's commentary to *Gomez* (Smith, J.C. (1993) Case Commentary, *R* v *Gomez*. Crim LR 304 – learn the key quote from this commentary) and Professor A.T.H. Smith's comments (Smith, A.T.H. (2001) Theft and sharp practice: who cares now? CLJ 21).
- Explain how the 'gifts cases' extended the scope of appropriation.
- You could offer a brief discussion of the remaining actus reus elements to further demonstrate the importance of the mens rea elements.　▶

- Relate each paragraph back to the question and explain how the case law supports the assertion.
- Critically evaluate the effect that this has on the mens rea. Explain that liability is consequential upon the jury's interpretation of 'honesty'.

! Don't be tempted to . . .

- Confuse the distinction between the *ratio* in *Lawrence* and the *obiter* statement in *Morris*.
- When discussing consent and appropriation, do not mention section 2(1) of the Theft Act 1968 and dishonesty. Students often confuse appropriation and dishonesty, because while consent is irrelevant to appropriation, an honest belief in consent may negate the dishonesty aspect (s. 2(1)(b), Theft Act 1968). These are two entirely distinct issues. Appropriation is an actus reus element and should be considered in isolation from the mental state of the defendant.
- Recite the facts of *Lawrence*, *Morris*, *Gomez* and *Hinks* in laborious detail. If you need to refer to the facts, do so briefly. Remember that as this essay requires an evaluation of the law, the principles from the cases are far more important.
- Go through the law relating to dishonesty and intention to permanently deprive in detail. Do not simply write everything you know on theft.

? Question 2

After checking her pay slip, Samantha notices that she has been overpaid by £200. She arranges an appointment to see her line manager, Thomas, the following day in order to report the error. However, later that day an email is sent to all staff detailing proposals for pay cuts for all employees. Angry at this, Samantha decides to keep the £200 overpayment.

In the evening, Samantha goes shopping for an outfit for her friend's birthday party. She decides to splash out on a designer dress with matching shoes and handbag. The outfit costs £1,000 at full price, but Samantha removes a '50% off' label from a different dress and places it on the outfit she wants to buy. She takes this to the cashier and pays £500 for the whole outfit. At the cash desk, Samantha notices a catalogue. Believing it to be free, she takes one. In fact, the catalogue costs £3.50.

On her way out of the shop, Samantha notices a £10 note on the floor. After looking around to see who might have dropped it, she picks it up and puts it in her purse.

Discuss Samantha's liability for the offence of theft.

Answer plan

→ Define theft and state where it comes from.

→ Discuss whether Samantha is liable for theft of the overpayment. In particular, you should consider section 5(4) of the Theft Act 1968.

→ Consider the theft arising from Samantha's conduct in placing a '50% off' label on the outfit. This requires consideration of appropriation.

→ Discuss whether Samantha has stolen the catalogue. Section 2(1) of the Theft Act 1968 will be important here.

→ Consider whether there was a theft of the £10 note. Who does this belong to? Is Samantha dishonest?

Diagram plan

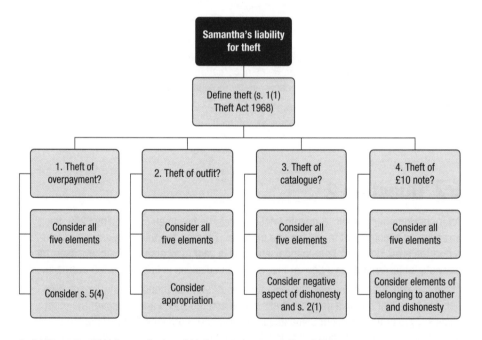

A printable version of this diagram plan is available from **www.pearsoned.co.uk/lawexpressqa**

Answer

[1] As the question asks
specifically about theft, you
should restrict your answer
to theft. You will gain no
extra marks for discussing
the offences of burglary or
fraud. If the question is more
general and asks you simply
to discuss the relevant party's
criminal liability, then you
should consider all offences
which arise in the question.
See the mixed questions in
Chapter 13 for examples.

[2] Use a logical and clear
structure, dealing with each
incident of theft in turn and use
headings to maintain focus.

[3] Set out the law relating
to appropriation briefly and
cite the relevant statutory
provision and any relevant
case law.

[4] This demonstrates to
an examiner that you are
aware of the two different
appropriations, the first of
which is an innocent one, the
second will form the basis of
the conviction for theft.

[5] Deal with the actus reus
elements first, before
considering whether the mens
rea is satisfied.

Samantha could be liable for theft of the £200 overpayment, the outfit, the catalogue and the £10 note.[1] Theft is defined under section 1(1) of the Theft Act 1968 as the dishonest appropriation of property belonging to another with the intention to permanently deprive the other of it. The prosecution must prove all five elements in order to secure a conviction: *Lawrence* v *MPC* [1971] 2 All ER 1253.

The £200 overpayment[2]

By keeping the £200, Samantha may have committed theft. She has appropriated the money. Appropriation is partially defined under section 3(1) of the Theft Act 1968 as assuming the rights of the owner. The case of *Morris* [1983] 3 All ER 288 confirmed that the defendant need not assume all of the owner's rights, but any single right will do.[3] When Samantha takes possession of the money, she appropriates it. She assumes a further right of the owner (that of possession) by keeping the money.[4] Whether or not Samantha has the consent of her employers in respect of either of these assumptions is irrelevant to appropriation: *Lawrence* v *MPC* and *Gomez* [1993] 1 All ER 1. The £200 is property under section 4(1) of the Theft Act 1968, as it is a 'thing in action' – Samantha has a right to payment by her bank of £200. The property belongs to her employers because, under section 5(4) of the Theft Act 1968, it is property obtained by mistake. Thus, the actus reus elements of theft are satisfied.[5]

Although at first Samantha intends to pay back this money, her intention changes after she receives the email. At this stage, she forms the intention to permanently deprive her employer of the money by keeping it. The remaining question then is whether Samantha is dishonest. Dishonesty is not defined in the Theft Act 1968. Section 2(1) does provide a partial definition of the negative aspect of dishonesty, but

[6] As it does not apply, you should not go through all of the paragraphs under section 2(1). It is still worth mentioning the section though in order to demonstrate to the examiner that you have considered and rejected the provision.

[7] Set out the *Ghosh* test in full. Students often misstate the test, so ensure that you learn the full test and explain it accurately.

[8] Once you have set out the law relating to dishonesty, apply it to the problem scenario.

[9] If you want to mention the facts of *Morris* here in order to acknowledge the similarity between them and those in the problem scenario, do so very briefly.

this is unlikely to apply here.[6] Therefore, the test for dishonesty under *Ghosh* [1982] 2 All ER 689 should be applied (recently approved in *Cornelius* [2012] EWCA Crim 500). This test requires the jury to consider: (i) whether the honest and reasonable person would regard what Samantha did as dishonest; and (ii) whether Samantha realised that the honest and reasonable person would regard her conduct as dishonest.[7] The first limb is objective and the second is subjective. Samantha's conduct is likely to be dishonest according to *Ghosh* because the honest and reasonable person would regard keeping the money as dishonest and the fact that Samantha initially intends to report the overpayment indicates that she probably realises this.[8] Thus, the mens rea is likely to be satisfied.

The outfit

Samantha is likely to be guilty of theft of the outfit. She appropriates it when she picks it up and then again when she places the '50% off' label on it. This is an assumption of a right of the owner: section 3(1); *Morris*. This scenario is similar to that in *Morris*, where the defendant swapped the labels on goods in a shop.[9] Although Samantha had the consent of the shop to pick up the outfit, she had no consent to put the label on the outfit. Nevertheless, consent is not relevant to appropriation: *Lawrence* and *Gomez*. The outfit is personal property under section 4(1) and it belongs to the shop: section 5(1). Thus, the actus reus elements of theft are satisfied.

Samantha clearly intends to permanently deprive the shop of the full cost of the outfit. The negative aspect of dishonesty under section 2(1) is unlikely to apply here. Applying *Ghosh*, the honest and reasonable person would regard Samantha's act of applying the '50% off' label to the outfit in order to pay half the cost dishonest. Samantha must have realised this or she would have simply asked for the discount. Thus, the mens rea elements of theft are satisfied.

The catalogue

In relation to the catalogue, Samantha may have a defence to a charge of theft. The actus reus elements of the offence are clearly satisfied, but the mens rea might be disputed. Samantha has appropriated the catalogue by taking and keeping it. This amounts to an assumption of a right of the owner – that of possession: section 3(1); *Morris*.

Whether or not she had consent to take the catalogue is irrelevant to the question of appropriation: **Gomez**. The catalogue is personal property under section 4(1) and it belongs to the shop. Thus, the actus reus elements are satisfied.

Samantha intended to permanently deprive the shop of the catalogue. However, in respect of dishonesty, she may be able to rely upon section 2(1)(a) or (b) in her defence.[10] Under section 2(1)(a), Samantha will not be dishonest if she honestly believed that she had a right in law to take the catalogue. She may have such a belief if she honestly thought that the catalogues were free for customers. Alternatively, under section 2(1)(b), Samantha will not be dishonest if she honestly believed that she had the consent of the shop to take the catalogue. It is likely that at least one of these provisions will apply. However, if they do not, the jury will determine dishonesty using the **Ghosh** test.[11] It is unlikely that Samantha was dishonest here.

[10] If you think that *both* of these provisions might apply, mention them both. However, as section 2(1)(c) does not apply here, do not mention that provision.

[11] You should still mention the fact that the *Ghosh* test will apply in the absence of the provision under section 2(1) in order to demonstrate to the examiner that you understand the way in which section 2(1) and *Ghosh* work in practice.

The £10 note

By keeping the £10 note, Samantha may have committed theft. She appropriates it when she picks it up and assumes the right of possession: section 3(1); **Morris**. Under section 4(1), property includes money. It is difficult to know who the £10 belongs to. The owner has lost it, but this is unlikely to be abandoned property. It is very difficult to abandon property, because this requires an indifference to the property. The owner is unlikely to be indifferent to the money. Thus, the £10 must belong to somebody for the purposes of theft. Under section 5(1), property belongs to anybody in possession or control of it. By taking it into her possession, Samantha has acquired a right of possession of the £10. The shop may also have possession or control of the £10 if it demonstrates an intention to exercise control over the shop and the things in it: **Hibbert v McKiernan** [1948] 2 KB 142 and **Parker v British Airways** [1982] QB 1004.

[12] Ensure that you read the precise wording of section 2(1)(c) and understand it. Students often make the mistake of thinking that reasonable steps actually have to be taken, when they do not. The defendant must merely hold an *honest belief* that the owner could not be found *if* reasonable steps *were* taken.

If the actus reus elements are satisfied, consideration must be given to the mens rea. Samantha clearly intends to permanently deprive the owner of the money as she intends to keep it, but is she dishonest? She might argue that she honestly believed she had a right in law to the money (s. 2(1)(a)), or that she honestly believed that the owner could not be found even if all reasonable steps were taken (s. 2(1)(c)).[12] If either of these apply, she will not be dishonest. If they do not, the **Ghosh** test will be applied. If the jury think that the honest and reasonable man would regard keeping the £10 as dishonest, and that Samantha knew this, she will be convicted of theft.

 Make your answer stand out

- Adopt a clear structure. Use headings if necessary in order to ensure you remain focused on the potential theft in question. Headings may also assist the examiner by adding clarity to your answer.

- You should deal with each of the incidents of theft in turn and consider whether the actus reus is satisfied before moving on to the mens rea.

- Cite only the relevant principles of law and do not use your answer to regurgitate everything you know about theft.

- Apply the law to the problem scenario as you go. As a general guide you should try to apply the law every time you state a relevant principle of law.

- Refer to any relevant academic opinion. In particular, you could mention the key quote describing appropriation from Professor J.C. Smith's commentary to *Gomez* (Smith, J.C. (1993) Case Commentary, *R* v *Gomez*. Crim LR 304). You should also make reference to any judicial comment which may be relevant.

! Don't be tempted to . . .

- Set out all of the relevant law on theft in the first half of your answer and do not leave your application of the law to the problem scenario until the end of your answer. This practice of simply writing everything you know about theft and adding a cursory paragraph of application at the end of your answer will gravely affect your chances of passing the exam.

- Neglect correctly stating and applying both the objective and the subjective limbs of the *Ghosh* test.

- Forget that section 2(1)(c) of the Theft Act 1968 does not actually require the defendant to take reasonable steps to find the owner. He/she must merely hold an honest belief that the owner could not be found if reasonable steps were taken.

❓ Question 3

Bernard is a 94-year-old man who is very frail and housebound. Andrew, a family friend, has been a regular visitor to Bernard's house for the past three years. When Andrew visits Bernard he also brings round some food and does a few odd jobs around the house for Bernard. They often sit and play cards together and Andrew listens to Bernard's stories about life during the Second World War. Andrew notices that Bernard has recently become more forgetful and very easily confused. One day, Andrew does some gardening jobs for Bernard. Bernard is so pleased with Andrew's work that he hands Andrew a jewel-encrusted gold brooch which once belonged to Bernard's mother, and insists that Andrew takes the brooch as a 'thank you' present. Andrew has had his eye on the brooch for some time as he thinks that it is worth around £5,000, but he suspects that Bernard is unaware of its true value. He decides to accept the present from Bernard.

After admiring his own work in Bernard's garden, Andrew decides to go home and work on his garden too. Remembering that his lawnmower is broken, Andrew decides to borrow Bernard's lawnmower. He thinks that Bernard probably wouldn't notice the lawnmower is missing and he decides not to bother asking Bernard for permission. However, Andrew forgets to return the lawnmower and six months later he is too embarrassed to return it, so he abandons it outside a charity shop where a passer-by decides to take it.

Discuss the liability of Andrew and the passer-by for the offence of theft.

Answer plan

➜ Define theft and state where it comes from.

➜ Discuss whether Andrew is liable for theft of the gift of the jewel-encrusted gold brooch. You should consider whether, and in what circumstances, it is possible to steal a gift.

➜ Consider the theft arising from Andrew's conduct in borrowing the lawnmower without asking permission and leaving it outside a charity shop. This requires consideration of the meaning of appropriation, dishonesty and intention to permanently deprive.

➜ Discuss whether the passer-by has stolen the lawnmower. The meaning of belonging to another will need to be considered here.

Diagram plan

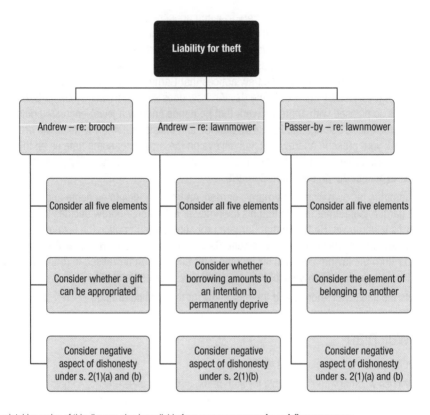

A printable version of this diagram plan is available from **www.pearsoned.co.uk/lawexpressqa**

Answer

[1] As with the problem question on theft above, this question specifically asks about theft, so you should restrict your answer to theft. You will gain no extra marks under the circumstances for discussing burglary.

Andrew might be liable for theft of the brooch given to him as a 'thank you' present, and the lawnmower. The passer-by might also be liable for theft of the lawnmower from outside the charity shop. Theft is defined under section 1(1), of the Theft Act 1968 as the dishonest appropriation of property belonging to another with the intention to permanently deprive the other of it.[1] The prosecution must prove all five elements in order to secure a conviction: *Lawrence* v *MPC* [1971] 2 All ER 1253.

Gift of the brooch[2]

By taking the brooch, Andrew may very well be convicted of theft.[3] It is first necessary to establish the actus reus elements. Andrew has appropriated the brooch. Appropriation is partially defined under section 3(1) as an assumption of the rights of the owner. According to **Morris** [1983] 3 All ER 288, the defendant need not assume all the owner's rights, just one single right. He appropriates it by assuming the right of possession: section 3(1); **Morris**. According to **Hinks** [2001] 2 AC 241, it is possible to appropriate a valid gift. While Andrew has Bernard's consent to take the brooch, consent is irrelevant to appropriation: **Lawrence** and **Gomez** [1993] 1 All ER 1. The brooch is property under section 4(1) as it is 'personal property'. The property clearly belongs to another, namely Bernard, as it is a family heirloom. Thus, the actus reus elements of theft are satisfied.

The prosecution may rely upon **Hinks** to argue that Andrew is guilty if he dishonestly accepts the gift. Andrew intends to permanently deprive Bernard of the brooch as he intends to keep it (and possibly sell it). However, he might argue that he honestly believed he had a right in law to keep the brooch as it was a gift (s. 2(1)(a)), or that he honestly believed he had Bernard's consent to take the brooch (s. 2(1)(b)). If so, he is not dishonest. If section 2(1) does not apply, **Ghosh** [1982] 2 All ER 689 will be applied (recently approved in **Cornelius** [2012] EWCA Crim 500). If the jury thinks that the honest and reasonable man would regard keeping the brooch as dishonest, and that Andrew knew this, he will be guilty of theft. As Bernard is forgetful and easily confused and Andrew clearly knows this, he may be objectively dishonest for taking the brooch. Andrew's conduct is objectively dishonest in light of the fact that he has had his eye on the brooch for some time and he suspects that Bernard is not aware of its value when he gives it to Andrew. Andrew also probably realises that the honest and reasonable man would regard his conduct as dishonest, and thus he is likely to be convicted of theft of the brooch.

Borrowing the lawnmower

Andrew is likely to be guilty of theft of the lawnmower. He appropriates it when he takes possession of it. This is an assumption of a right of the owner: section 3(1); **Morris**. Andrew has no consent to take the lawnmower, but consent is not relevant to appropriation: **Gomez**. If

Andrew is not guilty of theft at this stage, there is arguably a later appropriation of the lawnmower, either when Andrew forgets to return the lawnmower or when he leaves it outside the charity shop. A later appropriation occurs under section 3(1) where a person 'has come by the property (innocently or not) without stealing it, any later assumption of a right to it by keeping or dealing with it as owner'.[4] Thus, Andrew may still be guilty of theft provided that the other elements of the theft are present at the time of a later appropriation. The lawnmower is clearly property for the purposes of theft as it is 'personal property' under section 4(1). The property belongs to another, namely Bernard. Thus, the actus reus elements of theft are satisfied.

[5] Set out the law relating to whether borrowing amounts to an intention to permanently deprive briefly and cite the key statutory provision.

[6] Where there are two conflicting lines of authorities, apply both in the alternative to demonstrate to the examiner your knowledge of the area.

[7] Be specific about the name of the judge if you can. You should remember to use Lord Lane CJ in respect of *Lloyd*.

It is now necessary to establish whether the mens rea elements are present. Initially, Andrew borrows the lawnmower. Under section 6, a borrowing or lending may amount to such an intention where it is equivalent to an outright taking or disposal.[5] According to *DPP v Lavender* [1994] Crim LR 297, 'to dispose of' means 'to deal with', thus dealing with property could be sufficient. This is a wide approach under which Andrew has the necessary intention. By contrast,[6] in *Lloyd* [1985] QB 829, Lord Lane CJ[7] gave this element a narrow interpretation, stating that what was required was an intention to return the thing in such a changed state that it can be said that all its goodness or virtue has gone. As Andrew initially plans to return the lawnmower with most of its goodness and virtue, Andrew does not have the necessary intention under the narrow approach. However, having forgotten to return the lawnmower, Andrew then leaves it outside a charity shop. This is evidence that he intended to permanently deprive Bernard of the lawnmower (*Vinall* [2012] 1 Cr App R 29).

Dishonesty is not defined in the Theft Act 1968. However, section 2(1) provides a partial definition of the negative aspect of dishonesty. Under section 2(1)(b), a defendant is not dishonest if he honestly believes he would have had the consent of the owner. Andrew could argue that he honestly believed that he would have had Bernard's consent to borrow the lawnmower. This is a purely subjective test; hence it does not matter if his belief was not reasonable or mistaken. If Andrew had no such belief, section 2(1) will not apply and the test for dishonesty under *Ghosh* should be applied. This test requires the jury to consider: (i) whether the honest and reasonable person would regard what Andrew did as dishonest; and (ii) whether Andrew realised that the honest and reasonable person would regard his

[8] As with the answer to question 2 above, you should set out the *Ghosh* test in full and accurately.

[9] This sentence demonstrates that you understand the distinction between the two limbs of the *Ghosh* test.

[10] Use the facts given in the problem scenario to justify your conclusions.

conduct as dishonest.[8] The first limb is objective and the second is subjective.[9] Andrew's conduct is likely to be dishonest according to *Ghosh* if the honest and reasonable person would regard borrowing the lawnmower as dishonest. Since Andrew and Bernard seem to have a close relationship, one would have thought that Andrew would ask Bernard's permission to borrow the lawnmower. The fact that he does not do this indicates that his conduct may be objectively dishonest. If the objective limb is satisfied, Andrew will only be dishonest if he realises that his conduct is objectively dishonest. He probably does since he doesn't tell Bernard he has borrowed it either at the time of borrowing it or later, and in fact he becomes so embarrassed about returning it that he leaves it outside the charity shop.[10] Thus, the mens rea is likely to be satisfied. Even if Andrew is not dishonest at the time of borrowing the lawnmower, he becomes dishonest when he leaves it outside the charity shop as he cannot claim that he honestly believed that Bernard would consent to this (s. 2(1)(b)), the honest and reasonable person would find leaving someone else's property which you borrowed without asking them outside the charity shop dishonest and he probably realises this (*Ghosh*) since his embarrassment prevents him from returning it.

Passer-by takes lawnmower

The passer-by is likely to be guilty of theft of the lawnmower. He appropriates it when he takes possession of it. This is an assumption of a right of the owner: section 3(1); *Morris*. The passer-by has no consent to take the lawnmower, but consent is not relevant to appropriation: *Gomez*. The lawnmower is personal property under section 4(1). The lawnmower either belongs to Bernard in the sense that he owns it, or it belongs to the charity shop which has possession or control over it (*R (Ricketts)* v *Basildon Magistrates' Court* [2011] 1 Cr App R 15). Thus, the actus reus elements of theft may be satisfied.

[11] Refer back to the discussion of section 2(1)(b) above re honest belief in consent.

The passer-by intends to permanently deprive Bernard or the shop of the lawnmower. The negative aspect of dishonesty is likely to apply. Under section 2(1)(a), the passer-by may honestly believe he has a right in law to take the property or that he had consent to take it (s. 2(1)(b)).[11] If section 2(1) does not apply, *Ghosh* will be applied. The honest and reasonable person would probably regard the passer-by's conduct as dishonest, and the passer-by is likely to have realised that his conduct was objectively dishonest. Thus, the mens rea elements of theft are probably satisfied.

Make your answer stand out

- It is important that you structure your answer clearly. Plan your answer before you begin to write so that you know in advance whether you are going to conclude that Andrew or the passer-by is likely to be guilty of the theft of each item or not. This helps you to focus and avoid waffle and a muddled answer.

- Use any key quotes from cases that are relevant. It is worth learning key quotes from cases such as *Gomez*, *Hinks*, *Lloyd*, and *Ghosh* along with the name of the relevant judge so that you can cite them where relevant.

- Where the facts are vague, allowing for different possibilities, you should apply the law to each variable. For instance, the facts do not expressly state whether or not Andrew honestly believed that Bernard would have consented to him taking the lawnmower – you should apply the law to both variables.

- You should incorporate some academic opinion where possible. As this question involves the theft of a gift, you could include reference to Shute, S. (2002) Appropriation and the law of theft. Crim LR 445.

! **Don't be tempted to . . .**

- Speculate about matters which are not relevant to the specific problem scenario.

- Forget to discuss the negative aspect of dishonesty under section 2(1) of the Theft Act 1968 before applying *Ghosh*. Even where section 2(1) is unlikely to apply, you should state this (albeit briefly) in order to demonstrate to the examiner that you fully understand the law relating to dishonesty.

- Forget that section 2(1) is assessed on a purely subjective basis. Do not be tempted to apply an objective test to the negative aspect of dishonesty as you will lose marks for this.

Question 4

'The Law Commission recently commented that it found the criticisms of the present law [on dishonesty] "compelling". It was suggested that *Ghosh* was not so much a definition as a way of coping with the absence of a definition' (Ormerod, D. and Williams, D. (2007) *Smith's Law of Theft*, 9th edn. Oxford: Oxford University Press, p. 115).

To what extent do you agree that the test for dishonesty in *Ghosh* is in need of reform?

Diagram plan

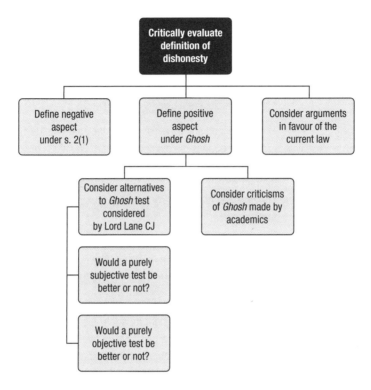

A printable version of this diagram plan is available from **www.pearsoned.co.uk/lawexpressqa**

Answer plan

➡ Define theft and state where it comes from.

➡ Explain the law relating to dishonesty using both the negative aspect under section 2(1) of the Theft Act 1968 and the positive aspect from *Ghosh*.

➡ Consider the judgment of Lord Lane CJ in the Court of Appeal in *Ghosh*.

➡ Set out the criticisms which have been made of the *Ghosh* test by academics.

➡ Put forward any arguments in favour of the current law on dishonesty.

➡ Conclude by providing your own informed opinion on the law and address the quote by commenting as to whether you agree with it or not.

Answer

This question requires a critical evaluation of the law relating to dishonesty. The quote suggests that there is validity in the criticisms of the current law and that the **Ghosh** [1982] 2 All ER 689 test is not a satisfactory way of dealing with the absence of a statutory definition of dishonesty. The **Ghosh** test has been subject to much criticism, but no suitable alternative has been found.[1]

Theft is defined under section 1(1) of the Theft Act 1968. Dishonesty is one of the mens rea elements of theft. The actus reus elements of theft are widely interpreted; this means that liability for theft hinges on the prosecution's ability to prove that the defendant was dishonest.[2] The question of dishonesty is one of fact, and thus is left to the jury to determine.

[2] This sentence demonstrates that you appreciate the importance of the role of dishonesty in a defendant's liability for theft.

There is no definition of dishonesty in the Theft Act 1968. However, the Act does provide three scenarios in which a defendant is not dishonest. This is the negative aspect of dishonesty.[3]

[3] Deal first with section 2(1), Theft Act 1968 rather than jumping straight to the *Ghosh* test. Section 2(1) is considered first in practice because if any of the scenarios within section 2(1) (a)–(c) applies, *Ghosh* need not be considered.

Under section 2(1), a defendant is not dishonest if: (a) he honestly believes that he had a right in law to the property; (b) he honestly believes that he had or would have had the owner's consent had the owner known about the circumstances; or (c) he honestly believes that the owner could not be found even if all reasonable steps were taken to try to find him. It should be noted that reasonable steps do not actually have to be taken. This negative, partial definition of dishonesty is subjectively assessed.[4] Where section 2(1) applies, no consideration need be given to **Ghosh**. However, where none of the scenarios under section 2(1) apply, then the **Ghosh** test is considered.

[4] Acknowledge that section 2(1) is very different from the *Ghosh* test in the sense that it provides a negative, partial definition of dishonesty which is subjectively assessed, whereas *Ghosh* provides a positive, part-objective and part-subjective test.

The positive aspect of dishonesty comes from **Ghosh**. The **Ghosh** test has two limbs. The first, objective limb came from **Feely** [1973] QB 530 and requires the jury to consider whether the honest and reasonable person would regard what the defendant did as dishonest. If this is answered in the affirmative, the second, subjective limb requires the jury to question whether the defendant himself realised that the honest and reasonable man would regard what the defendant did as dishonest. This is called the subjective limb, but it contains an objective element and calls for the defendant's recognition of his

[5] This sentence demonstrates that you understand the second limb of the test as Lord Lane CJ intended it, although it should be noted that academic commentary has debated this second limb (see Campbell (1994) The test of dishonesty in *Ghosh*. 43 CLJ 349).

[6] Professor Griew is probably the most famous critic of the *Ghosh* test, so you should (at the very least) refer to his articles and opinion.

[7] You should address aspects of the quote directly throughout your answer to ensure that you are engaging with the question.

[8] This is a famous example and you should discuss it here.

[9] You should also consider the alternative 'Robin Hood defence' argument.

objective dishonesty.[5] Only if both the objective and the subjective questions are answered in the affirmative, can the defendant be found to be dishonest.

The **Ghosh** test has been severely criticised by academics, most notably by Professor Griew[6] (Griew, E.J. (1985) Dishonesty: the objections to **Feely** and **Ghosh**. Crim LR 341.) and the arguments against the test are indeed compelling.[7] The dishonesty element in theft has become increasingly important in the assessment of a defendant's liability, especially since appropriation has been very widely interpreted by the courts (**Hinks** [2001] 2 AC 241). However, Lord Lane CJ demonstrated in **Ghosh** that the test does provide a compromise between the unsatisfactory alternatives of a purely subjective or a purely objective approach.

As Lord Lane CJ suggests in **Ghosh**, if dishonesty is meant to categorise a state of mind, then a purely objective test of dishonesty would not be suitable because the knowledge and belief of the defendant are at the root of the problem. His Lordship provides the example[8] of a man who comes to England from a country where public transport is free and travels by bus without paying. His mind is clearly honest, although his conduct, objectively speaking, is dishonest. Thus, an objective test of dishonesty would convict this man and Lord Lane CJ takes the view that this is not what Parliament could have intended. His Lordship notes that section 2(1) is drafted in subjective terms and relates to the belief of the defendant rather than his conduct and concludes that this subjective, partial definition could not be made to work with an objective test.

Consideration should also be given to the suitability of a subjective test. Lord Lane CJ criticises the objection that a subjective test would 'abandon all standards but that of the accused himself, and to bring about a state of affairs in which 'Robin Hood would be no robber'. The objection suggests that on a subjective approach a defendant could argue that he himself did not believe his conduct to be dishonest, and thus that he is not dishonest. This is known as the 'Robin Hood defence'.[9] However, His Lordship states that this objection 'misunderstands the nature of the subjective test' which incorporates an objective element such that the defendant is judging his knowledge or belief of the objective standard of dishonesty. Thus, His Lordship was satisfied that the **Ghosh** test would not provide the 'Robin Hood defence'.

While the **Ghosh** test has been applauded for adding clarity to the law (see Smith, J.C. (1982) Commentary, **R v Ghosh**. Crim LR 608), it has also been strongly criticised. Griew argues that there is no ordinary standard of honesty; he calls this the 'fiction of community norms'. What one person regards as honest another might regard as dishonest. Similarly, what might be regarded as honest in one part of the country might be deemed dishonest in another. Thus, the standard of honesty has too many variables. The test also assumes that jurors are themselves honest.

[10] You should try to refer to a number of different academics' opinions.

Griew further argues that leaving the question of dishonesty to the jury leads to inconsistent verdicts and uncertainty in the law, as well as longer and more expensive trials as defendants are more likely to plead not guilty and take their chances with a jury. Griew suggests that dishonesty is a question of law which should not be left to the jury. Spencer argues that the test is too complicated for juries and that it provides a defence of mistake where a defendant can argue that he did not realise that honest and reasonable people would regard his conduct as dishonest (Spencer, J.R. (1982) Dishonesty: what the jury thinks the defendant thought the jury would have thought. CLJ 222). Campbell argues that the second limb of the test is not necessary where the jury is directed to consider all the circumstances under the first limb (Campbell, K. (1994) The test of dishonesty in **Ghosh**. 43 CLJ 349).[10]

[11] Refer back to the quote in your conclusion and offer your own opinion in respect of the *Ghosh* debate.

In conclusion, the **Ghosh** test is by no means perfect, but despite its critics, the test has survived. The criticisms of it may very well be compelling: views of jurors as to what is honest differ, the test may fail to offer consistency, the law might be uncertain in this respect and inaccessible as a defendant does not know if his conduct will be deemed dishonest until after the jury's verdict. The law must be flexible enough to adapt to changing views in society, but should also provide consistency and certainty. However, the alternatives suggested so far are less than satisfactory, and it seems that the **Ghosh** test is currently the best definition that we have, albeit not a perfect one.[11]

Make your answer stand out

- Refer to academic opinion as much as possible in order to demonstrate that you have engaged with the academic debate.

- You should read the articles referred to in the answer and get to grips with the arguments being made by different academics: Smith, J.C. (1982) Commentary, *R* v *Ghosh*. Crim LR 608; Griew, E.J. (1985) Dishonesty, the objections to *Feely* and *Ghosh*. Crim LR 341; Spencer, J.R. (1982) Dishonesty: what the jury thinks the defendant thought the jury would have thought. CLJ 222; and Campbell, K. (1994) The test of dishonesty in *Ghosh*. 43 CLJ 349.

! **Don't be tempted to . . .**

- Use the first person (the word 'I'), although you are asked to give your opinion in this question. You should adopt a more formal style of writing when writing academic answers. You could take guidance on writing style from good textbooks and academic journals.

- Forget that section 2(1) is based upon the honest belief of the defendant, and thus is subjectively assessed.

- Misstate the *Ghosh* test. Do not be tempted to shorten the test – you must set it out in full.

- Recite the facts of *Ghosh*. This question is asking you about the academic debate surrounding the test and the facts of the case are not relevant to this.

 Try it yourself

Now take a look at the question below and attempt to answer it. You can check your response against the answer guidance available on the companion website (**www.pearsoned.co.uk/lawexpressqa**).

Critically evaluate the overlap between civil law and criminal law in the offence of theft.

www.pearsoned.co.uk/lawexpressqa

 Go online to access more revision support including additional essay and problem questions with diagram plans, You be the marker questions, and download all diagrams from the book.

Other property offences

8

How this topic may come up in exams

Other property offences, such as burglary, aggravated burglary, robbery, handling stolen goods and criminal damage are often examined by way of problem questions. Such questions might examine just one or two property offences, while others might require exploration of a mixture of property offences including theft and fraud.

Burglary and robbery are often assessed as part of the same problem question, as they are closely related, both being found under the Theft Act 1968. When answering a question on burglary you should also be aware of the possible existence of the offence of aggravated burglary appearing in the question.

Before you begin

It's a good idea to consider the following key themes of other property offences before tackling a question on this topic.

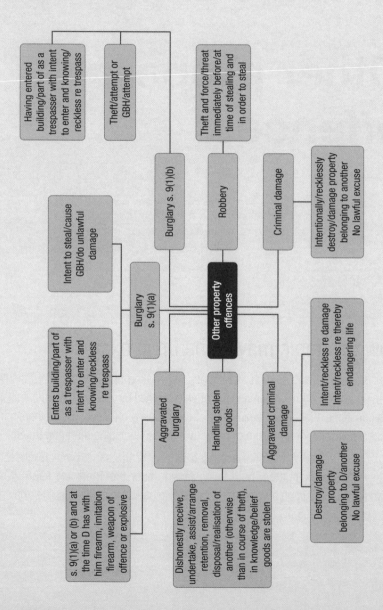

? Question 1

Rhonson is a career criminal who has vowed to retire from a life of crime and lead an honest life. He plans to retire to Spain where he will buy a large and luxurious villa to live in. In order to fund his retirement plans, Rhonson decides to carry out one last heist. He has heard about a rare and beautiful ruby which is on display at a museum in London and he is confident that he can gain access to it. After much deliberation, Rhonson plans to take the ruby one evening as the museum is closing. He hides an iron bar in his jacket, pays for a ticket and enters the museum before closing time. He then hides in a cleaning cupboard until closing time. Once the museum has closed, Rhonson emerges from the cupboard and finds the room holding the ruby. He sees a security guard standing by the ruby and he strikes him on the back of the head with the iron bar, knocking him unconscious. Rhonson then grabs the ruby and escapes.

Discuss Rhonson's criminal liability.

Diagram plan

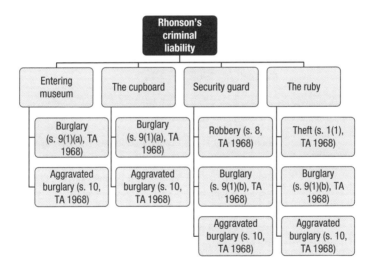

A printable version of this diagram plan is available from **www.pearsoned.co.uk/lawexpressqa**

Answer plan

➡ Identify the offences in the question including the two different offences of burglary under section 9(1)(a) and (b) of the Theft Act 1968.

➡ Discuss Rhonson's liability for burglary under section 9(1)(a) and aggravated burglary under section 10 when he enters the museum.

➡ Explore Rhonson's liability for burglary under section 9(1)(a) and aggravated burglary under section 10 when he enters the cupboard and then when he leaves the cupboard after closing time.

➡ Discuss Rhonson's liability for robbery under section 8, burglary under section 9(1)(b) and aggravated burglary under section 10 in respect of Rhonson's attack on the security guard.

➡ Consider whether Rhonson is guilty of theft, burglary under section 9(1)(b) and aggravated burglary under section 10 when he takes the ruby.

Answer

[1] Listing the relevant offences at the start demonstrates that you have properly considered and understood the question before commencing your answer.

Rhonson could be guilty of burglary under section 9(1)(a) and (b) of the Theft Act 1968, aggravated burglary under section 10 of the Theft Act 1968, robbery under section 8 of the Theft Act 1968, and theft.[1] There are two offences of burglary under section 9(1)(a) and (b) of the Theft Act 1968.[2]

[2] This demonstrates that you are aware that there are two distinct offences of burglary.

[3] Ensure that your structure is clear and logical. Go through the scenario chronologically.

Entering the museum[3]

Rhonson is guilty of burglary under section 9(1)(a) when he enters the museum before closing time. Under section 9(1)(a), a defendant commits burglary if he enters a building or part of a building as a trespasser with the intention to steal, inflict GBH or do unlawful damage (s. 9(2)). It is clear that Rhonson enters a building when he pays for a ticket and goes into the museum. According to **Collins** [1973] QB 100, entry must be 'effective and substantial', although in **Brown** [1985] Crim LR 212 it was held that entry need only be 'effective'. In **Ryan** [1996] Crim LR 320, simply leaning through a window constituted sufficient entry. Rhonson has clearly entered the museum here. While Rhonson seemingly has permission to enter the building at this point, he is a trespasser for the purposes of section 9(1) if he entered the museum in excess of the permission granted to him (**Jones and Smith** [1976] 1 WLR 672). Since Rhonson entered the museum in order to steal the ruby, he has entered the museum in excess of the permission granted to him, and thus as a trespasser. Rhonson has the requisite mens rea for burglary under section 9(1)(a) because he knows that he is trespassing[4] and he does so with the intention to steal the ruby. Thus, at this stage, he is guilty of burglary under section 9(1)(a).

[4] Do not forget to set out and apply the mens rea relating to the trespass.

Rhonson might also be guilty of aggravated burglary under section 10 of the Theft Act 1968. This offence requires proof of a burglary while at the time of the burglary the defendant has with him a firearm, imitation firearm, weapon of offence or explosive. When Rhonson first enters the museum and commits burglary under section 9(1)(a), he has the iron bar with him. The iron bar can be classed as a 'weapon of offence', which includes any article intended for use for causing injury to or incapacitating a person (s. 10(1)). If Rhonson has the iron bar with him in order to injure somebody he will have the requisite intention (***Kelly*** (1993) 97 Cr App R 24). Where aggravated burglary is charged in respect of a burglary under section 9(1)(a), the time at which the defendant must be proved to have the weapon of offence with him is upon entry.[5] Here, Rhonson does have the iron bar with him on entry, thus he may be convicted of aggravated burglary.

[5] Demonstrate that you understand the distinction between an aggravated offence under section 9(1)(a) and an aggravated offence under section 9(1)(b) by drawing on the importance of the meaning of 'at the time'.

Cupboard

When Rhonson enters the cupboard he is guilty of burglary under section 9(1)(a), because he enters a part of a building as a trespasser (***Walkington*** [1979] 1 WLR 1169). Rhonson has clearly entered the cupboard and he is a trespasser at this stage because, as a visitor to the museum he is not supposed to walk into cleaning cupboards, and he knows that he is trespassing. However, it is also necessary to establish that he had an ulterior intention under section 9(1)(a) upon entry. As Rhonson does not intend to steal anything inside the cupboard, this element may not be satisfied.[6] Since there is no burglary at this stage, there can be no aggravated burglary. However, when Rhonson emerges from the cupboard after closing time, he is likely to be guilty of burglary under section 9(1)(a). At this stage, he enters a part of a building (Walkington) as a trespasser because he should not be in the museum after closing time, and he knows that he is trespassing.[7] He also has the ulterior intent necessary under section 9(1)(a) at this point because he intends to steal the ruby from the museum (the part of the building that he has just entered). Rhonson will also be

[6] This sentence illustrates a good understanding of the law on burglary.

[7] This sentence shows your application of the law to the facts of the problem scenario.

guilty of aggravated burglary under section 10 here, because at the time of entry he has with him a weapon of offence, namely the iron bar.

Security guard

Under section 8 of the Theft Act 1968, Rhonson will be guilty of robbery if it can be established that immediately before or at the time of stealing, and in order to steal, he used force on any person or put or sought to put any person in fear of being then and there subjected to force. Rhonson strikes the security guard with the iron bar, thus the use of force is clear. It is also clear that this use of force takes place immediately before or at the time of stealing the ruby. It is also clear that Rhonson uses force 'in order to steal'.[8] Thus, Rhonson is likely to be guilty of robbery.

Section 9(1)(b) requires that, having entered a building or part of a building as a trespasser, the defendant steals or attempts to steal or inflicts or attempts to inflict GBH on a person. Rhonson may also be guilty of burglary under section 9(1)(b). When he strikes the security guard with the iron bar, it is likely that he inflicts GBH on the security guard. Thus, Rhonson may be guilty of burglary under section 9(1)(b) if the infliction of GBH can be established. Rhonson might also be guilty of aggravated burglary when he strikes the security guard, if he commits a section 9(1)(b) burglary at this stage with the iron bar. According to *O'Leary* (1986) 82 Cr App R 341, it is necessary to prove that the defendant had the weapon with him at the time of the ulterior offence, which Rhonson did.

Ruby

Rhonson may be guilty of theft of the ruby. When he picks up the ruby, Rhonson appropriates it under section 3 of the Theft Act 1968 because he assumes a right of the owner. The ruby is clearly personal property under section 4 and it belongs to another under section 5.[9] He would be dishonest if the honest and reasonable man would regard taking the ruby as dishonest and he realises this (*Ghosh* [1982] QB 1053). It is also clear that he intends to permanently deprive the owner of the ruby, as his reason for picking it up is to keep it.

At this stage, Rhonson is also guilty of burglary under section 9(1)(b) as having entered the museum as a trespasser, he steals the ruby.

[8] This paragraph demonstrates a good understanding of the elements of robbery.

[9] As this question encompasses a number of offences, you will probably not have time to go through all of the elements of theft in detail. However, mentioning the elements demonstrates that you are aware of them.

If he is guilty of burglary here, he will also be guilty of aggravated burglary under section 10 as he has a weapon of offence (the iron bar) with him at the time of the theft.

✓ **Make your answer stand out**

- You should demonstrate to the examiner that you are aware of the differences between the offence of burglary under section 9(1)(a) and that under section 9(1)(b) of the Theft Act 1968.
- Make sure that you apply the law to the facts of the problem scenario throughout. An examiner does not simply want you to recite everything you know about the relevant offences, but they want to know why these offences are relevant.
- Use a separate paragraph for each offence that you discuss so as to avoid confusing the examiner and in order to maintain your focus.
- Ensure that you correctly apply the offence of aggravated burglary and accurately identify the burglary that the aggravated offence applies to.

! **Don't be tempted to . . .**

- Simply recite the relevant sections from the Theft Act 1968 verbatim. The examiner wants to know that you understand the law and can apply it well, rather than that you can memorise the words of the sections.
- Confuse the elements of burglary under section 9(1)(a) and (b), Theft Act 1968.
- Spend too much time discussing the elements of theft at the expense of other property offences. The instruction line of this question does not restrict your answer to theft, and thus requires a wider exploration of property offences.

📝 Question 2

'Determining whether there has been an entry has proved more difficult than might be envisaged . . . The Act gives no express guidance and it seems to have been assumed in Parliament that the common law rules would apply. The courts have, however, adopted inconsistent approaches . . . ' (Ormerod, D. and Williams, D. (2007) *Smith's Law of Theft*, 9th edn. Oxford: Oxford University Press, p. 249).

Critically evaluate the law relating to entry in burglary.

Answer plan

→ Outline the old common law meaning of entry.

→ Discuss the approach taken more recently by the courts.

→ Consider academic opinion on the meaning of entry.

Diagram plan

A printable version of this diagram plan is available from **www.pearsoned.co.uk/lawexpressqa**

Answer

Burglary requires the defendant to enter a building or part of a building as a trespasser (s. 9(1)(a) and (b), Theft Act 1968). However, the word 'entry' has not been defined under the Act. This has proved more of a problem than perhaps might have been expected and the courts have adopted inconsistent approaches. As a result, the law is confused. Under the common law, the insertion of any part of the body (however small) into the building was sufficient (Ormerod, D. (2011) *Smith and Hogan Criminal Law*, 13th edn. Oxford: Oxford University Press, p. 953). According to **Davis** (1823) Russ & Ry 499, the insertion of the forepart of the forefinger was sufficient.[1] The Theft Act 1968 does not assist on the meaning of entry as it provides no definition of 'entry'. Parliament assumed that the old common law would apply (Ormerod (2011), pp. 953–4). However, it seems the task of interpreting 'entry' has fallen to the courts which have adopted inconsistent approaches.

[1] Mention the facts of the case very briefly just to provide an example of the way in which the old common law rule was applied.

In **Collins** [1973] QB 100, Edmund Davies LJ stated that the crucial issue was where exactly the defendant was at the time that the victim invited him in.[2] Applying the common law rule, if any part of D's body had been inserted into the building before she invited him in, he had entered the building as a trespasser. However, if no part of his body had been inserted into the building before she invited him in, he would have entered lawfully. Instead, Edmund Davies LJ stated that

[2] Rather than recite the facts of the case in detail, you should focus on the key issue in the case.

the defendant's entry must be 'effective and substantial'. No further guidance was given. 'Effective' might mean that the defendant must be able to carry out his ulterior intent, but this interpretation would conflict with the common law rule which merely requires the insertion of part of the body. 'Substantial' might mean that most of the defendant's body must be inserted through the window. This would also conflict with the common law rule which only requires the insertion of any part of the body, *howsoever small*.[3]

In **Brown** [1985] Crim LR 212, the Court of Appeal still failed to apply the common law rule. Professor Griew comments that 'The court might in **Brown** have supported **Collins** by adopting the same simple rule. It did not do so; and its judgment is explicable only on the basis that the rule has not survived. If that is right, we are left in need of further authority, preferably in firm terms that will make for uniformity of decision' (Griew, E. (1986) *The Theft Acts 1968 and 1978*. London: Sweet & Maxwell, p. 91). Instead, the court modified the test in **Collins** and held that entry need not be 'substantial', but had to be 'effective'. It was unclear whether this meant that while the defendant need not insert most of his body into the building, he must be able to carry out his ulterior intent.[4] In **Ryan** [1996] Crim LR 320, the defendant became stuck and unable to steal anything. Nevertheless, the Court of Appeal held that his entry was effective. This renders the word 'effective' meaningless.

As the law stands, entry has to be effective but not substantial, yet the defendant does not have to be able to carry out the ulterior offence. Ormerod argues that we should revert to the common law position: 'It is unsatisfactory that such a crucial *actus reus* element of a serious offence should be left for a jury to determine; the best course would be to accept the continued existence of the common law rule' (Ormerod (2011), p. 954). Although this is a much wider approach,[5] it is a simple one which provides clarity and accessibility. The current law is unsatisfactory because it is confusing on the meaning of 'entry': the cases are inconsistent.[6]

It is also unclear whether the insertion of other objects, such as a child under ten or an animal, into a building is sufficient to constitute entry. A child will not be convicted if he/she is under ten years old as he/she will have a defence of infancy. The adult who causes the child to enter might be guilty of burglary under the doctrine of innocent agency

7 Compare various academic views to show your wider knowledge.

8 You would not be expected to remember long quotes verbatim, but you should be able to at least paraphrase the academic view.

(*Michael* (1840) 9 C & P 356); however, there is no recent authority directly on this point. There is conflicting academic opinion about the application of the doctrine of innocent agency to burglary.[7] Professor Williams states that 'At common law one could enter through an innocent agent, e.g. through a small child (under the age of responsibility) who was put into the premises to steal. There is little social need for this construction of the offence, since few people would feel alarmed by the entry of a small child . . . However, the courts will probably continue the old rule if the question arises' (Williams, G. (1983) *Textbook of Criminal Law*. London: Stevens & Sons, p. 840).[8] Ormerod comments that 'This is probably not burglary under the 1968 Act' (Ormerod (2011), p. 955). Griew acknowledges that there is no authority on the point but argues that the doctrine of innocent agency should apply to burglary (Griew (1986), p. 92).

It is difficult to distinguish the insertion of an inanimate object, such as a pole or hook or even a bomb thrown or a bullet shot through a window, into a building for the purpose of the commission of an ulterior offence. Ormerod (2011) states that the courts may not be willing to preserve the old technical rules regarding instruments because they lead to 'outlandish results' (p. 954). Ormerod also argues that this does not constitute entry in the simple language of ordinary men in which the Act was said to be written (Ormerod (2011), p. 954). Ormerod suggests perhaps the defendant must be at least present at the scene – 'on the job' (Ormerod (2011), p. 954). Perhaps there is arguably a distinction between the defendant causing an instrument to enter a building (e.g. by throwing something), and where an instrument represents an extension of the defendant's body (e.g. a pole). Ormerod comments that there have not been problems in practice due to the sensible CPS charging guidance that where there are factual difficulties, the CPS should consider charging a different offence (e.g. theft) (Ormerod (2011), p. 955).

There is no clear and settled meaning of entry, and as such, the law is not accessible and is ambiguous.[9] It is arguable that this runs contrary to the rule of law which requires that 'The law must be open and adequately publicised. If it is to guide people they must be able to find out what it is' (Raz, J. (1977) The Rule of Law and its virtue. 93 LQR 195).

[10] Suggest an approach that the courts and/or Parliament could take in order to remove the confusion which currently exists.

While Parliament could intervene here, it is submitted that a simpler, and preferable, approach would be for the courts to follow the common law rule.[10] It is true that the common law rule adopted a very wide approach to entry, but it was at least clear and accessible.

✓ **Make your answer stand out**

■ You should explore the criticisms of the old common law approach in more detail. This approach is obviously much wider than the approach taken by the courts. Consider why this might not be preferable.

■ You could also consider other cases on entry as a trespasser, including: *Walkington* [1979] 1 WLR 1169 (going behind a moveable counter amounts to entry of a part of a building) and *Jones and Smith* [1976] 1 WLR 672 (going into father's house with the intention of taking the TV exceeds the implied permission of D's entry).

■ You could incorporate further academic opinion into your answer, particularly relating to burglary via the insertion of animate or inanimate objects into a building.

■ You might also expand upon the requirement of clarity and accessibility under the rule of law and the particular implications of violating the rule of law in relation to the criminal law.

! **Don't be tempted to . . .**

■ Merely recite the facts of the three main cases on 'entry'. You really need to analyse the inconsistent approaches, rather than set out the facts.

■ Explore the other elements of burglary in detail. The examiner here is looking for your evaluation of the meaning of 'entry' and reference to academic critique in relation to that element.

Question 3

Bill is heavily in debt, having spent thousands of pounds on credit cards and taken out various bank loans. He borrows a further £300 from Reg, promising to pay the money back within a month. After a month, Bill is unable to repay the debt. This angers Reg who threatens to kill Bill unless he pays him £1,000 immediately. To show Bill that he is serious, Reg throws a brick through the front windscreen of Bill's car just as Bill starts to drive away. Bill swerves and crashes into a brick wall.

Later that evening, Reg still hadn't received the £1,000 from Bill, so he decided to drive to Bill's house to scare Bill again. Once at Bill's house, Reg pulls up the flowers in Bill's front garden and pours petrol through Bill's letterbox and sets fire to it. The fire spreads throughout Bill's house and to the neighbour's house before the fire brigade manage to put it out.

Discuss whether Reg is criminally liable for any property offences.

Answer plan

→ Consider the offences of blackmail under section 21 of the Theft Act 1968, and criminal damage, aggravated criminal damage and arson under the Criminal Damage Act 1971.

→ Examine Reg's liability for blackmail under section 21 of the Theft Act 1968 in respect of the threat to kill Bill.

→ Explore Reg's liability for simple criminal damage and aggravated criminal damage under section 1(1) and 1(2) of the Criminal Damage Act 1971 when he throws the brick through the windscreen of the car.

→ Discuss Reg's liability for criminal damage to the flowers in Bill's garden under section 1(1) of the Criminal Damage Act 1971.

→ Consider Reg's liability for aggravated criminal damage by fire under section 1(2) and (3) of the Criminal Damage Act 1971 when he sets Bill's house on fire.

Diagram plan

Reg's liability for blackmail for the threat to kill – s. 21, Theft Act 1968

Reg's liability for criminal damage for throwing the brick – s. 1(1) and 1(2), Criminal Damage Act 1971

Reg's liability for criminal damage to the flowers in Bill's garden – s. 1(1), Criminal Damage Act 1971

Reg's liability for aggravated criminal damage by fire for setting Bill's house on fire – s. 1(2) and (3), Criminal Damage Act 1971

A printable version of this diagram plan is available from **www.pearsoned.co.uk/lawexpressqa**

Answer

This question requires consideration of the property offences of which Reg might be convicted. Reg could be guilty of blackmail under section 21 of the Theft Act 1968, aggravated criminal damage under section 1(2) of the Criminal Damage Act 1971, simple criminal damage under section 1(1) of the Criminal Damage Act 1971, and aggravated criminal damage by fire (arson) under sections 1(2) and (3) of the Criminal Damage Act 1971. Reg's liability for these offences will be explored in chronological order.[1]

Threat to kill

Reg may be guilty of blackmail under section 21 of the Theft Act 1968. The actus reus requires proof that the defendant made a demand with menaces.[2] This is satisfied because Reg threatens to kill Bill unless he repays him the £1,000. A threat to kill would satisfy the requirement of menaces as it would be likely to influence the mind of an ordinary person of normal stability and courage (*Clear* [1968] 1 QB 670). The mens rea requires proof that the demand was unwarranted and that the demand was made with a view to gain or intention to cause loss. The demand was unwarranted unless Reg believes that he has reasonable grounds for making the demand (s. 21(1)(a)), and that the use of the menaces is a proper means of enforcing the demand (s. 21(1)(b)). Reg is unlikely to believe that demanding a payment of £1,000 to cover a debt of £300 is reasonable, and he most likely does not believe that the threat to kill is a proper means of enforcing the demand, so the demand is unwarranted. Finally, by making the demand, Reg intends to gain the money which he does not already have (s. 34(2)(a)(i)).

The car windscreen

When Reg throws the brick through the windscreen of the car, he commits simple criminal damage of the window, the car, and the brick wall (if any damage is caused to the car and brick wall upon crashing) under section 1(1) of the Criminal Damage Act 1971. Simple criminal damage requires proof that the defendant intentionally or recklessly destroyed or damaged property belonging to another without lawful excuse. The damage need not be permanent (***Gayford v Chouler***

[1898] 1 QB 316), but must be more than trivial (*A (a juvenile)* v *R* [1978] Crim LR 689). What constitutes damage is a matter of fact and degree (*Roe* v *Kingerlee* [1986] Crim LR 735). The windscreen is permanently damaged and personal property (s. 10(1), Criminal Damage Act 1971) which belongs to another (s. 10(2), Criminal Damage Act 1971). The same can be said for the car and brick wall if they indeed sustain any damage. Reg has no lawful excuse for causing the damage as he cannot argue that he honestly believed that he had (or would have had) the consent of the owner under section 5(2)(a) of the Criminal Damage Act 1971 and he did not honestly believe that the property was in need of immediate protection under section 5(2)(b) of the Criminal Damage Act 1971.[3] It is likely that Reg intended to cause the damage, thus the offence of simple criminal damage is established. Even if he does not intend to cause damage to the car or the brick wall, he is at the very least reckless in this regard. Recklessness is subjectively assessed under *G* [2003] UKHL 50, and requires Reg to have considered the risk that his conduct might cause damage, but to have taken that risk anyway. The risk is certainly an unjustifiable one.[4]

> [3] Although the defence of lawful excuse does not apply here, this sentence demonstrates that you understand when the defence under section 5(2) is available.

> [4] Set out and apply the current subjective test of recklessness where appropriate. There is no need to apply the old law under *MPC* v *Caldwell* [1982] 1 AC 341 in a problem scenario.

It is also necessary to consider whether Reg might also be guilty of aggravated criminal damage under section 1(2) of the Criminal Damage Act 1971. This offence contains an extra mens rea requirement. In order to successfully convict Reg of aggravated criminal damage, the prosecution must also prove that Reg thereby[5] intended to or was reckless as to endangering the life of another. The fact that Reg threw the brick directly at the windscreen of a car, which might be likely to crash as a result, is evidence from which it could be inferred that he thereby intended to endanger life. However, at the very least he must have been reckless as to whether life would be endangered. Thus, Reg is likely to be convicted of aggravated criminal damage under section 1(2).

> [5] The inclusion of this word 'thereby' is crucial and demonstrates that you understand the law. There must be an intention or recklessness *by* the damage or destruction to endanger life.

The flowers in the garden

Reg could be charged with simple criminal damage with respect to pulling the flowers out in Bill's garden. This would be charged under section 1(1) of the Criminal Damage Act 1971. There would need to be some investigation into the damage caused to the flowers – it is not clear from the facts whether the flowers were pulled out with their roots or not or if any other damage was caused. Even if the damage to the flowers is not permanent, it will still be damage for the purposes of criminal damage provided that the damage is more than trivial. The flowers are property (s. 10(1), Criminal Damage Act 1971) and they belong to another person, namely Bill. Reg has no defence of lawful excuse. Consequently, the actus reus of simple criminal damage is satisfied. The mens rea of simple criminal damage requires proof that Reg intended or was reckless as to causing such damage. It is quite clear that Reg intended to cause the damage here.[6]

[6] Do not forget to state and apply the mens rea elements of the offence. You could also consider the offence of theft here.

Setting fire to the house

Reg might be guilty of aggravated criminal damage by fire (arson) when he sets the house on fire. Aggravated criminal damage by fire is an offence under sections 1(2) and 1(3) of the Criminal Damage Act 1971.[7] Burning the house down will amount to destruction of property by fire. The house is property (s. 10(1), Criminal Damage Act 1971) and it belongs to another under section 10(2) of the Criminal Damage Act 1971. Reg has no lawful excuse for causing the damage to the house. The mens rea of aggravated criminal damage by fire requires an intention or recklessness as to the damage. Reg clearly intended to damage the house here. Aggravated criminal damage by fire also contains an extra mens rea requirement, namely that Reg thereby intended to or was reckless as to endangering the life of another. By setting fire to a house, it can be inferred that Reg thereby intended to endanger life, or that he was at the very least reckless. Thus, Reg is likely to be convicted of aggravated criminal damage by fire under sections 1(2) and 1(3).

[7] Where criminal damage is committed by fire, the offence is charged contrary to both section 1(1) (or s. 1(2) if dealing with aggravated criminal damage) and section 1(3), Criminal Damage Act 1971.

 Make your answer stand out

■ Think carefully about your structure where you have more than one defendant. You should adopt a structure which is clear and logical. It may be better to deal with events chronologically; alternatively, it may make more sense to deal with each defendant in turn.

■ Ensure that you apply the law to the problem question every time you cite a legal principle.

■ Ensure that you always identify and apply the specific mens rea of all relevant offences.

! Don't be tempted to . . .

- Waste valuable time in the exam by reciting large chunks of statute. Instead, you should at times paraphrase the relevant section you wish to refer to and apply the law to the scenario.

- Misstate the tests on lawful excuse in criminal damage under section 5(2) of the Criminal Damage Act 1971. Ensure that you are familiar with the subjective/objective nature of the tests so that you apply the law accurately.

- Forget to spend time discussing the mens rea of offences. Having explored and applied the actus reus elements, students often then forget to do the same for the mens rea. If you do this, you are really only providing part of an answer and this will gravely affect your performance in the exam.

@ Try it yourself

Now take a look at the question below and attempt to answer it. You can check your response against the answer guidance available on the companion website (**www.pearsoned.co.uk/lawexpressqa**).

> 'Despite the fact that s. 1 appears to be clear, precise and not dependent on context, criminal damage remains somewhat ambiguous in scope and applicability with some (albeit limited) scope for graffiti artists to argue they fall outside it' (Edwards, I. 'Banksy's Graffiti: A not-so-simple case of criminal damage?' (2009) 73 JCL 345).
>
> Critically evaluate the scope of criminal damage.

---

www.pearsoned.co.uk/lawexpressqa

Go online to access more revision support including additional essay and problem questions with diagram plans, You be the marker questions, and download all diagrams from the book.

Offences under the Fraud Act 2006

9

How this topic may come up in exams

Fraud could be examined by way of an essay or in a problem question. Essay questions on fraud may ask you to compare the law under the Fraud Act 2006 with the old deception offences which the Act replaced. You may be asked for a critical evaluation of the law and to consider whether the scope of the Act is problematic. You should prepare by reading the academic opinion surrounding fraud. Problem scenarios might ask you to discuss fraud only or you might be required to identify a number of different property offences in a mixed problem question.

■ Before you begin

It's a good idea to consider the following key themes of offences under the Fraud Act 2006 before tackling a question on this topic.

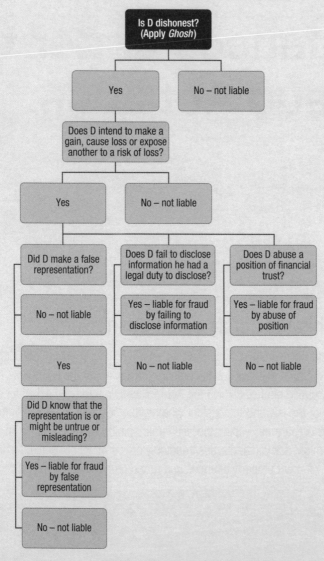

A printable version of this diagram is available from **www.pearsoned.co.uk/lawexpressqa**

❓ Question 1

Karis has recently taken over caring for her elderly grandmother who has become housebound. Karis visits her grandmother every day and carries out daily tasks for her, such as preparing her meals and going shopping for food. One day, her grandmother asks Karis to collect her pension. Karis goes to the post office with her grandmother's pension book, she decides that she will spend half of her grandmother's pension and then tell her that the payment has been reduced. However, the cashier refuses to hand over the pension payment because Karis is not authorised to collect the money.

Later that day, Karis applies for a job. One of the questions asks Karis to declare any unspent previous convictions. Karis has a recent conviction for theft, but she is concerned that she will not get the job if she puts this on the form, so she leaves it out of her application.

After completing the application form, Karis decides to buy a can of lemonade from a vending machine. However, she uses a fake pound coin as part of her payment. The vending machine rejects the fake coin and dispenses it into the change compartment.

Discuss Karis' criminal liability for the offence of fraud.

Diagram plan

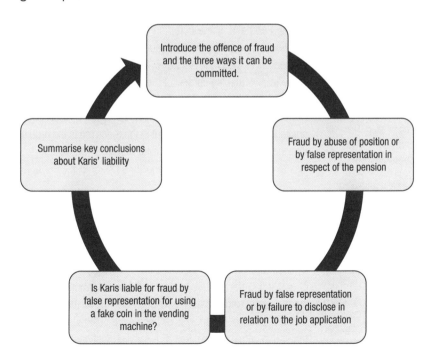

A printable version of this diagram plan is available from **www.pearsoned.co.uk/lawexpressqa**

Answer plan

➜ Introduce the offence of fraud and the three ways it can be committed.

➜ Consider fraud by abuse of position or fraud by false representation in respect of Karis's attempt to collect her grandmother's pension.

➜ Consider fraud by false representation or fraud by failure to disclose in relation to the job application.

➜ Consider whether Karis is liable for fraud by false representation for using a fake coin in the vending machine.

[1] Be clear to show that you are aware that there is only one offence of fraud under section 1 of the Fraud Act 2006.

[2] This demonstrates that you are aware that there is just one offence of fraud which may be committed in three ways.

[3] Make a brief mention of the common elements at the start of your answer in order to demonstrate to the examiner that you are aware of the relationship between the different ways in which fraud can be committed. However, do not write out everything you know about these.

[4] Adopt a clear and logical structure. Use headings in order to ensure that you focus on one incident at a time.

[5] This sentence demonstrates a wider understanding of the law relating to fraud. It shows the examiner that you have not merely learnt the provisions of the Fraud Act 2006, but that you are also aware of what is missing from the Act.

Answer

Karis could be criminally liable for fraud in relation to her attempt to collect her grandmother's pension, her job application, and in respect of her use of the vending machine. Fraud is an offence under section 1 of the Fraud Act 2006.[1] It may be committed in one of three ways: by false representation (s. 2), by failing to disclose information (s. 3) or by abuse of position (s. 4).[2] Although sections 2–4 provide for three distinct methods of committing fraud, each of these types of fraud contains some common elements.[3] Dishonesty is a mens rea element common to each fraud. As the term 'dishonesty' is not defined under the Fraud Act 2006, the courts will look to the meaning of the term within the context of theft. The negative aspect of dishonesty under section 2(1) of the Theft Act 1968 does not apply to fraud. However, the positive aspect under **Ghosh** [1982] 2 All ER 689 will be applied. Another common element in the mens rea is the requirement that the defendant intends to gain for himself or another, or to cause loss to another or to expose another to a risk of loss.

Pension[4]

In respect of her attempt to collect her grandmother's pension, Karis may be guilty of fraud by abuse of position under section 4 or fraud by false representation under section 2. In respect of fraud by abuse of position, unfortunately neither of the terms 'abuse' and 'position' were defined under the Fraud Act 2006.[5] Nevertheless, it is likely that this offence will apply here because a position of financial trust may arise within the context of a familial relationship. By acting as a carer to her grandmother and agreeing to pick up the pension, it could be said that Karis 'occupies a position in which [s]he is expected to safeguard, or not to act against, the financial interests of another person'[6] (s. 4(1)(a)). The offence requires that she abuses that position under section 4(1)(b). Karis does so by trying to obtain the money with the aim of spending half of it. There is no requirement that Karis must actually obtain the money. The mens rea of this offence requires proof that Karis has been dishonest in abusing her position (s. 4(1)(b)) and the **Ghosh** test of dishonesty will be applied here. Applying the first objective limb of **Ghosh**, the honest and reasonable person would certainly regard Karis's conduct as dishonest and Karis is very likely to realise this. The final mens rea element which needs to be established is that Karis intended to make a gain for herself or another or to cause loss to another or to expose another to a risk of loss (s. 2(1)(b)). Karis clearly intends, by means of the abuse of her position, to make a gain for herself, as she wishes to spend half of the pension money (s. 4(1)(c)). Under section 5(2), gain and loss extend only to gain or loss of money or other property. Property includes real or personal property, things in action and other intangible property. The property she intends to gain is the money. Therefore, Karis is likely to be guilty of fraud by abuse of position in respect of the pension.[7]

7 Conclude in relation to each incident of fraud as you go along. There is no need to write a long conclusion detailing Karis's liability for each scenario again at the end.

Karis might also be guilty of fraud by false representation in respect of the pension. The actus reus of this offence requires that Karis makes a false representation, which she does when she represents to the post office cashier that she has the authority to collect the money and when she tells her grandmother that she will collect her pension for her. Under section 2(3), a representation includes a representation as to fact, which this is. This is a false representation under section 2(2)(a) because it is untrue to say that she has the authority to make the transactions to the cashier, and in respect of her grandmother, and Karis intends to spend half of the pension payment.

The mens rea requires that Karis knows that the representation is or might be untrue or misleading under section 2(2)(b). Karis probably knows that she should not collect the money, so she probably knows that that representation is untrue. She certainly knows that she intends to spend half of the money, so the representation made to her grandmother is untrue. The offence of fraud also requires proof of dishonesty, thus the **Ghosh** test must be applied again. The honest and reasonable person would regard her conduct as dishonest. The second limb is subjective and requires consideration of whether Karis realised that the honest and reasonable person would regard this as dishonest. If she did, then she would be dishonest. Finally, Karis intended to make a gain for herself or another or cause loss to another or to expose another to a risk of loss (s. 2(1)(b)) and she intended to gain the money.

Job application form

Karis might be guilty of fraud by false representation or fraud by failing to disclose information in respect of the job application form. In respect of the fraud by false representation, Karis makes a false representation when she represents to the company that she has no unspent previous convictions. This is a representation as to fact (s. 2(3)). This is a false representation under section 2(2)(a) because it is an untrue statement. The mens rea requires that Karis knows that the representation is or might be untrue or misleading under section 2(2)(b). Karis knows that she has a recent conviction for theft, so she knows that the representation is untrue. The offence of fraud also requires proof of dishonesty, thus the **Ghosh** test must be applied again. The honest and reasonable person would regard her declaration as dishonest. The second limb is subjective and requires consideration of whether Karis realised that the honest and reasonable person would regard this as dishonest. If she did, then she would be dishonest. Finally, Karis intended to make a gain for herself or another or to cause loss to another or to expose another to a risk of loss (s. 2(1)(b)), as she intended to gain a salary or payment from the job.

[8] Set out any possible alternative offences which Karis might be charged with.

Alternatively, Karis might be charged with fraud by failing to disclose information under section 3.[8] By ticking the box marked 'no', she is not only making a false representation, but is also failing to disclose the conviction. The actus reus of this offence requires that the defendant fails to disclose information which he/she has a legal obligation to disclose. The mens rea elements require that Karis is dishonest and has an intention to make a gain or cause loss. Thus, Karis is likely to be guilty of fraud by false representation and may also be guilty of fraud by failing to disclose information.

Vending machine

By using the fake coin in the vending machine, Karis may be guilty of fraud by false representation under section 2. She makes a false representation of fact to the vending machine that the coin is legitimate currency. Under section 5(2), a representation is made if it 'is submitted in any form to any system or device designed to receive, convey or respond to communications (with or without human intervention)'.[9] Thus, using the coin in the vending machine will be sufficient. The representation is false because it is 'untrue' or at the very least 'misleading' (s. 2(2)(a)). It makes no difference that the machine failed to dispense the lemonade, as the representation does not need to operate on the machine.

The mens rea of the offence requires that Karis knows that the representation is or might be false under section 2(2)(b). Karis knows that the representation that she is making to the machine is false. Karis clearly has an intention to gain property, namely the can of lemonade, for herself. The **Ghosh** test of dishonesty must be applied: the honest and reasonable person would find the use of a fake coin in a vending machine as dishonest. If Karis's conduct is objectively dishonest, then she will be convicted of fraud by false representation if she realised this.

✓ **Make your answer stand out**

- Deal with each incident of fraud as it occurs in order to maintain a logical structure.
- Ensure that you consider whether Karis might be guilty of fraud via any of the three methods for each scenario.
- Set out the relevant sections from the Fraud Act 2006 where appropriate.
- Refer to academic opinion to make your answer really stand out. You could make reference to leading articles on fraud such as Ormerod, D. (2007) The Fraud Act 2006 – criminalising lying? Crim LR 193.
- Refer to other sources, such as the Explanatory Notes to the Fraud Act 2006 and Farrell, S., Yeo, N. and Landenberg, G. (2007) *Blackstone's Guide to the Fraud Act 2006*. Oxford: Oxford University Press, both of which provide examples of the application of the Fraud Act 2006.

! **Don't be tempted to . . .**

- Merely write out everything you know about each of the types of fraud without applying the law.
- Make the mistake of applying section 2(1) of the Theft Act 1968 to the meaning of dishonesty, but do set out and apply both limbs of the *Ghosh* test. ▶

■ Gloss over the elements which are common to each type of fraud, namely dishonesty and an intention to gain or cause loss. Even though these are common to each type of fraud, you must apply the law relating to these elements in each different scenario.

🖋 Question 2

The old deception offences were problematic and in need of reform. The Fraud Act 2006 has removed many of the problems with the former law, but it has been criticised for being far too wide in scope. To what extent do you agree that the offence of fraud is too broad?

Answer plan

→ Outline the elements of fraud and the three ways it can be committed.

→ Discuss criticisms of the deception offences and the rationale behind the Fraud Act 2006.

→ Examine whether the Act resolved the problems with the old law.

→ Analyse the scope of the Fraud Act 2006.

Diagram plan

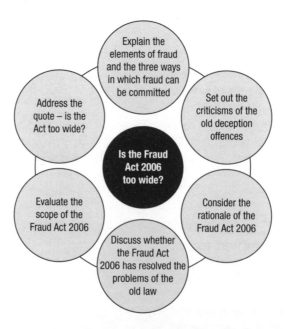

A printable version of this diagram plan is available from **www.pearsoned.co.uk/lawexpressqa**

Answer

This question requires discussion of the effect of the Fraud Act 2006 and the scope of the offence of fraud. The Act came into force on 15 January 2007 and it created a general offence of fraud which can be committed in three ways: (s. 1) by false representation; (s. 2) by failing to disclose information; or (s. 3) by abuse of position. This single offence replaced the old deception offences which had been problematic for a number of reasons. In doing so, the Act eliminated many of the problems with the former law. However, the Act has been the subject of much academic criticism.

One important criticism of the old law was that there were too many complicated offences of deception. Professor Ormerod describes the deception offences as 'notoriously technical' and 'over-particularised' (Ormerod, D. (2007) The Fraud Act 2006 – criminalising lying? Crim LR 193).[1] These offences were very specific and narrowly defined. The actus reus of the deception offences required proof that deception had been caused and that either property, services, a pecuniary advantage or a money transfer had been obtained. The offences were heavily dependent upon proof of actus reus elements. Many defendants who should have been convicted secured acquittals due to technicalities, such as being charged with the wrong offence. Thus, the deception offences had a detrimental effect on the effectiveness of the criminal justice system.

[1] Incorporate academic opinion into your answer. You should refer directly to this leading academic article on fraud as this demonstrates that you have read widely in your revision.

The old offence of obtaining property by deception (s. 15, Theft Act 1968) was inadequate in dealing with cases in which the defendant had obtained a money transfer by deception. Problems arose in the case of **Preddy** [1996] AC 815. The House of Lords held that where a person transferred money from one bank account to another, he could not be convicted of obtaining property by deception as the debit leaving one bank account did not amount to the same property belonging to another as the credit which entered the other bank account. A new offence of obtaining a money transfer by deception under section 15A of the Theft Act 1968 was created.[2]

[2] Cite *Preddy* and explain the problems highlighted by this case in order to demonstrate your knowledge of the technical problems with the old deception offences.

The old offences required proof of causation. This created a further difficulty for the prosecution. If the causative link between the obtaining and the deception was not proved, no conviction could result. It was also unclear whether an omission was sufficient under the old

3 This sentence compares the
position under the new Fraud
Act 2006.

deception offences or whether a conviction was dependent upon an act (**Firth** (1989) 91 Cr App R 217). It is now clear under the Fraud Act 2006 that an offence of fraud may be committed by an omission to disclose information which one has a legal duty to disclose (s. 3) and by abuse of position (s. 4).[3]

The old deception offences were also criticised for failing to meet the requirements of an offence of fraud in today's technological and internet-focused age. The offences did not allow for a deception to be practised against a machine. It was only possible to practise a deception against a person (**Davies v Flackett** [1974] RTR 8). Thus, the deception offences were inadequate to deal with fraud via a machine. The Fraud Act 2006 deals with this by providing that a false representation may be made if it 'is submitted in any form to any system or device designed to receive, convey or respond to communications (with or without human intervention)' (s. 2(5)).

A further criticism of the old deception offences was that they were difficult for juries to understand. As the tribunal of fact, jurors must be able to understand the elements of the offences, otherwise there is a risk of an unfair trial and the integrity of the criminal justice system is compromised.

The Fraud Act 2006 eliminated these problems by creating one single offence of fraud. The offence is not heavily focused on actus reus elements. For instance, instead of requiring proof of anything having been obtained (an actus reus element), fraud requires proof of an intention to make gain for himself or another, or to cause loss or to expose another to a risk of loss (a mens rea element). There is no longer any requirement of proof that the obtaining caused a deception to be practised. Instead, fraud simply requires a form of conduct to be proved, such as the making of a false representation, a failure to disclose information, or abuse of position. The offence of fraud focuses on the mens rea, which simply requires dishonesty and the intention to gain or cause loss.

While the provisions of the Theft Act 1968 have been heavily criticised by many academics, such as Professor Ormerod and the judiciary (see Lord Goff's opinions in **Preddy**), the new Fraud Act 2006 has also been subject to criticism. One criticism of the Fraud Act 2006 is that it has created an offence in which the actus reus is too wide, to the extent that liability is too heavily dependent upon proof of dishonesty.[4]

4 This sentence draws the
answer back to the criticisms
of the Fraud Act 2006 and
thus the title of the question.

The Act relies upon the **Ghosh** ([1982] 2 All ER 689) test of dishonesty which is used in theft cases and which has itself been the subject of much discomfort within the criminal law (see the criticisms made by Professor Griew (in Griew, E.J. (1985) Dishonesty: the objections to *Feely* and *Ghosh*. Crim LR 341) and Professor Spencer (Spencer, J.R. (1982) Dishonesty: what the jury thinks the defendant thought the jury would have thought. CLJ 222). It has been claimed that the test assumes a fictional standard of honesty and leaves too much in the hands of the jury, leading to inconsistent verdicts.

Although the objective of the Fraud Act 2006 was to expand the scope of fraud in order to ensure the successful prosecution of fraudsters, the Fraud Act 2006 has gone too far. The offence of fraud is so widely drafted that it overlaps with the offence of theft and catches behaviour which should not really be regarded as fraud. It creates criminal liability where a matter could be dealt with by civil law (e.g. providing bad references) or internal procedure, or where no civil court would deem the matter actionable (e.g. trade puffs).

 Make your answer stand out

- Refer to other academic opinion, such as: Withey, C. (2007) The Fraud Act 2006 – some early observations and comparisons with the former law. 71 JCL 220; Allgrove B. and Sellers, S. (2009) The Fraud Act 2006: is breach of confidence now a crime? 4 JIPLP 278; Monaghan, C. (2010) To prosecute or not to prosecute? A reconsideration of the overzealous prosecution of parents under the Fraud Act 2006. 74 *Journal of Criminal Law* 259.
- You should explore further examples of the types of conduct which the Fraud Act 2006 criminalises unnecessarily.
- You should also refer to the Law Commission (2002) Report, *Fraud* (No. 276) and the Explanatory Notes to the Fraud Act 2006.
- You could further explore the criticisms of the old law and elaborate on the problems caused by the case of *Preddy*.

! Don't be tempted to . . .

- Describe all of the old deception offences from the Theft Acts 1968 and 1978 in detail as these are now redundant.
- Simply write everything you know about the Fraud Act 2006 as you will not be addressing the question which asks you to critically evaluate whether the Fraud Act 2006 has improved the law relating to fraud.
- Forget to address the quote directly in your answer.

@ Try it yourself

Now take a look at the question below and attempt to answer it. You can check your response against the answer guidance available on the companion website (**www.pearsoned.co.uk/lawexpressqa**).

> Critically evaluate the extent to which the Fraud Act 2006 overlaps with the Theft Act 1968.

www.pearsoned.co.uk/lawexpressqa

 Go online to access more revision support including additional essay and problem questions with diagram plans, You be the marker questions, and download all diagrams from the book.

Defences

10

How this topic may come up in exams

General defences could be examined by way of essay questions on individual defences or on a mixture of the defences, or by a problem question. Essay questions might require you to critically evaluate a particular general defence, such as intoxication or self-defence. Alternatively, an essay question might take a more general approach and ask you to consider a certain category of defences, such as those concerned with the capacity of the defendant (e.g. insanity and automatism). Problem scenarios could require you to identify and apply the law relating to one or more general defences.

Before you begin

It's a good idea to consider the following key themes of defences before tackling a question on this topic.

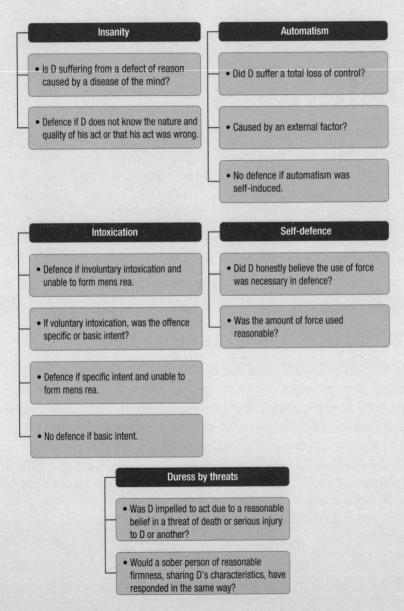

Insanity

- Is D suffering from a defect of reason caused by a disease of the mind?

- Defence if D does not know the nature and quality of his act or that his act was wrong.

Automatism

- Did D suffer a total loss of control?

- Caused by an external factor?

- No defence if automatism was self-induced.

Intoxication

- Defence if involuntary intoxication and unable to form mens rea.

- If voluntary intoxication, was the offence specific or basic intent?

- Defence if specific intent and unable to form mens rea.

- No defence if basic intent.

Self-defence

- Did D honestly believe the use of force was necessary in defence?

- Was the amount of force used reasonable?

Duress by threats

- Was D impelled to act due to a reasonable belief in a threat of death or serious injury to D or another?

- Would a sober person of reasonable firmness, sharing D's characteristics, have responded in the same way?

A printable version of this diagram is available from **www.pearsoned.co.uk/lawexpressqa**

? Question 1

Florian decides to have a party at his house. He hires some strobe lights and some powerful speakers and invites his friends, including Lisa, round. Lisa, who is 35 years old, suffers from epilepsy. While she had frequent seizures as a child, in her adult years she has only had one or two seizures. However, after a few hours of dancing Lisa complains about feeling 'a bit funny'. She suffers an epileptic seizure during which she lashes out at Florian who is trying to help her. She strikes Florian several times in the head, causing severe bruising. Lisa is charged with assault occasioning actual bodily harm contrary to section 47 of the Offences Against the Person Act 1861.

Advise Lisa as to her criminal liability. Would your answer be any different if instead of being epileptic, Lisa is diabetic and:

(a) She failed to take her insulin before attacking Florian?

(b) she had taken her insulin, but suffered the attack because she failed to eat sufficiently after taking the insulin?

Answer plan

➡ Discuss the defence of insanity in relation to Lisa's epileptic seizure.

➡ Consider the defence of insanity in respect of the hyperglycaemic attack.

➡ Consider the defence of automatism in relation to the hypoglycaemia.

➡ Examine whether Lisa's automatism was self-induced and the effect of this.

Diagram plan

Elements of the offence

AR – proof of battery which causes ABH

MR – mens rea of battery

Lisa's epileptic seizure

Insanity (*M'Naghten* rules (1843))

Epilepsy – internal factor (*Sullivan* (1984))

(a) Lisa's hyperglycaemic attack

Insanity (*M'Naghten* rules (1843))

Hyperglycaemia – internal factor (*Hennessy* (1989))

(b) Lisa's hypoglycaemic attack

Non-insane automatism

Hypoglycaemia – external factor (*Quick* (1973))

Self-induced automatism? (*Bailey* (1983))

A printable version of this diagram plan is available from **www.pearsoned.co.uk/lawexpressqa**

Answer

This question requires consideration of the defences of automatism and insanity. However, before exploring these it is necessary to discuss the elements of the offence charged. The prosecution will be able to establish that Lisa has the actus reus of assault occasioning actual bodily harm contrary to section 47 of the Offences Against the Person Act 1861.[1] The offence may be committed by either an assault or a battery which causes actual bodily harm. In this case, Lisa inflicts unlawful force on Florian, which is the actus reus of a battery (see **Collins v Wilcock** [1984] 1 WLR 1172). Lisa is clearly both the factual and legal cause of Florian's injuries. Actual bodily harm is widely defined in **Miller** [1954] 2 WLR 138 so as to include 'any hurt or injury calculated to interfere with health or comfort' (per Lynskey J). Florian suffers severe bruising, which is most likely to be sufficient for actual bodily harm. The prosecution will also need to establish the mens rea of assault occasioning actual bodily harm, namely that Lisa had the requisite mens rea for battery – intention or recklessness in relation to the infliction of unlawful force.[2] It is unclear here whether Lisa has the necessary mens rea as there is no evidence as to whether she was aware of her actions.

As stated above, two defences might be available to Lisa. These are insanity (also known as insane automatism) and automatism (also known as non-insane automatism). Non-insane automatism is a preferable defence, due to the fact that a successful plea results in a complete acquittal and the burden of proof is on the prosecution.[3] By contrast, a successful plea of insanity results in a verdict of not guilty by reason of insanity (s. 1, Criminal Procedure (Insanity) Act 1964) and the burden of proving the elements of insanity is on the defence. However, although Lisa would prefer to rely upon the defence of non-insane automatism in the first given scenario, this would be unlikely to succeed due to the fact that the factor which caused Lisa's attack was an internal factor (her epilepsy) rather than an external factor which is required for non-insane automatism.[4] This means that Lisa will be left with the defence of insanity as an available alternative.

Insanity is governed by the **M'Naghten** rules (**M'Naghten** (1843) 10 Cl & F 200), which were set down by the House of Lords. These

[1] As the question asks you about Lisa's liability, you will need to briefly discuss whether the elements of the offence charged are satisfied.

[2] Do not forget that the mens rea of assault occasioning ABH is the mens rea of an assault or a battery. No additional mens rea is required: *Savage; Parmenter* [1992] 1 AC 699.

[3] This shows that you know more than just the elements of the defences, but that you can advise a client as to the implications of the defences and which would be preferable.

[4] If this defence obviously does not apply here, then rule it out concisely, explaining why and move on to the more appropriate defence.

rules state that every man is presumed sane, but he may rebut that presumption by proving, on a balance of probabilities, that at the time of the offence he was suffering from a defect of reason caused by a disease of the mind, and that he did not know the nature and quality of his act or that he did not know that the act he was doing was wrong. A defect of reason involves proof that Lisa was deprived of her power of reasoning and not mere absentmindedness (*Clarke* [1972] 1 All ER 219). The defect of reason must be caused by a disease of the mind, which must affect the ordinary mental faculties of reason, memory and understanding (per Devlin J in *Kemp* [1957] 1 QB 399).[5] Lisa suffers from epilepsy and this is deemed to be a disease of the mind, which is an internal factor (*Bratty v A-G for Northern Ireland* [1963] AC 386 and *Sullivan* [1984] AC 156). Thus, in this scenario, the only defence available to Lisa would be the defence of insanity.[6]

Lisa would also be required to prove either that she did not know the nature and quality of her act or that she did not know that the act was wrong. The first of these two alternatives is a denial of the mens rea of the offence – Lisa must prove that she did not know the physical nature of the act she was doing (*Codere* (1917) 12 Cr App R 21). Alternatively, Lisa must prove that she did not know that the act was legally wrong. There is little evidence of either of these elements on the facts, but one is necessary for the plea of insanity to be successful.[7]

Looking at the alternative set of facts in part (a), Lisa suffers from diabetes and has had a hyperglycaemic attack. According to the case of *Hennessy* [1989] 1 WLR 287, a defendant who commits an offence during a hyperglycaemic attack may only plead insanity. Lord Lane CJ held that 'hyperglycaemia . . . caused by an inherent defect, and not corrected by insulin is a disease, and if . . . it does cause a malfunction of the mind, then the case may fall with *M'Naghten rules*'. Thus, as hyperglycaemia is caused by the condition of diabetes itself, an internal factor, the defence of insanity is the only option available to Lisa here. Again, she would have to prove that she did not know the nature and quality of her act or that she did not know that the act was wrong.

In part (b), the attack is due to the fact that Lisa had taken her insulin but had failed to eat sufficiently after doing so. In this case, Lisa would not be forced to plead insanity, but she would instead be advised

[5] You should learn the key parts of leading judgments so that you can cite them in your answer.

[6] Set out your conclusion as to the most likely defence along with your reasoning.

[7] If there is no evidence on a particular point, then say so. Do not ignore these elements as they are a necessary part of the defence.

[8] This is a very widely cited quote that you should ensure that you are fully aware of and prepared to refer to.

to try to plead non-insane automatism on the basis that the insulin (an external factor) caused the reaction. Non-insane automatism has been defined by Lord Denning as 'an act which is done by the muscles without any control by the mind, such as a spasm, a reflex action or a convulsion; or an act done by a person who is not conscious of what he is doing, such as an act done whilst suffering from concussion or whilst sleepwalking' (*Bratty v Attorney General for Northern Ireland*).[8] This defence involves a total loss of voluntary control due to an external factor. A defendant who commits an offence during a hypoglycaemic attack may rely on the defence of non-insane automatism (*Quick and Paddison* [1973] QB 910 and *Bingham* [1991] Crim LR 433). However, in this particular scenario, Lisa has failed to eat sufficiently after taking her insulin. If she is deemed to be reckless in doing so (i.e. it is necessary to question whether or not she knew that by failing to eat properly she was running the risk of unpredictable or aggressive conduct),[9] then her non-insane automatism may be said to be self-induced (*Bailey* [1983] 1 WLR 760). If there is evidence that Lisa's automotive state was self-induced and that she was at fault, then she will have no defence to a basic intent offence such as assault occasioning actual bodily harm because the necessary recklessness for the mens rea of that offence will have been established.[10]

[9] Explain what recklessness would mean here in plain language.

[10] This demonstrates that you can distinguish between specific and basic intent offences in context and apply the law accurately.

✓ Make your answer stand out

■ Where a problem scenario gives you alternative sets of facts, ensure that you address all alternatives and that you do so in a logical, structured and clear way so that the examiner can follow your answer easily.

■ Where a question requires consideration of a number of defences, you should deal with the most appropriate defences in the most detail and rule out any inappropriate ones concisely.

■ Ensure that you use authorities to support every principle of law that you rely upon.

■ Make reference to relevant quotes from judgments where appropriate to show the depth of your knowledge.

■ You could refer to academic opinion on the point of whether insanity is an appropriate defence in relation to epilepsy or not. For instance, see Mackay, R.D. and Reuber, M. (2007) Epilepsy and the defence of insanity – time for a change. Crim LR 782.

! Don't be tempted to . . .

■ Forget to address the elements of the offence he/she has been charged with as well as the defences, where a question on defences asks you to consider the liability of the defendant. A defendant's liability is obviously dependent upon both the elements of the offence being established as well as the success of any defences.

■ Simply set out everything you know about the defences. You must ensure that you apply the law to the particular facts of the question.

■ Make the mistake of failing to answer the parts that give you alternative facts. Ensure that you manage your time well so that you are able to deal with all parts that require answering. You will lose valuable marks by not addressing the alternative scenarios.

🖎 Question 2

'It remains deeply unsatisfactory for the law [on insanity] to remain so ill-defined as to leave exposed to the risk of such a verdict a person with a mental condition of what may be a trivial nature and who poses no real future risk to society' (Ormerod, D. (2008) *Smith and Hogan Criminal Law*, 12th edn. Oxford: Oxford University Press, p. 283).

Discuss with reference to case law.

Answer plan

➜ Consider the *M'Naghten rules*.

➜ Consider examples of a 'disease of the mind'.

➜ What are the implications of a successful plea of insanity?

➜ Discuss automatism and diminished responsibility as alternatives.

➜ Conclude with the Law Commission review of insanity.

Diagram plan

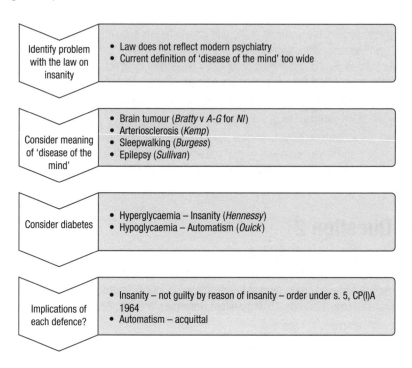

Identify problem with the law on insanity
- Law does not reflect modern psychiatry
- Current definition of 'disease of the mind' too wide

Consider meaning of 'disease of the mind'
- Brain tumour (*Bratty* v *A-G* for *NI*)
- Arteriosclerosis (*Kemp*)
- Sleepwalking (*Burgess*)
- Epilepsy (*Sullivan*)

Consider diabetes
- Hyperglycaemia – Insanity (*Hennessy*)
- Hypoglycaemia – Automatism (*Ouick*)

Implications of each defence?
- Insanity – not guilty by reason of insanity – order under s. 5, CP(I)A 1964
- Automatism – acquittal

A printable version of this diagram plan is available from **www.pearsoned.co.uk/lawexpressqa**

Answer

[1] Identify the key problem with the law at the very start in your own words.

[2] Citing the Law Commission in your opening paragraph demonstrates that you are aware that this is an area which was recently considered by the Commission. You should paraphrase this rather than remember the quote verbatim.

The law on insanity has been subject to much criticism and there have been many calls for reform. The law is outdated and fails to reflect modern psychiatric views of mental disorders.[1] As the Law Commission has recognised, the main problem is the fact that 'the key concept of "disease of the mind" has no agreed psychiatric meaning. As interpreted by the courts, it has even come to include conditions that are not mental disorders, such as epilepsy and diabetes' (Law Commission (2010), Consultation Paper, *Unfitness to Plead and the Insanity Defence*.[2] As the title suggests, the rules on insanity are ill-defined and 'deeply unsatisfactory' in today's society.

The law on insanity is governed by the *M'Naghten rules* (1843) 10 Cl & F 200), in which the House of Lords stated that there is a general presumption that every man is sane, such that if he wishes to raise insanity as a defence, he must rebut that presumption by proving insanity on a balance of probabilities. Thus, the burden of proving the defence is on the defendant. The defendant must prove that at the time of the offence he was suffering from a defect of reason caused by a disease of the mind, and that he did not know the nature and quality of his act or that he did not know that the act he was doing was wrong.

The first element, 'a defect of reason' involves proof that the defendant was deprived of his power of reasoning and not merely absentminded (*Clarke* [1972] 1 All ER 219). The defect of reason must be caused by a disease of the mind. The term 'disease of the mind' is not a medical one but a legal one.[3] The types of conditions which are covered by the term are wide in scope, ranging from a brain tumour to sleepwalking. According to Devlin J in *Kemp* [1957] 1 QB 399, a disease of the mind must affect the 'mind' (i.e. the ordinary mental faculties of reason, memory and understanding) rather than just the 'brain' in the physical sense. A closer reference to case law illustrates the types of conditions which have been deemed to constitute a 'disease of the mind'. In the case of *Kemp*, arteriosclerosis was held to constitute a disease of the mind, and it is likely that a brain tumour would amount to a disease of the mind after Lord Denning suggested as much in *Bratty v A-G for Northern Ireland* [1963] AC 386 (although it should be noted that this *obiter* comment conflicts with the decision in *Charlson* (1955) 39 Cr App R 37)[4]. More controversially, epilepsy has been deemed to constitute a disease of the mind (see *Bratty v A-G for Northern Ireland* and *Sullivan* [1984] AC 156). In *Bratty v A-G for Northern Ireland*, Lord Denning defined a disease of the mind as 'any mental disorder which has manifested itself in violence and is prone to recur'. This term has been further extended to sleepwalking in the case of *Burgess* [1991] 2 QB 92. These cases demonstrate that a defendant who commits a criminal offence during an epileptic seizure or while sleepwalking is deemed to be legally 'insane'. Mackay and Reuber take the view that it is 'surely no longer acceptable to use the label "insanity" for any case of epileptic automatism' (Mackay, R.D. and Reuber, M. (2007) Epilepsy and the defence of insanity – time for a change. Crim LR 782).[5] These

[3] Once again, reiterate the fact that the problem with the law is the fact that the rules have been developed by lawyers rather than experts in psychiatry.

[4] Ensure that you are aware of which comments are *obiter dicta* and which statements are binding *ratio decidendi*. Drawing such a distinction demonstrates the detailed level of your knowledge.

[5] Incorporate some academic opinion into your answer. This means that you will need to read more than just your textbook and module guide.

cases are highly controversial and 'deeply unsatisfactory', and as the title suggests, they expose individuals with relatively trivial conditions who pose no real future risk to society to the risk of a verdict of not guilty by reason of insanity.[6]

An area of confusion in the law on insanity is the way in which the law deals with defendants with diabetes. According to the case of **Hennessy** [1989] 1 WLR 287, a defendant who commits an offence during a hyperglycaemic attack may plead insanity. However, a defendant who commits an offence during a hypoglycaemic attack may plead the more favourable defence of automatism. A successful plea of insanity leads to a verdict of not guilty by reason of insanity and the disposal options available to a judge are a hospital order, a supervision and treatment order or an absolute discharge (s. 5, Criminal Procedure (Insanity) Act 1964). A plea of insanity is not favoured by defendants who fear being labelled as 'insane' and would prefer a successful plea to lead to acquittal rather than a hospital or supervision and treatment order. By contrast, a successful plea of automatism leads to no such label and a complete acquittal. On first glance it seems odd that the fate of a defendant with diabetes, whose condition is linked to his commission of an offence, will depend upon whether at the time of the offence he was suffering from hyperglycaemia or hypoglycaemia. The distinction made by the law is grounded in the direct causes of these different states. Hyperglycaemia (high blood sugar level) is

[7] Draw on judicial comment where you can in order to support your arguments.

caused by a lack of insulin. In **Hennessy**, Lord Lane CJ held that 'hyperglycaemia . . . caused by an inherent defect, and not corrected by insulin is a disease, and if . . . it does cause a malfunction of the mind, then the case may fall within the **M'Naghten** *rules*'.[7] Thus, as hyperglycaemia is caused by the condition of diabetes itself, an internal factor, the defence of insanity is the only available option. However, hypoglycaemia (low blood sugar level) is caused by excess insulin in the body. A defendant who commits an offence during a hypoglycaemic attack may rely on the defence of automatism because the cause of hypoglycaemia is an external factor, namely the insulin which has been administered to the defendant (see **Quick and Paddison** [1973] QB 910 and **Bingham** [1991] Crim LR 433). Although these conditions are caused by different factors, the distinction made seems improper and inappropriate.

It is clear from the cases mentioned that the term 'disease of the mind' has been given a wide interpretation to the extent that it now encompasses many trivial conditions which should not fall within the remit of insanity. Unfortunately, the law has developed so that such defendants are left with no suitable alternative defence.[8] Automatism has been ruled out in the above cases as this defence is deemed to apply where the automaton state is caused by an external factor. The only alternative which might apply to some of the above defendants is the defence of diminished responsibility, but this is not a general defence (it only applies to murder) and it is a partial defence (reducing liability rather than absolving a defendant of liability). The law is in a 'deeply unsatisfactory' state and reforms are necessary.[9]

[8] It is prudent to give some consideration to alternative defences that might be available, but do not spend too much time on this.

[9] Refer back to the title directly at the end of your answer.

✓ Make your answer stand out

- You should refer to further academic opinion by the leading academics in this field. In particular, you should read Mackay, R.D. (1990) Fact and fiction about the insanity defence. Crim LR 247; Mackay, R.D. (1998) *Mental Condition Defences in Criminal Law*. Oxford: Oxford University Press; Mackay, R.D. and Kearns, G. (1999) More fact(s) about the insanity defence. Crim LR 714; and Mackay, R.D., Mitchell, B. and Howe, L. (2006) Yet more facts about the insanity defence. Crim LR 399.

- You could also refer to the proposals for reform made by the Butler Committee in 1975. Read Home Office/DHSS (1975) Report of the Committee on Mentally Abnormal Offenders (The Butler Report). Cmnd. 6244.

- You might also make reference to the terminology used in the Mental Health Act 2007 in respect of the meaning of 'mental disorder'.

- You should also refer to Law Commission (2013) Discussion Paper, *Insanity and Automatism*. http://www.lawcom.gov.uk/wp-content/uploads/2015/06/insanity_discussion.pdf

! Don't be tempted to . . .

- Set out the facts of all the cases that you refer to. Your knowledge of the principles of law from each case and your analysis of the law are far more important and will earn you higher marks.

- Spend too much time considering the other elements of insanity. This question is about the meaning of 'disease of the mind', so you should focus on that rather than merely set out your knowledge of the other elements of insanity.

- Forget to address the quote directly in your answer.

❓ Question 3

Raymond works for an investment bank. As a result of the recession, the bank decides to make several compulsory redundancies and Raymond loses his job. After being told that he is being made redundant, Raymond goes to the nearest pub to drown his sorrows. After drinking several pints of beer with a bottle of whisky, Raymond begins flirting with the barmaid. As she walks past him when collecting empty glasses, Raymond slaps her bottom. The landlord of the pub witnesses the event and throws Raymond out of the pub.

On his way home, Raymond passes the bank. He picks up a newspaper seller stand and throws it at the bank window. The window shatters. When he arrives home, Raymond realises that he has lost his house keys. He breaks into a house, believing it to be his own home. However, he actually breaks into his next door neighbour's house, causing damage to the front door.

The following week, Raymond finds that he is struggling to get to sleep. He decides to take a dose of sleeping pills which had been prescribed to his wife. When Raymond goes to bed he repeatedly beats his wife over the head with a vase, killing her. Raymond has no recollection of this.

Discuss Raymond's possible defences to charges of sexual assault, criminal damage and murder.

Diagram plan

Sexual assault

- Voluntary intoxication (*Majewski*)
- Basic intent offence (*Heard*)
- No defence

Damage to window

- Voluntary intoxication (*Majewski*)
- Basic intent offence
- No defence

Breaking into house

- Intoxicated mistake (*Jaggard* v *Dickinson*)

Murder/manslaughter

- Involuntary intoxication?
- Apply *Hardie*? Was D reckless?
- Guilty of basic intent offence of manslaughter
- Intoxication may negate intention for specific intent offence of murder

A printable version of this diagram plan is available from **www.pearsoned.co.uk/lawexpressqa**

Answer plan

➡ Consider the fact that Raymond was voluntarily intoxicated and the *DPP* v *Majewski* [1977] AC 443 rules.

➡ Can Raymond rely on his intoxication in respect of the sexual assault?

➡ Can Raymond rely on his intoxication in respect of the basic intent offence of criminal damage?

➡ Consider Raymond's intoxicated mistake in breaking into the house.

➡ Discuss whether Raymond's intoxication in respect of the murder is voluntary or not.

➡ Discuss whether Raymond may rely on his intoxication in respect of the murder.

Answer

This question requires consideration of whether Raymond has any defences to the charges of sexual assault, criminal damage and murder. Raymond is intoxicated throughout the scenarios. For policy reasons, intoxication is not a defence *per se*, but in certain circumstances evidence of intoxication may be used to negate the mens rea of an offence.[1] The effect of raising evidence of intoxication will be explored in respect of each charge.

[1] You should recognise the fact that intoxication itself is no defence, but that intoxication is really evidence of a mistake or a denial of the mens rea elements of an offence.

Sexual assault of the barmaid

The first potential offence that Raymond may be charged with is sexual assault under section 3 of the Sexual Offences Act 2003. It is important to note that where the defendant does have the necessary intention for the offence, the fact that he is intoxicated will provide no defence because a drunken intent is still an intent:[2] ***Sheehan and Moore*** [1975] 1 WLR 739. So, if there is any evidence that Raymond intended the sexual assault, he will be guilty of the offence irrespective of any intoxication. However, it is not clear in this scenario whether Raymond had the necessary intention, thus it is necessary to explore his intoxication.

[2] Before you discuss the rules relating to voluntary intoxication, you should address the principle that an intoxicated intent is sufficient mens rea.

There are two types of intoxication: voluntary intoxication and involuntary intoxication. At this stage in the scenario, Raymond is voluntarily intoxicated.[3] The rules which apply to voluntary intoxication are set out by the House of Lords in ***DPP* v *Majewski*** [1977] AC 443. In this case, it was held that voluntary intoxication is no defence to crimes of

[3] Ensure that you distinguish between voluntary and involuntary intoxication and state which applies to this part of the question.

basic intent, although it may be evidence which goes towards negating the mens rea in a specific intent offence. A specific intent offence is one which requires proof of intention as the mens rea element of the offence. A basic intent offence is one which requires proof of a lesser form of mens rea, such as recklessness. Lord Elwyn-Jones held that voluntarily becoming intoxicated is a reckless course of conduct to take.[4] Thus, a voluntarily intoxicated defendant is automatically reckless and therefore he has the mens rea for every basic intent crime. However, this distinction between specific and basic intent offences has been criticised for being illogical and confusing. At first glance, it is difficult to categorise sexual assault as a specific or basic intent offence. The Court of Appeal has held that sexual assault is a basic intent offence, despite the fact that intentional touching is a requisite element of the offence: see *Heard* [2007] EWCA Crim 125.[5] On this interpretation, Raymond's voluntary intoxication will not negate the mens rea of sexual assault, thus it will provide no defence to the charge of sexual assault.

[4] Refer to specific judges' names from leading judgments in your answer to a problem question to show that you have actually read the case in question.

[5] Where there is a more recent case dealing with the specific issue in the question, you must ensure that you refer to this.

Breaking the window of the bank

In respect of breaking the window of the bank, Raymond will be charged with criminal damage under section 1(1) of the Criminal Damage Act 1971. If Raymond does have the necessary intention for the offence, the fact that he is intoxicated will provide no defence because a drunken intent is still an intent: *Sheehan and Moore*. If there is evidence proving beyond reasonable doubt that Raymond intended the criminal damage, he will be guilty. Further to this, any evidence that Raymond's intoxication was 'Dutch courage' to give him the confidence to commit the offence will provide no defence to the charge: *Attorney General for Northern Ireland v Gallagher* [1963] AC 349.

Criminal damage is a basic intent offence because the mens rea requires proof of either intention or recklessness as to causing damage, thus Raymond will not be able to rely on evidence of his voluntary intoxication in his defence. In light of Lord Elwyn-Jones's opinion in *Majewski*, evidence of voluntary intoxication is evidence of recklessness, thus in this scenario Raymond's intoxication provides evidence of the mens rea required for criminal damage.

Breaking into the wrong house

In respect of the act of breaking into the wrong house, Raymond will again be charged with criminal damage. He may attempt to plead lawful excuse under section 5(2) of the Criminal Damage Act 1971 if he honestly believed that he had consent to damage the property. In this case, as he honestly believed it to be the house he shared with his wife, he may have honestly believed that he had her consent to damage the property in order to gain entry. Despite the fact that he made a mistake due to his intoxication, he may still rely upon lawful excuse as a defence: *Jaggard* v *Dickinson* [1981] QB 527. Bizarrely, in such situations, the *Majewski* rule does not apply. Ormerod acknowledges the anomalous result here: 'Where the defendant did not intend any damage to property (but was reckless) he may be held liable because he was drunk; but where he did intend damage to property but thought the owner would consent he is not liable, however drunk he may have been' (Ormerod, D. (2011) *Smith and Hogan Criminal Law*, 13th edn. Oxford: Oxford University Press, pp. 323–4).[6]

[6] If you can incorporate some academic opinion into your answer to a problem question you should do so.

Killing his wife

Raymond may be charged with murder for killing his wife. At this stage, Raymond's intoxication is due to the sleeping pills that he has taken. It is necessary to ascertain whether Raymond is voluntarily or involuntarily intoxicated. Raymond will argue that his intoxication was involuntary due to the fact that he took prescription drugs which should have a sedative effect on him and that he was unaware of the effect the tablets would have on him.[7] Involuntary intoxication may provide a defence to any offence provided that the defendant did not have the requisite mens rea for the offence (i.e. an intention to kill or cause GBH in this case). However, in this case Raymond took tablets which were prescribed to his wife.[8] The facts here are similar to those in *Hardie* [1985] 1 WLR 64, in which the Court of Appeal held that consideration must be given to whether the defendant's conduct in taking the non-dangerous drug was reckless. If his conduct was not reckless, he could rely on evidence of his involuntary intoxication to negate his mens rea for murder. Consideration should be given to the fact that the drug Raymond took is lawful in prescribed quantities and that he was unaware of the effect the drug would have on him, as well as the fact that the normal effect of taking the drug is sedative. In these circumstances, Raymond's intoxication is likely to be treated

[7] This sentence sets out the argument that the defendant will seek to put forward in his defence and explain the rationale behind it.

[8] This sentence sets out the counterargument (which the prosecution will seek to rely on).

as involuntary. Thus, it may provide evidence to negate the mens rea of murder and any lesser charge of manslaughter.

[9] Briefly summarise the conclusions you reached in respect of each offence.

In conclusion,[9] Raymond's voluntary intoxication is likely to provide no defence to the sexual assault and the criminal damage of the window of the bank. However, he may rely on evidence of his intoxication in defence of criminal damage to the house and murder.

✓ **Make your answer stand out**

- You should include references to academic opinion to make your answer stand out.
- You could also refer to judicial comment in *DPP* v *Majewski*, *Heard* or *Hardie*.
- Ensure that you apply the law to the specific facts of the problem scenario each time you set out a legal principle.
- You could also refer to the Law Commission (2009) Report, *Intoxication and Criminal Liability* (No. 314), which makes a number of recommendations on reforming the law.

! **Don't be tempted to . . .**

- Confuse the rules relating to voluntary intoxication from *Majewski* with those relating to involuntary intoxication.
- Recite the facts of *Majewski*. Although *Majewski* is the leading case on voluntary intoxication, the principle of law derived from this case is of more relevance in an answer than the specific facts of the case.
- Forget to ensure that you revise the effect that intoxication has on specific defences, such as mistaken belief in lawful excuse (*Jaggard* v *Dickinson*), mistaken belief in self-defence (*O'Connor* [1991] Crim LR 135; *O'Grady* [1987] QB 995), etc.

 Question 4

'If a man of his own volition takes a substance which causes him to cast off the restraints of reason and conscience, no wrong is done to him by holding him answerable criminally for any injury he may do while in that condition. His course of conduct in reducing himself by drugs and drink to that condition . . . supplies the evidence of mens rea . . . ' (Lord Elwyn-Jones, *DPP* v *Majewski* [1977] AC 443).

To what extent is the law on voluntary intoxication in a satisfactory state?

Answer plan

➜ Analyse criticisms of *Majewski*.

➜ Consider the distinction between specific and basic intent.

Diagram plan

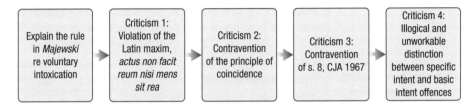

A printable version of this diagram plan is available from **www.pearsoned.co.uk/lawexpressqa**

Answer

[1] This sentence provides a justification for the statement in the first line.

The courts frown upon defendants using evidence of their intoxication as a defence. The courts must not be seen to be condoning drunken behaviour which culminates in the commission of an offence by permitting defendants to escape liability due to intoxication.[1] Therefore, intoxication is said to be no defence *per se*; however, evidence of intoxication may be sufficient to deny the mens rea of an offence. The quote refers to the rule in **DPP v Majewski**, the leading authority on voluntary intoxication from the House of Lords. According to Lord Elywn-Jones in **Majewski**, voluntary intoxication is no defence to crimes of basic intent, but it may be a partial defence to crimes of specific intent if the defendant lacks the requisite intention for the offence.[2] A specific intent offence is one which requires proof of intention as the mens rea element of the offence. By contrast, the mens rea of a basic intent offence may be satisfied by proof of a lesser form of mens rea, such as recklessness.[3] As the quote above demonstrates, Lord Elywn-Jones took the view that voluntarily becoming intoxicated is a reckless course of conduct to take. Thus, a voluntarily intoxicated defendant is automatically reckless and therefore he has the mens rea for every basic intent crime. This means that a defendant will be guilty of a basic intent offence if he then performs the actus reus of a basic intent crime. However, where the defendant does have the necessary intention for the offence, the fact that he is intoxicated will

[2] You should explain the quote in the title (and therefore the rule in *Majewski*) in your own words to demonstrate that you fully understand the rule.
[3] Demonstrate your understanding of the distinction between specific intent and basic intent offences.

provide no defence because a drunken intent is still an intent: *Sheehan and Moore* [1975] 1 WLR 739.

[4] This sentence addresses the second part of the title directly and ensures that you (and the examiner) remain focused on the point in issue.

The decision of *Majewski* has been criticised for a number of reasons, and thus it may be argued that the law is not in a satisfactory state.[4] As stated above, *Majewski* was a decision dictated by policy reasons as the courts did not want to be seen to be condoning drunken behaviour which could be harmful to society. The criticisms of *Majewski* are 'aimed at the decision of the House [of Lords] to compromise fundamental principles of criminal law for reasons of policy' (Monaghan, N. (2016), *Criminal Law Directions*, 4th edn. Oxford: Oxford University Press, p. 366). The main criticisms are that the rule in *Majewski* violates fundamental principles of criminal law such as the Latin maxim *actus non facit reum nisi mens sit rea* ('an act does not make a man guilty of a crime, unless his mind be also guilty,' per Lord Hailsham in *Haughton v Smith* [1975] AC 476), the principle of coincidence of actus reus and mens rea and section 8 of the Criminal Justice Act 1967 and justifies compromising these principles for policy reasons.[5]

[5] Summarise the criticisms by listing them before explaining them in further detail below.

The principle that 'an act does not make a man guilty of a crime, unless his mind be also guilty' is compromised because *Majewski* does not require proof of the defendant's state of mind, which is instead presumed to be guilty. Where, at the time of the offence, the defendant is completely unaware of what he is doing due to his intoxicated state (although he is not suffering a disease of the mind), he is nonetheless guilty of any relevant basic intent offence (Monaghan (2016), p. 367).

The rule in *Majewski* also ignores the principle that the actus reus and the mens rea of an offence must coincide in order for the defendant to be guilty of an offence. Lord Elwyn-Jones regards a defendant who becomes intoxicated as reckless. This mens rea is formed as the defendant becomes intoxicated and before the actus reus of the offence is performed. Subjective recklessness requires that a defendant recognises the risk of a consequence (the actus reus) occurring but goes on to take that risk anyway. However, '[t]he "recklessness" of the defendant which is presumed under *Majewski* is not related to the defendant's actus reus as it arises prior to his performance of the actus reus' (Monaghan (2016), p. 367).

The effect of the rule in **Majewski** is that where a defendant voluntarily becomes intoxicated, there is a presumption that he is reckless. Ormerod refers to this as a 'form of "prior fault"' (Ormerod,
D. (2011) *Smith and Hogan Criminal Law*, 13th edn. Oxford: Oxford
University Press, p. 315).[6] It can be argued that this presumption of
mens rea contravenes section 8 of the Criminal Justice Act 1967,
which requires a jury to decide whether the defendant foresaw the
result of his actions (i.e. was subjectively reckless) by reference to all
the evidence.

[6] Refer to academic opinion
to demonstrate that you have
read beyond your module
guide/lecture notes.

The use of the distinction between specific intent and basic intent
offences has also been criticised for being confusing and unclear.
Ormerod comments that '[i]n view of the rule in **Majewski**, the
nature of "specific intent" is a matter of great importance but a care-
ful scrutiny of the authorities, particularly **Majewski** itself, fails to
reveal any consistent principle by which specific and basic are to be
distinguished' (Ormerod (2011), p. 317). Thus, it would appear that
the distinction between basic and specific intent offences lacks any
logical rationale.

These principles have been compromised in the interest of policy
considerations. However, the policy aims, that the rule was designed
to tackle, remain problematic in cases where there is no lesser basic
intent offence of which to convict the defendant (e.g. theft is a specific
intent offence to which voluntary intoxication could be a defence, but
there is no lesser offence that the defendant could be convicted of).[7]

[7] Illustrate your point here with
an example.

It is interesting to note that new offences created today are more
frequently avoiding the traditional intention/recklessness approach
to the mental element of the offence.[8] This has been seen with the
Sexual Offences Act 2003, under which offences such as rape and
sexual assault no longer include the word recklessness. The Serious
Crime Act 2007 also prefers intention and belief over recklessness.
Consequently, it must be questioned to what extent the basic/specific
intent offence distinction is still useful. In **Heard** [2007] EWCA Crim
125, the Court of Appeal stated that the use of the terms 'specific
intent' and 'basic intent' might not be suitable for every offence. This
case involved an allegation of sexual assault which requires intentional touching, yet the court held that basic intent was required and
thus the defendant's intoxication could not negate the mens rea. The
approach taken was that 'specific intent' offences require proof of

[8] This paragraph demonstrates
your wider knowledge of
criminal law.

purpose or consequence. This case conflicts with the approach taken in **Majewski** and appears to add to the confusion already created by the House of Lords.

[9] Refer back to the question in your conclusion and use this final paragraph to briefly summarise your findings.

In conclusion, the law on voluntary intoxication is not in a satisfactory state[9] as it compromises fundamental principles of criminal law in the name of policy and provides an illogical and confusing manner of distinguishing offences which is becoming increasingly inappropriate for modern day offences. The law is in need of significant reform in this area.

✓ Make your answer stand out

- Refer to further academic opinion, such as Gough, S. (2000) Surviving without *Majewski*. Crim LR 719; and Simester, A. (2009) Intoxication is never a defence. Crim LR 3.
- Refer to the recommendations for reform in the Law Commission (2009) Report, *Intoxication and Criminal Liability* (No. 314) and the Draft Criminal Law (Intoxication) Bill. These recommendations seek to clarify the terminology used.
- You could expand your discussion of the case of *Heard*.
- You could also refer in more detail to judicial comment on the distinction between specific intent and basic intent offences.

! Don't be tempted to . . .

- Merely set out everything that you know about voluntary and involuntary intoxication. This question is specifically asking you to critically analyse the rule relating to voluntary intoxication.
- Recite the facts of cases in detail. If you do think that certain facts of a case are particularly relevant to the point you are making then you should refer to them briefly. For example, see the (very brief) reference to the facts of *Heard* in the answer above.
- Forget to address the quote directly in your answer.

? Question 5

One night, Caleb, who lives alone, is asleep in his house when he hears noises coming from downstairs that wake him up. Caleb suspects that someone has broken into his house so he picks up his cricket bat and creeps downstairs. He sees the silhouette of a man moving around in the living room and he notices that the man is holding a gun. He swings the cricket bat at the person, striking him hard in the torso. The blow knocks the man to the floor, causing him serious bruising and fractured ribs. Caleb turns on the light and realises that the man is in fact his brother, Bert, who tells Caleb that he was looking for somewhere to sleep as his girlfriend had thrown him out of his house. Bert was not holding a gun but in fact had a torch in his hands, and he tells Caleb that the batteries had run out. Bert explains that he did not want to wake Caleb up so he used the key he has to Caleb's house to let himself in.

Consider whether Caleb has a defence available to him. Would it make a difference to your answer if Caleb was drunk at the time?

Diagram plan

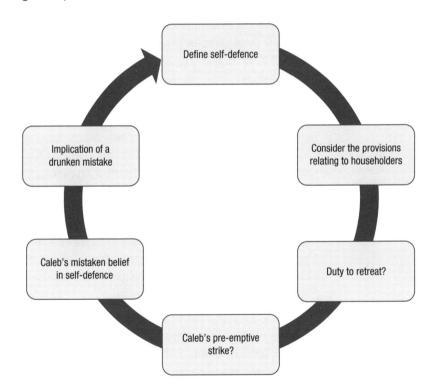

A printable version of this diagram plan is available from **www.pearsoned.co.uk/lawexpressqa**

Answer plan

→ Briefly give the definition of self-defence with authorities.

→ Assess whether Caleb's pre-emptive strike precludes the defence.

→ Consider the effect of Caleb's mistaken belief in self-defence.

→ Consider the provisions relating to householders under the Criminal Justice and Immigration Act 2008 (as amended by the Crime and Courts Act 2013).

→ Examine the implication of a drunken mistake.

Answer

[1] Explain briefly what self-defence is before then elaborating on this and setting out the tests from the authorities.

Caleb might have the defence of self-defence available to him. Self-defence is a common law defence which permits a defendant to use reasonable force to protect himself if he honestly believes that the use of force is necessary.[1] It is a general defence to any offence and if Caleb successfully pleads the defence, he will be completely acquitted. Some principles of law related to the defence have been put on a statutory footing by section 76 of the Criminal Justice and Immigration Act 2008. The objective of this section is to clarify the law relating to self-defence: section 76(9).[2]

[2] This demonstrates to the examiner that you are aware of recent legislation and its purpose.

The leading authority of **Palmer v R** [1971] AC 814 sets out the two limbs necessary for a successful plea of self-defence. Applying these to Caleb, the first limb provides a subjective question which asks whether Caleb honestly believed that the use of force was necessary. The second limb is objective and asks whether the amount of force that Caleb used was reasonable. This test was later reiterated in **Oatridge** (1992) 94 Cr App R 367.[3] While Caleb bears an evidential burden in respect of self-defence (i.e. the defendant must raise some evidence of self-defence in order to make the issue a live one), the prosecution bears the legal burden of disproving self-defence beyond reasonable doubt: **Lobell** [1957] 1 QB 547.

[3] Summarise the two main limbs of self-defence and identify which limb is subjective and which is objective.

In order to ascertain Caleb's chances of successfully pleading self-defence, it is necessary to apply the two limbs from **Palmer v R** to the problem scenario. In respect of the first limb, it must be questioned whether Caleb honestly believed that force was necessary to defend himself. A defendant may not rely on self-defence if he acts out of revenge or for any other reason than the defence of himself. In this scenario, Caleb acts because he sees a silhouette of a man moving around downstairs in his house in the middle of the night. Since Caleb lives alone and is not expecting anyone to be present downstairs in his house, he is understandably concerned. However, at no point does the man directly confront him, so it could be argued that there was no

[4] Identify the facts in the scenario that relate to the first limb and ensure that you apply the law to the facts.

threat to Caleb's personal safety. Caleb also thinks that he sees a gun in the man's hands. This element is only satisfied if Caleb is acting out of an honest belief that it is necessary to act to defend himself.[4]

Common law has long recognised that a defendant may act in defence of his property (**Hussey** (1925) 18 Cr App R 160). This is also recognised in s. 76(2)(aa), Criminal Justice and Immigration Act 2008 (as amended by s. 148, Legal Aid, Sentencing and Punishment of Offenders Act 2012). Thus, Caleb would have this defence available to him if he was in fact protecting his property.

It is clear that he has made a mistake because the man was actually his brother. Nevertheless, Caleb's mistake does not preclude him from relying upon self-defence provided that his belief that force was necessary was honestly held: **Williams (Gladstone)** [1987] 3 All ER 411 (confirmed in section 76(4) of the Criminal Justice and Immigration Act 2008). Thus, Caleb will be judged according to the circumstances as he honestly believed them to be. As he honestly believed that the man posed a threat to him and that he was defending himself, the first limb is satisfied.[5]

[5] After stating this further principle re mistake, ensure that you also apply the law to the facts and conclude in relation to the first limb.

There is a requirement that the danger to the defendant must be sufficiently imminent (**Devlin v Armstrong** [1971] NI 13). It is questionable whether the danger was sufficiently imminent in this scenario as there is no evidence that the man had confronted or noticed Caleb. Consideration should also be given to the fact that Caleb struck Bert first and before any violence from Bert. Such a pre-emptive strike does not preclude Caleb from relying upon self-defence: see **Beckford v R** [1988] AC 130, in which Lord Griffiths held that a man 'does not have to wait for his assailant to strike the first blow'.[6] There is also no duty on a defendant to retreat: **Bird** [1985] 2 All ER 513. Thus, there is no duty on Caleb to retreat.

[6] Try to memorise a few key quotes from leading judgments.

Provided that the first limb of self-defence is not disproved by the prosecution, consideration should be given to the second limb of the test from **Palmer v R**. This requires that the amount of force actually used by the defendant was reasonable. This is objectively assessed and is a question for the jury to determine. Where a defendant uses excessive or disproportionate force, his defence of self-defence will not be successful: **Clegg** [1995] 1 AC 482 (see section 76(6) of the Criminal Justice and Immigration Act 2008).[7] Although this limb carries an objective test, there is a subjective element to the question

[7] Where appropriate, make reference to the provisions of the Criminal Justice and Immigration Act 2008, which purports to clarify the law. This adds further support to your arguments.

because the defendant must use reasonable force in the circumstances as he believed them to be: **Owino** [1996] 2 Cr App R 128 (also reiterated under s. 76(3) of the Criminal Justice and Immigration Act 2008). In this scenario, Caleb strikes the man with a cricket bat in the torso. There is only evidence that he struck him once and he did not strike him in the head, which is evidence from which it can be inferred that his intention was to defend himself.[8] Some leeway is given to defendants who act in 'the heat of the moment'. In **Palmer v R**, the Privy Council recognised the fact that a defendant may not be expected to 'weigh to a nicety the exact measure of his necessary defensive action' (placed onto a statutory footing by section 76(7) of the Criminal Justice and Immigration Act 2008). Thus, in this scenario, the fact that Caleb may have been taken a bit by surprise, having just woken up in the middle of the night, may be taken into account here.

The more lenient provisions relating to householders also apply to Caleb as Caleb uses force while in a building that is a dwelling, and he is not trespassing in that dwelling at the time, but he believes the man to be a trespasser (s. 76(8A), Criminal Justice and Immigration Act 2008, as amended by s. 43(2), Crime and Courts Act 2013). This means that the defence of self-defence will not be available to Caleb if his use of force was grossly disproportionate in the circumstances. However, the provisions also state that this only applies to the defence of the person and not to the defence of property.

If Caleb was drunk at the time of the incident, the answer would be different.[9] This is because, although an honest but mistaken belief does not preclude self-defence (**Williams (Gladstone)**), a mistake which is made due to intoxication will preclude the defence. This was stated *obiter* in **O'Grady** [1987] QB 995 and confirmed by the Court of Appeal in **O'Connor** [1991] Crim LR 135 and more recently in **Hatton** [2005] EWCA Crim 2951. This has also been clarified by section 76(5) of the Criminal Justice and Immigration Act 2008. Thus, if Caleb's mistake in perceiving Bert to be a threat was made due to his intoxicated state, he would not be able to rely upon the defence of self-defence.

[8] Identify key words within the facts of the scenario and use them to support your answer.

[9] Do not forget to deal with the alternative scenario at the end of your answer, otherwise you will lose valuable marks.

Make your answer stand out

- Problem scenarios on self-defence can be quite difficult to structure due to the fact that there are several important principles of law from key authorities which need to be addressed and applied. So, ensure that you adopt a clear structure and are aware which principle relates to the subjective limb and which to the objective limb.

- Whenever you set out a legal principle, ensure that you state the relevant authority and apply the principle to the facts of the problem scenario.

- Identify brief quotes from key judgments which you can rely upon to support your arguments.

- Be aware of which cases have been put onto a statutory footing by section 76 of the Criminal Justice and Immigration Act 2008 and refer to both the case and provision together to demonstrate your knowledge of this.

! **Don't be tempted to . . .**

- Merely provide a textbook recitation of the law on self-defence. The examiner does not want to read a narrative of the law but is looking to see whether you can identify relevant principles of law and apply these appropriately to the facts in the question.

- Confuse the subjective and the objective limbs of the test and ensure that you distinguish clearly between these.

- Provide the facts of the cases unless these are directly relevant to the question. If they are, you should then only set out material facts briefly.

Question 6

'The existing law as it relates to self-defence generally, and specifically in relation to self-defence against home intruders, is clear and easily understood by jurors . . . The [reforms introduced by the Crime and Courts Act 2013] will make the law of self-defence generally (i.e. not simply in home intruder cases) confused and unworkable, and will very likely lead to a number of expensive appeals . . . There is a risk that the creation of a new legal test may send out a message that it is acceptable for people to take the law into their own hands and engage in acts of vigilantism' (Law Society, Parliamentary Brief, Crime and Courts Bill, HC Second Reading, Monday 14 January 2013 at Paras. 14–17).

With reference to the above quote, critically evaluate the legislative reforms to the law on self-defence since 2008.

Diagram plan

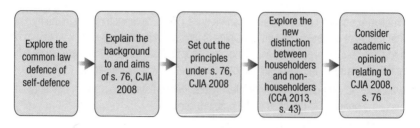

A printable version of this diagram plan is available from **www.pearsoned.co.uk/lawexpressqa**

Answer plan

➜ Refer to the common law on self-defence.

➜ Discuss the reforms introduced by section 76 of the Criminal Justice and Immigration Act 2008.

➜ Consider the reforms introduced by section 43 of the Crime and Courts Act 2013.

➜ Compare and contrast academic critique on the legislative reforms.

Answer

[1] Set out the aim of the reforms at the start of your answer. There is no need to go into much detail in your introduction as this is something you will explore later in your answer.

Until relatively recently, the law on self-defence was found at common law. In 2008, most of the leading cases were put onto a statutory footing by the enactment of section 76 of the Criminal Justice and Immigration Act 2008 (CJIA 2008). It is clear from the 2008 Act that section 76 was intended to improve understanding of the practical application of the law on self-defence and the prevention of crime (s. 76(9)).[1] More recently, this provision has been amended by subsequent legislation, firstly by section 148 of the Legal Aid, Sentencing and Punishment of Offenders Act 2012, and then by section 43 of the Crime and Courts Act 2013. The first of these amendments relates to the common law defence of property, while the latter amendment creates a legal distinction between the use of self-defence by a householder and a non-householder. This amendment creates a new test for the degree of force that is deemed to be reasonable in cases involving householders. Section 76 has been criticised by academics

[2] Cite academic opinion to support your answer as well, to demonstrate that you have read widely.

and described as 'pointless' (Dennis, I. (2008) A pointless exercise. Crim LR 507) and 'patchy in its coverage' (Padfield, N. (2008) The Criminal Justice and Immigration Act 2008. *Archbold News* 5).[2] Thus, it must be questioned whether this provision was at all necessary to clarify the common law position.

Self-defence is a general defence which may be pleaded by a defendant who uses reasonable force in order to protect himself from an attack which he honestly believes he will be subjected to. It is derived from the common law, although many of the key cases on self-defence now have a statutory footing, and recent legislation has since expanded the scope of the defence for householders. Self-defence is a complete defence which leads to acquittal if pleaded successfully. The defendant bears an evidential burden in respect of self-defence. The prosecution bears the legal burden of disproving self-defence beyond reasonable doubt: *Lobell* [1957] 1 QB 547.

[3] You should use the leading authority on self-defence to set out the test under the common law.

The defence is both subjectively and objectively assessed. According to the leading authority of *Palmer v R* [1971] AC 814, the Privy Council confirmed that self-defence requires proof that the defendant honestly believed that the use of force was necessary (the subjective limb) as well as proof that the amount of force used by the defendant in his own defence was reasonable (the objective limb).[3] A defendant's mistaken belief that he is acting in self-defence does not preclude him from relying upon the defence, provided that his belief was honestly held. Thus, the defendant is judged according to the circumstances as he honestly believed them to be. This principle has since been confirmed by section 76(4), CJIA 2008. However, where the defendant's mistake is due to his intoxication, the defence will not be available to him: *O'Grady* [1987] QB 995, *O'Connor* [1991] Crim LR 135 and *Hatton* [2005] EWCA Crim 2951. This has since been put onto a statutory footing by section 76(5), CJIA 2008. According to *Clegg* [1995] 1 AC 482, the use of excessive or 'disproportionate' force precludes the defence. This has since been given statutory effect in section 76(6), CJIA 2008. The 'reasonable force' limb of self-defence also contains a subjective element because the defendant must use reasonable force in the circumstances as he believed them to be: *Owino* [1996] 2 Cr App R 128. This has also since been confirmed by section 76(3), CJIA 2008. Under the common law, the defendant has been given a degree of leeway in the amount of force used. The Privy Council in *Palmer v R* [1971] AC 814 recognised the fact that a defendant may not be expected to 'weigh to a nicety the exact measure of his necessary defensive action'. This has also been codified by section 76(7), CJIA 2008.

10 DEFENCES

[4] Explain what led to the enactment of section 76, CJIA 2008.

[5] Provide an example of a significant case which provided some impetus behind the enactment of section 76, CJIA 2008.

[6] Summarise the effect of the amendment in a short sentence.

[7] This sentence provides some criticism of the section.

[8] You must provide evidence to support the criticism of section 76, CJIA 2008 that you make in this paragraph.

Section 76 was enacted largely as a result of media pressure on Parliament to clarify the law on self-defence.[4] This media pressure arose due to high profile cases, such as the case of *Martin (Anthony)* [2002] 2 WLR 1, in which the defendant shot two burglars who had broken into his property.[5] The case raised questions about the use of self-defence by householders who attack intruders, such as how much force householders may use in dealing with an intruder and whether a householder is permitted to use pre-emptive action. This issue has recently been tackled by an amendment to section 76, CJIA 2008. Section 76(5A), CJIA 2008 (as inserted by section 43(2), Crime and Courts Act 2013) makes specific provision for cases involving householders. It provides that householders who use 'grossly disproportionate' force in the circumstances may not avail themselves of self-defence. Thus, householders are afforded more leniency than a non-householder.[6] Prior to this amendment, section 76 could be criticised for doing no more than restating the law on self-defence. It certainly did not address the questions which arose in the wake of the case of *Martin (Anthony)*. However, where the amendment by the Crime and Courts Act 2013 attempts to address this issue, it offers limited guidance on what exactly constitutes grossly disproportionate force. As such, it is difficult to see how the amended section 76 clarifies the law for members of the public.[7]

Further criticism of the section is that it fails to codify all of the principles of law relating to self-defence. Padfield states that the section is 'patchy in its coverage of the complexities of the "defence"' (Padfield (2008), p. 8). Dennis comments that '. . . the more critical practitioner might well ask what is the point of setting out a partial codification of these principles' (Dennis (2008), p. 5). Dennis lists several principles of law that the section fails to codify, including all the purposes for which force may lawfully be used, the meaning of the word 'force', acts preparatory to the use of force or pre-emptive conduct, the use of force against a police officer, the fact that there is no duty to retreat, etc. The following principles of self-defence are enshrined in common law: the danger to the defendant must be sufficiently imminent (*Devlin v Armstrong* [1971] NI 13) and a pre-emptive strike does not preclude the defendant from relying upon self-defence (*Beckford v R* [1988] AC 130). There is no mention of these in the CJIA 2008.[8]

The purpose of section 76 was to 'improve the understanding of the practical application' of the defence (Explanatory Notes to the CJIA 2008, Para. 532). However, Ormerod states 'it might be doubted whether the section has done much to clarify anything' (Ormerod, D. (2009) Case comment *R* v *Drane (Paul)*: self-defence: summing up – subjective element. Crim LR 202). In fact, he goes so far as to state that the enactment of the section was a 'waste of valuable parliamentary time which could have been spent on more pressing issues of criminal justice' (Ormerod, D. (2009), p. 203).[9] Thus, while section 76 purports to have 'clarified' the law on self-defence, it appears that it has added very little to the law. The creation of a new test for householders does little to clarify the law and, indeed, raises more questions since the distinction between 'disproportionate' force and 'grossly disproportionate' force is unclear. The codification of the law on self-defence is a half-hearted attempt which failed to incorporate all the key principles of common law which have developed over the years. As such, the section does not improve the law and may in fact have served to complicate the law by creating new problems for the courts and jurors to decipher.

[9] Draw on further academic commentary in order to offer more critique of the provision.

✓ **Make your answer stand out**

■ Incorporate more academic criticism of section 76, CJIA 2008 into your answer.

■ Consider the compatibility of section 76(6) on the proportionality of the defendant's response with Article 2 of the European Convention on Human Rights. In particular, see Ormerod, D. (2009) Cheating the public revenue. Crim LR 202.

■ Explore the defences under section 3(1), Criminal Law Act 1967 (prevention of crime and protection of another).

■ Discuss the extent to which section 76(8), CJIA 2008 permits the characteristics of the defendant to be taken into account. Compare the common law position in *Martin (Anthony)*.

■ Consider the amendment introduced by section 148, Legal Aid, Sentencing and Punishment of Offenders Act 2012.

> **! Don't be tempted to . . .**
>
> - Merely set out verbatim the wording of section 76, CJIA 2008. You need to explain the effect of the section and consider whether it has clarified and improved the law.
> - Set out the facts of the cases, as these are not directly relevant to the question and you will waste valuable time.
> - Simply provide an emotive narrative of your views on how much force a householder should be permitted to use in attacking an intruder or in defence of his property.

? Question 7

Answer **BOTH** parts.

Discuss which defences, if any, are available to the parties in the following scenarios:

(a) Mike and Dave are members of a criminal gang known for its violent methods. Mike tells Dave that he must shoot the leader of a rival gang. Dave, who has a particularly low IQ, initially refuses to carry out the shooting. Mike then threatens Dave that he will kidnap and torture Dave's wife and children unless Dave shoots the rival gang leader. Dave agrees to shoot the rival gang leader and does so.

AND

(b) Bob confides in a work colleague, Ernie. Bob tells Ernie that he is homosexual and that he is petrified that their boss, who is openly homophobic, might find out and fire him. Ernie, who is heavily in debt, threatens to reveal Bob's secret to their boss unless Bob gives him £1,000 by the end of the week. Bob is terrified that Ernie will carry out his threat, so the following day he drinks half a bottle of vodka to steady his nerves and then robs a post office. He gives £1,000 to Ernie.

Diagram plan

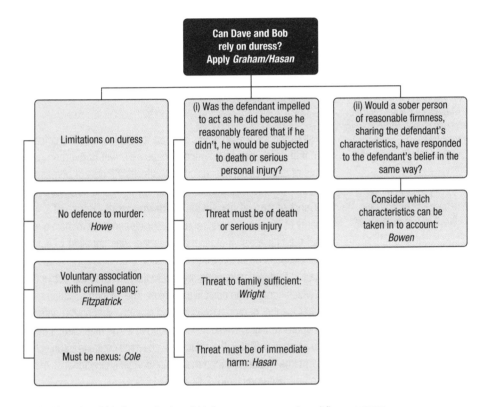

A printable version of this diagram plan is available from **www.pearsoned.co.uk/lawexpressqa**

Answer plan

→ Outline the test for duress from *Graham* (1982) 74 Cr App R 235 and *Hasan* [2005] UKHL 22.

→ Consider the effect that Dave's voluntary association with a criminal gang has on a plea of duress.

→ Examine the availability of duress as a defence to murder (i.e. if the shooting is fatal).

→ Consider the fact that there must be a threat of death or serious violence and the effect that the other threats directed at Bob will have on a plea of duress.

→ Address Bob's intoxication ('Dutch courage').

Answer

[1] At the very start you should briefly identify the main issues before exploring the question in more detail.

This question requires consideration of whether Dave and Bob will be able to rely on the defence of duress in respect of the offences that they have committed. A further issue is the effect of Bob's intoxication.[1]

[2] Where a question is divided into parts, deal with each part separately, using headings to highlight the division in your answer.

[3] You should state the result of a successful plea of the defence as this is obviously an important factor which influences your advice to a defendant.

[4] Before applying the law to the facts, you should set out the two limbs of the test and cite supporting authorities.

Part (a)[2]

Duress by threats is a complete defence available where the defendant commits a criminal offence because his will is overborne by threats of death or serious violence. A successful plea of duress will result in a complete acquittal.[3] The test for duress is now set out in the Court of Appeal decision in **Graham** and the House of Lords authority of **Hasan**. The test requires consideration of two main questions:[4] the first asks whether the defendant was impelled to act as he did because he reasonably feared that, if he didn't, he would be subjected to death or serious personal injury? This is the subjective limb which contains an objective element. The second question asks whether a sober person of reasonable firmness, sharing the defendant's characteristics, would have responded to the defendant's belief in the same way. This is the objective limb which contains a subjective element (the reasonable man may share certain characteristics of the defendant: **Bowen** [1996] 2 Cr App R 157).

Dave will seek to plead duress as a defence in respect of the shooting. However, there are some limitations on the defence and it is not clear on the facts in the scenario what offence Dave has been charged with.

[5] If the facts are unclear or some important information is omitted from the facts, then say so. This demonstrates your awareness of which issues are important.

It is also unclear whether the shooting of the rival gang leader leads to the death of that gang leader.[5] If Dave is charged with murder, he will not be able to rely upon the defence of duress because duress is no defence to murder: **Howe** [1987] AC 417. Even if the gang leader does not die, duress may not be a defence to Dave if he is charged with attempted murder: **Gotts** [1992] 2 AC 412. Duress will be a defence if Dave is charged with an offence such as wounding or inflicting GBH under section 20, Offences Against the Person Act (OAPA) 1861, or wounding or causing GBH with intent under section 18, OAPA 1861.

Applying the subjective question to the facts in part (a), the threat here was of violence to Dave's family. This is a sufficient threat for the

⁶ Apply the law by explaining why the threat is sufficient in this case.

purposes of duress because according to the case of **Wright** [2000] Crim LR 510, the threat of death or serious injury need not be directed at the defendant himself, but may be directed at his immediate family or someone close to him.[6] This has also been confirmed in **Hasan**. Thus, the threats towards Dave's family are sufficient. The law also requires that the threats be of immediate harm so that the defendant cannot take evasive action. According to **Hasan**, the harm must reasonably be expected to follow immediately or almost immediately. It is not clear here how immediate the harm is on the facts. Any delay between the threat and Dave carrying out the shooting will rule out the defence of duress.

⁷ Adopt an appropriate structure, dealing with the subjective limb in one paragraph and then the objective limb in a separate paragraph.

The second question which must be addressed is the objective limb of duress.[7] This asks whether a sober person of reasonable firmness, sharing the defendant's characteristics, would have responded to the defendant's belief in the same way. According to **Graham**, the defendant's age and sex can be taken into account. In **Bowen**, this was extended to include other characteristics, such as pregnancy, serious physical disability, recognised mental illness or a psychiatric condition. The facts indicate that Dave has a particularly low IQ. This is not a relevant factor and may not be taken into account, unless Dave's IQ is so low that he may be deemed to be suffering from a mental illness. Whether this is the case is unclear on the facts. Duress may be successful here if the jury is satisfied that a reasonable man would have acted in the same way. However, if there is any psychiatric evidence that Dave is suffering from some mental illness or impairment, this could be taken into account in respect of whether it renders him more susceptible to pressure and threats.

⁸ Do not forget to deal with any facts which may limit the defence, such as voluntary associations with criminal gangs.

A further issue requiring consideration is the fact that Dave has voluntarily associated with a gang known to use violent methods. According to the House of Lords, Dave's defence of duress will fail where he has voluntarily associated himself with a criminal gang: **Hasan**.[8] Dave has exposed himself to the risk of being forced to commit a crime by associating with a criminal gang: see **Fitzpatrick** [1977] NILR 20 and **Sharp** [1987] QB 853.

Part (b)

Bob will be charged with robbery and will seek to plead duress as a defence. As stated above, the test for duress is set out in **Graham** and **Hasan**. The test requires consideration of two questions: (i) was the defendant impelled to act as he did because he reasonably feared that if he didn't he would be subjected to death or serious personal injury? (ii) would a sober person of reasonable firmness, sharing the defendant's characteristics, have responded to the defendant's belief in the same way? It is worth pointing out at this stage that the defence of duress requires a threat of death or serious injury. However, on the facts, Ernie has threatened to reveal Bob's sexuality and has made no threats of death or serious injury, thus the defence of duress is not available here: *Baker and Wilkins* [1997] Crim LR 497.[9] In *Valderrama-Vega* [1985] Crim LR 220, the Court of Appeal held that threats to disclose homosexual orientation alone are insufficient for the defence of duress. In addition to this, on the facts it is clear that Ernie did not actually tell Bob to rob the post office, but merely told him to give him £1,000. Thus, there is an insufficient nexus between the threat and the offence of robbery, and the defence of duress is not available: see *Cole* [1994] Crim LR 582.

[9] If on the facts it is clear that the defence is not available, then you should state this early on after setting out the test for duress.

Bob's intoxication is unlikely to provide any defence to a charge of robbery. Although the intoxication is voluntary and under the rule in *DPP v Majewski* [1977] AC 443 evidence of voluntary intoxication may negate the mens rea in a specific intent offence. Here Bob's intoxication is 'Dutch courage'. Intoxication as a result of 'Dutch courage' is no defence in law: see *Attorney General for Northern Ireland v Gallagher* [1963] AC 349. Although the intoxication is voluntary here, a drunken intent is still an intent: *Sheehan and Moore* [1975] 1 WLR 739 and there is clear evidence of intention on the facts. Bob still had the mens rea for robbery at the time and thus he will be guilty: *Kingston* [1995] 2 AC 355.

✓ Make your answer stand out

- Use a range of different authorities to support the principles you rely upon.
- There are many principles of law and authorities which you may rely upon in respect of duress, thus it is important that you ensure that you structure your answer in a logical and coherent way.
- Add reference to judicial comment to your answer. For instance, you could refer to Lord Bingham's opinion in *Hasan*.
- You could also try to incorporate some academic opinion in your answer, particularly in relation to the leading House of Lords' decision in *Hasan*.

! Don't be tempted to . . .

- Merely cite *Hasan* as an authority on duress because it is the most recent leading authority. *Hasan* draws upon previous case law, thus you should demonstrate your knowledge of other earlier cases too.
- Forget to apply every principle of law which you cite. The examiner is not just looking for your knowledge of legal principles, but also for your ability to apply the law appropriately to the facts of a question.

@ Try it yourself

Now take a look at the question below and attempt to answer it. You can check your response against the answer guidance available on the companion website (**www.pearsoned.co.uk/lawexpressqa**).

'. . . many defendants whose mental condition may undercut any culpability for the offence charged choose to plead guilty or defend themselves on [grounds other than insanity]' (Simester, Spencer, Sullivan and Virgo, *Simester and Sullivan's Criminal Law Theory and Doctrine* (2010), Hart Publishing, p. 701).

Critically evaluate the defence of insanity in light of the above statement.

www.pearsoned.co.uk/lawexpressqa

Go online to access more revision support including additional essay and problem questions with diagram plans, You be the marker questions, and download all diagrams from the book.

11

Inchoate offences

How this topic may come up in exams

Inchoate offences might be examined by essay questions or problem questions. Problem questions on inchoate offences lend themselves easily to simultaneous examination of accessorial liability; you may find these two topics mixed in a problem question. Problem questions will require you to have knowledge of other offences, such as burglary, theft and offences against the person. Essay questions might require you to critically evaluate a particular element of an inchoate offence, such as the actus reus of attempt, or it might require consideration of wider issues, such as the overlap between the Serious Crime Act 2007 and accessorial liability.

◾ Before you begin

It's a good idea to consider the following key themes of inchoate offences before tackling a question on this topic.

A printable version of this diagram is available from **www.pearsoned.co.uk/lawexpressqa**

❓ Question 1

Shaun and Grant are career criminals. Grant owes Shaun a favour and Shaun asks Grant for a considerable sum of money because he is in debt to a dangerous criminal gang. Shaun asks Grant if he will commit a robbery of a security van which delivers cash to the local banks as the vans carry large amounts of cash, and share the money with him. Shaun tells Grant that he has been monitoring the movements of a particular security van for the past few months and he believes that this van could be an easy target, due to the fact that the security guards who drive the van do not follow security procedures properly. He also promises Grant that he will obtain all the security details that Grant will need in exchange for a third of the cash seized.

Shaun obtains security information for Grant regarding the arrival time of the van, the number of security guards with the van and the positioning of the guards during a delivery of cash. Grant then decides that he will commit the robbery and persuades his friend Kane to help. Grant and Kane meet to discuss how best to approach the crime and together they come up with a plan to commit the robbery while armed and using disguises.

One week before the planned robbery, Shaun decides to commit the robbery of the security van himself so that he can keep all of the money seized. Shaun arrives at the bank and hides in a street round the corner to wait for the van. However, when the van shows up, Shaun runs away. The following week, following the original plan, Grant and Kane arrive at the scene of the planned robbery. When the van turns up, Grant and Kane approach the van shouting threats of violence, but a security guard activates an alarm and Grant and Kane make their escape.

Discuss the criminal liability of Shaun, Grant and Kane.

Answer plan

→ Refer to Shaun encouraging and assisting Grant to commit a robbery.

→ Discuss the conspiracy between Grant and Kane and any liability of Grant under the Serious Crime Act (SCA) 2007 for encouraging Kane to commit the robbery.

→ Consider whether Shaun may be liable for attempted robbery.

→ Consider whether Grant and Kane may be liable for attempted robbery.

Diagram plan

1. Shaun encourages and assists Grant to commit robbery	• Encouraging or assisting crime – Serious Crime Act 2007

2. Grant encourages Kane to commit robbery	• Encouraging crime – Serious Crime Act 2007

3. Grant and Kane conspire to commit robbery	• Conspiracy – s. 1, Criminal Law Act 1977

4. Shaun not guilty of attempted robbery	• Not more than merely preparatory under s. 1, Criminal Attempts Act 1981 • *Campbell* (1991) 93 Cr App R 350 and *Geddes* [1996] Crim LR 894

5. Grant and Kane commit attempted robbery	• Attempted robbery – s. 1, Criminal Attempts Act 1981 • *Jones* [1990] 1 WLR 1057

A printable version of this diagram plan is available from **www.pearsoned.co.uk/lawexpressqa**

Answer

[1] Keep your introduction short and to the point. Identify the topic and the potential offences which require discussion.

This scenario involves inchoate liability and requires consideration of the encouragement and assistance of robbery by Shaun, conspiracy to commit robbery between Grant and Kane, and attempts to commit robbery by Shaun initially and then by Grant and Kane.[1]

The first offence is committed by Shaun when he asks Grant to commit the robbery. This constitutes encouragement to commit robbery under Part 2, sections 44–46 of the Serious Crime Act 2007. When Shaun provides security details on the van he also assists a crime under sections 44–46. The actus reus of these offences is similar. Under sections 44 and 45, it must be proved that Shaun did an act capable of encouraging or assisting the commission of an offence. Section 46 applies where a defendant does an act capable of encouraging or assisting the commission of one or more of a number of offences (here there could be a robbery or theft). In this case, Shaun asking Grant to commit the offence and stating that he can provide security

[2] This sentence demonstrates wider knowledge of the law (including the old common law offence of incitement which the offences under the SCA 2007 replaced) and, in the absence of any authorities on the point, the way in which the courts are likely to apply the law.

details might constitute encouragement. The word 'encouraging' is not defined in the Act, but it is thought that the old common law meaning of incitement will apply.[2] In *Race Relations Board* v *Applin* [1973] 1 QB 815, Lord Denning defined incitement widely, as 'to spur on by advice, encouragement or persuasion'. Shaun's words will most likely constitute encouragement to commit robbery. By providing security details relating to the van, Shaun has done an act capable of assisting robbery. Thus, the actus reus elements of these offences are satisfied.

[3] Do not forget to apply the mens rea elements of the offences and to distinguish between sections 44 and 45, SCA 2007.

Shaun could be convicted under section 44 if it can be proved that he intentionally encouraged or assisted the commission of the robbery. This offence requires proof of various mens rea elements.[3] The first is an intention to do the acts of encouragement or assistance. This is clearly present here – it cannot be said that Shaun does not intend to provide advice or security details to Grant. It must also be proved that Shaun intended to encourage or assist the commission of an offence. On the facts, it seems clear that Shaun's purpose in providing advice and the security details is to encourage or assist the doing of an act capable of amounting to the commission of an offence: section 47(2). Shaun must also believe that, or be reckless as to whether, Grant will have the mens rea for robbery: section 47(5)(a). Here, in light of the fact that they are career criminals, Shaun probably believes that Grant has the mens rea for robbery. Shaun must also believe that, or be reckless as to whether, if the act is done, it will be done in the circumstances or with the consequences required for robbery: section 47(5)(b). It is likely that Shaun does believe that the circumstances and/or consequences of the offences will be present. Thus, the mens rea of section 44 is satisfied and Shaun could be guilty of intentionally encouraging or assisting the commission of robbery under section 44.

[4] In this scenario, this offence need only be dealt with briefly as the more serious offence under section 44, SCA 2007 applies.

If the prosecution has any difficulty proving the intention under section 44, the mens rea under section 45 will be satisfied in any event.[4] The mens rea under section 45 is a belief that the offence will be committed and a belief that his act will encourage or assist the commission of the offence. It is unlikely that the prosecution will need to charge Shaun with the offence under section 46 of encouraging or assisting offences believing that one or more offences will be committed, as this offence is really intended to cover situations where the defendant does not know (or has no belief as to) which offence will

5 If one of the offences does
not apply, state this and
briefly explain why.

be committed.[5] By contrast here, it can be said that Shaun does know
the offence which will be committed, namely robbery.

It could also be said that Grant is guilty of encouraging Kane to commit the robbery under section 44 of the SCA 2007. Grant performs
the actus reus of doing an act capable of encouraging or assisting
the commission of an offence by persuading Kane to help. He also
has the mens rea because he intends to persuade Kane to commit a
robbery and he believes that, or is reckless as to whether, Kane will
have the mens rea for robbery and that the act will be done in the
circumstances or with the consequences required for robbery.

There is a conspiracy between Kane and Grant to commit robbery.
Conspiracy is a statutory offence under section 1(1) of the Criminal
Law Act 1977. Conspiracy requires proof that there was an agreement
between two or more persons to pursue a course of conduct which
amounts to a criminal offence: section 1(1)(a). There is an agreement
between Grant and Kane to steal money from the security van using
the threat of force and this would amount to a robbery. Thus, the

6 Do not forget to address the
mens rea of conspiracy after
setting out and applying the
actus reus elements.

7 Make direct reference to
relevant facts in the problem
scenario in order to support
your argument.

actus reus of conspiracy is present. The mens rea requires proof that
Grant and Kane intended that the agreement be carried out and that
the robbery be committed: *Yip Chiu-Cheung* v *R* [1995] 1 AC 111.[6]
There is evidence on the facts that at the time of the agreement they
did intend that the agreement be carried out because they decided
to get guns and disguises, and they then did so.[7] The final mens
rea requirement under section 1(2), CLA 1977 is that the defendant
intended or knew the facts or circumstances which constitute the
actus reus of the robbery. This is unlikely to be an issue. Grant and
Kane will be convicted of conspiracy to commit robbery.

8 Do not forget that attempts
are charged contrary to the
CAA 1981 and not under
the statute which prescribes
the full substantive offence
(such as the Theft Act 1968).

When Shaun turns up to carry out the robbery a week earlier than
planned, he may be guilty of attempted robbery under section 1(1)
of the Criminal Attempts Act (CAA) 1981.[8] He clearly has the mens
rea of an attempt as he intends to commit the full offence of robbery,
by stealing money from the security guards, and immediately before
or at the time of stealing to use or threaten force in order to do so
(s. 8, Theft Act 1968). The actus reus of an attempt requires that the
defendant takes steps that are more than merely preparatory towards

[9] When applying the actus reus of an attempt, use factually similar cases to support your conclusion.

the commission of the offence. In **Campbell** (1991) 93 Cr App R 350, the defendant was not guilty of attempted robbery after he walked backwards and forwards outside the post office he planned to rob. It could be argued that by simply arriving at the scene of the crime, Shaun has not done enough to be guilty of an attempt.[9] Similarly, in **Geddes** [1996] Crim LR 894, the defendant's conviction for an attempted false imprisonment of a school pupil was quashed because he had not had any contact with a pupil. Rather, he had merely got himself in a position to commit the offence. On this basis, Shaun is unlikely to be convicted of attempted robbery. Although he has the mens rea of attempted robbery because he intends to commit a robbery, he does not have the actus reus, as arriving at the scene and hiding is likely to constitute mere preparation.

However, Grant and Kane get a little further and actually approach the van shouting threats of violence before the alarm is activated and they run off. By actually approaching the guards and threatening them, they have probably done acts more than merely preparatory. This is similar to the case of **Jones** [1990] 1 WLR 1057 in which pointing the gun at a person took the situation beyond mere preparation and into an attempt. They clearly have the intention to commit a robbery and will probably be convicted of an attempted robbery under section 1(1) of the CAA 1981.

 Make your answer stand out

- Ensure that you adopt a clear and logical structure when answering a problem question on inchoate offences. A chronological approach is usually most appropriate.
- Use authorities to support your argument as to whether the defendant has satisfied the actus reus of an attempt.
- Choose factually similar cases which reflect the steps taken by the defendant in the problem scenario. There are six key authorities which you should seek to apply where relevant: *Campbell*, *Geddes* and *Jones* (cited above), *Gullefer* [1990] 1 WLR 1063, *Boyle and Boyle* (1986) 84 Cr App R 270 and *Tosti* [1997] Crim LR 746.
- Ensure that you are familiar with the distinction between the offences under sections 44–46 of the SCA 2007.

> **! Don't be tempted to . . .**
>
> - Use terms such as conspiracy and attempt in the abstract. A defendant may not be guilty of 'conspiracy' or 'attempt', but may be guilty of 'conspiracy to steal' or 'attempted robbery'.
> - Forget that offences of conspiracy are charged contrary to the Criminal Law Act 1977 and attempts are charged contrary to the CAA 1981. Inchoate offences are not charged contrary to the legislative provision in which the full substantive offence is found (e.g. attempted robbery is charged contrary to the CAA 1981 and not the Theft Act 1968).
> - State the mens rea of inchoate offences incorrectly. The mens rea of conspiracy and the offences under the SCA 2007 are confusing and you must demonstrate a good knowledge of these elements.

Question 2

Patty is an employee at Greens Ltd, a garden supplies wholesaler. Her boss, Frank, is a bully and terrorises his staff with threats to withhold their pay and cancel their annual leave unless they achieve unrealistic sales targets. Patty often comes home from work in tears and tells her husband, Brian, about the awful things that Frank has said that day. Brian becomes angry with Frank and he decides to discuss with Patty a plan to kill Frank. Patty and Brian agree to use weedkiller to poison Frank by placing it in his coffee. Patty does not want to be actively involved in placing the weedkiller in Frank's coffee, so Patty and Brian consult Patty's colleague, Andreas, about their plan. Andreas, who also hates Frank, thinks that the plan is a good idea and agrees to poison Frank.

The following morning at work, Andreas goes to the warehouse at Greens Ltd and takes a packet of weedkiller off the shelf. He places a small quantity of the weedkiller into Frank's jar of coffee. However, Andreas doesn't place enough weedkiller in the coffee for the poison to have any effect on Frank. Later that day, having seen Frank still alive after drinking his coffee, Andreas decides to stab Frank to death. He arms himself with a knife and goes up to Frank's office. Approaching Frank's chair from behind, Andreas reaches out to stab Frank, but stops when he realises that Frank is already dead.

Discuss the criminal liability of Patty, Brian and Andreas.

Answer plan

→ Consider whether Patty and Brian can be guilty of conspiracy to kill (as husband and wife).

→ Examine the conspiracy to kill Frank between Brian and Andreas and Patty and Andreas.

→ Consider whether Andreas may be guilty of the attempted murder of Frank.

→ Discuss impossibility and attempts.

Diagram plan

A printable version of this diagram plan is available from **www.pearsoned.co.uk/lawexpressqa**

Answer

[1] Demonstrate that you have identified the key issues from the start by setting out briefly what you intend to address in your answer.

This question requires consideration of the liability of Patty, Brian and Andreas for inchoate offences in respect of Frank. There is initially a conspiracy to murder Frank and it will be necessary to explore who may be liable in respect of this conspiracy. Consideration of Andreas's liability for attempted murder will also require discussion, as will the issue of whether impossibility is a defence to an attempt.[1]

The first offence to consider is conspiracy to murder. Patty and Brian initially agree to kill Frank using weedkiller. Conspiracy is a statutory offence under section 1(1) of the Criminal Law Act 1977. According to section 1(1)(a), the actus reus of conspiracy requires proof that two or more people agreed to pursue a course of conduct which amounts to a criminal offence. However, under section 2(2)(a) of the Criminal Law Act, a husband and wife cannot be guilty of conspiracy to commit a crime[2] if they come to an agreement together about pursuing a course of conduct which amounts to an offence. However, Patty and Andreas may conspire to kill Frank, and Brian and Andreas may conspire to kill Frank; indeed, they have the actus reus of such conspiracies.[3]

[2] Do not forget to check the facts of the question to see if any of the limitations to conspiracy apply.

[3] Ensure that you apply this principle to the facts of the question after setting out the legal limitation.

The mens rea of conspiracy will be established if it is proved that Patty, Brian and Andreas intended to enter into the agreement and that they intended the agreement to be carried out and the substantive offence committed: **Yip Chiu-Cheung v R** [1995] 1 AC 111. This is likely to be satisfied on the facts. However, there is no requirement that the defendant intends to play an active part in carrying out the agreement: **Siracusa** (1990) 90 Cr App R 340. According to

O'Connor LJ in **Siracusa**, Patty could demonstrate an intention to play a part in carrying out the agreement by failing to stop the course of conduct. Thus, Patty will still be liable for conspiring with Andreas to kill Frank, even though she does not want to play an active part in putting the weedkiller in Frank's coffee.[4] There is a further mens rea requirement under section 1(2) which is that the defendant intends or knows of the facts or circumstances which constitute the actus reus of the killing. This is unlikely to be an issue here. Thus, Patty, Brian and Andreas are guilty of conspiring to kill Frank.

The next offence to take place is Andreas's attempt to kill Frank the following morning when he places the weedkiller in Frank's coffee jar. An attempt is a statutory offence under section 1(1) of the Criminal Attempts Act (CAA) 1981. The mens rea of an attempt is intention to commit the full offence and the actus reus requires the defendant to take steps which are more than merely preparatory towards the commission of the offence.[5] On these facts, if Andreas is to be charged with attempted murder, it must be proved that Andreas intended to commit the full offence of murder, i.e. that he intended to kill Frank: see **Whybrow** (1951) 35 Cr App R 141.[6] An intention to cause GBH is not sufficient. The Court of Appeal has also confirmed that intention under the CAA 1981 has the same meaning as it does under the common law: see **Pearman** (1985) 80 Cr App R 259. Thus, on a charge of attempted murder, the court might apply the meaning given to oblique intent in **Nedrick** (1986) 83 Cr App R 267: see **Walker and Hayles** (1990) 90 Cr App R 226. In this scenario, there is clear evidence that Andreas intends to kill Frank when he places the weedkiller in Frank's coffee.

The actus reus of an attempt involves taking steps that are more than merely preparatory towards the commission of the offence. Whether a defendant has taken such steps is a question of fact for the jury to decide: section 4(3) of the CAA 1981.[7] This must be determined on a case-by-case basis. To take the approach used by the Court of Appeal in **Jones** [1990] 1 WLR 1057, the events should be broken down and examined in turn.[8] On the facts, Andreas's conduct in going to the warehouse and picking up the weedkiller is merely preparatory.

5 When introducing a new offence, set out the source of law from which it derives and then define the actus reus and mens rea elements of the offence. This improves the structure of your answer.

6 As there is a specific authority on the mens rea of attempted murder, you should refer to this directly to demonstrate your knowledge to the examiner.

7 Show your knowledge of the relevant provisions of the legislation as well as of the practical aspects of prosecution.

8 This sentence demonstrates a good understanding of the approach taken by the Court of Appeal which can be applied to the facts of the problem scenario.

The key question is whether, when he places the weedkiller in the coffee jar, Andreas has taken steps which are more than merely preparatory. The approach adopted by the Court of Appeal in **Geddes** [1996] Crim LR 894, is that the question to be asked is whether the defendant 'has done an act which shows that he has actually tried to commit the offence in question or has he merely put himself in a position or equipped himself to do so?'[9] Here, Andreas has not gone as far as he could have gone by actually making the coffee for Frank and handing it to him. However, he has done more than merely put himself in a position to commit the murder as he has placed the weedkiller in the jar of coffee and has left the jar for Frank to use. Thus, the jury may very well decide on the evidence that Andreas is guilty of attempted murder here. The fact that Andreas has used inadequate means to try to kill Frank by placing too little of the weedkiller in the jar is irrelevant because impossibility through inadequate means is no defence to an attempt.[10]

After this unsuccessful attempt to kill Frank, Andreas tries to do so again later that day. At this stage, he could be charged with another offence of attempted murder under section 1(1) of the CAA 1981. The mens rea of attempted murder is present because Andreas clearly intends to kill Frank: **Whybrow**. The actus reus is also present because Andreas has taken steps that are more than merely preparatory by actually reaching out to stab Frank with the intention of killing him. According to the Court of Appeal in **Jones**, pointing a gun at the victim with the intention to kill him would be sufficient for attempted murder. The fact that Frank is already dead at this stage will provide Andreas with no defence because under section 1(2) of the CAA 1981, impossibility is no defence to an attempt: see also **Shivpuri** [1987] AC 1.[11]

In conclusion, although husband and wife cannot be guilty of a conspiracy alone, they will both be guilty of conspiracy to murder Frank contrary to section 1(1) of the Criminal Law Act 1977, along with Andreas. Andreas will also be guilty of two separate counts of attempted murder contrary to section 1(1) of the CAA 1981, to which impossibility will be no defence.

[9] If you can remember a relevant part of the judgment to cite, then do so as this will back up your argument.

[10] Do not forget to deal with this issue of impossibility due to inadequate means. Thus Andreas is likely to be guilty of attempted murder at this stage.

[11] You should deal with any factual impossibility briefly citing the correct statutory provision. Do not confuse the old common law approach with that under the statute.

Make your answer stand out

- You could address the conflict between the House of Lords' opinion in *Anderson* [1986] AC 27 and the preferred Court of Appeal decision in *Siracusa* on the mens rea of conspiracy.
- You could also explain how O'Connor LJ in *Siracusa* dealt with Lord Bridge's comments in *Anderson*.
- Refer to judicial comment or particular approaches taken by the courts in order to support your arguments. For instance, in *Jones*, the Court of Appeal broke down the events in the case. The same approach could be applied to a problem scenario.
- You could refer to academic opinion in support of your answer.

! Don't be tempted to . . .

- Confuse the position under the common law with that under the statute when dealing with whether impossibility is a defence to an attempt. As the defendant is charged with the offence of attempted murder under section 1(1) of the CAA 1981, the statutory rules on impossibility set out under section 1(2) of the same Act will apply rather than the common law position.
- Misstate the mens rea for attempted murder. Students often confuse the mens rea of attempted murder (intention to kill) with the mens rea for the full offence of murder (intention to kill or cause GBH). It may seem bizarre, but the mens rea for attempted murder is higher than the mens rea for the full offence of murder.

Question 3

'At common law the courts distinguished between acts that were merely preparatory . . . which could not be an attempt, and proximate acts, which could . . . Occasionally the judges construed the notion of a proximate act so narrowly that obvious rascals who had gone very far towards committing the intended offence were acquitted' (Williams, G. (1983) *Textbook of Criminal Law*. London: Stevens & Sons, pp. 410–11).

Critically evaluate the actus reus of an attempt.

Answer plan

→ Consider the actus reus of an attempt (common law and Criminal Attempts Act 1981).

→ Discuss the rationale for criminalising attempts.

→ Examine academic commentary on the scope of attempts.

Diagram plan

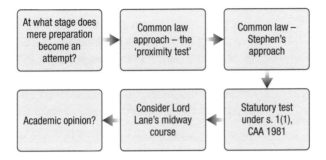

A printable version of this diagram plan is available from **www.pearsoned.co.uk/lawexpressqa**

Answer

[1] This sentence explains exactly what the problem with the law has been.

It has proved difficult to define with any precision and clarity a general test for the actus reus element of an attempt. The key question is: at what stage do acts intended to result in the commission of an offence go from being merely preparatory to an attempt in law?[1] At common law, the courts found it difficult to precisely articulate a definition of an attempt. The preferred approach, cited in many authorities, was known as the 'proximity test'. However, the proximity test was narrowly construed by judges in some cases, resulting in unjustified acquittals.[2] After the Law Commission made recommendations for reform, the task fell to Parliament to provide a statutory definition of an attempt under section 1(1) of the Criminal Attempts Act 1981 (CAA 1981). However, the statute failed to provide any clarification on the actus reus of an attempt.

[2] Make reference to the question in your introduction as this shows that you are focusing on the issue in the question rather than writing everything you know about the topic.

[3] Set out the test using the words from the judgment if you can.

Under the old common law, acts which were merely preparatory were not regarded as attempts, whereas proximate acts were. The proximity test was first elucidated in *Eagleton* (1855) Dears CC 515, in which Parke B stated that 'Acts remotely leading to the commission of the offence are not to be considered as attempts to commit it, but acts immediately connected with it are'.[3] Baron Parke elaborated by explaining that if 'any further step on the part of the defendant had been necessary [the act of the defendant] would not have been sufficiently proximate'. This was referred to as the 'last act' test. This was a restrictive approach which meant that defendants who had got 'very far' in their conduct towards the commission of the offence but had not quite reached the last act would be acquitted. The approach in **Eagleton** was approved in the case of **Robinson** [1915] 2 KB 342, in which it was held that acts 'remotely connected with the commission of the full offence' were not an attempt, while acts 'immediately connected with it' were. The proximity test was then also applied in **Comer v Bloomfield** (1971) 55 Cr App R 305 and by the House of Lords in **DPP v Stonehouse** [1977] 2 All ER 909. Lord Diplock in **DPP v Stonehouse** stated that the defendant must have 'crossed the Rubicon and burnt his boats' (i.e. gone so far that he would be unable to change his mind and retreat from his actions).

[4] This sentence demonstrates your awareness of the second line of authorities and demonstrates that you have read around the subject.

While the above authorities took the 'last act' approach, a second line of authorities took a different approach which was based on Stephen, J.F. (1887) *A Digest of the Criminal Law*. London: Macmillan.[4] This second approach was that 'An attempt to commit a crime is an act done with intent to commit that crime, and forming part of a series of acts which would constitute its actual commission if it were not interrupted'. This approach was approved in **Hope v Brown** [1954] 1 WLR 250 and **Davey v Lee** [1968] 1 QB 366.

Attempts are charged contrary to section 1(1), CAA 1981, according to which the actus reus of an attempt is satisfied when the defendant takes steps which are more than merely preparatory towards the commission of an offence. Although the judge will make an initial assessment as to whether there is sufficient evidence that the defendant did do an act which is more than merely preparatory, this is ultimately a question of fact to be decided by the jury: section 4(3), CAA 1981. According to Glanville Williams: 'There was nothing new in this [test]. It was simply an affirmation of the common law. This section does not try to tell us what such an act is, even by a very general formula' (Williams, G. (1991) Wrong turning on the law of attempt. Crim LR 416, p. 416).[5] The Act provides no further guidance as to what constitutes mere preparation and when a defendant has taken steps that go beyond merely preparing to commit an offence. Thus, whether the actus reus of an attempt is satisfied must be determined on a case-by-case basis.

[5] Refer to leading academic opinion on the issue to support your argument that the CAA 1981 was an unhelpful reform.

[6] Make reference to the Law Commission recommendations to show your knowledge of the background to the reforms.

In accordance with recommendations made by the Law Commission,[6] the Act avoids using the word 'proximate' in defining an attempt. Lord Lane has stated that the 'words of the Act seek to steer a midway course' between the two approaches under the old common law

(*Gullefer* [1990] 1 WLR 1063 at 1066). Lord Lane took the view that the attempt begins when the defendant 'embarks on the crime proper' or 'actual commission of the offence'. Smith argues that this approach 'would be as restrictive as demanding the defendant's "last act"' and that this midway course 'hardly advances the matter in any constructive fashion' (Smith, J.C. (1991) Proximity in attempt. Crim LR 576). Although on the face of it the wording of section 1(1) may not be as restrictive as the 'proximity test' under the old common law, the case law post-1981 appears to have taken a narrow approach to the interpretation of the section.[7] In *Campbell* (1991) 93 Cr App R 350, the defendant's conviction was quashed on the basis that 'A number of acts remained undone' (Watkins LJ)[8] despite the fact that the defendant was arrested outside a post office, equipped to commit robbery. The restrictive scope of the Act is confirmed by Williams (1991) who argues that requiring proximity is the same as requiring more than mere preparation: 'A proximate act was one that went beyond mere preparation, and an act that went beyond mere preparation was proximate'.

[7] Provide your interpretation of or opinion on the approach under the CAA 1981.

[8] Support your argument by reference to a specific case.

Smith (1991) criticises section 1(1) for leaving the courts to 'construe "more than merely preparatory" virtually unaided' and argues that the Court of Appeal should 'provide the lower courts with a collection of illustrations' on the matter.[9] Similarly, Dennis argues that the test was 'imprecise' and that it was 'undesirable to give no further guidance to either judge or jury on its application' and that this would 'carry risks of perverse and inconsistent verdicts' (Dennis, I.H. (1982) The Criminal Attempts Act 1981. Crim LR 5). The Law Commission rejected the 'substantial step' test adopted in the USA through fear that it would widen the law too much and because it was not capable of further elucidation (Law Commission (1980) Report, *Attempt: The Impossibility in Relation to Attempt, Conspiracy and Incitement* (No. 102)). However, Williams argues that 'this is not true of the substantial step test' and states that 'the commission's objection is impressively true of its own test . . . which is to be left without any statutory examples' (Williams, G. (1991), p. 422).

[9] After highlighting the criticisms of the CAA 1981, make suggestions as to how the law might have been improved. Use of academic opinion is appropriate to support your argument.

In conclusion, defining the actus reus of an attempt has been problematic and it would appear that Parliament's efforts to 'rationalise' the law with legislation has provided no general test which may be capable of uniform application. Thus, whether the actus reus of an attempt is satisfied must be determined on a case-by-case basis.

Make your answer stand out

■ Refer to further academic opinion, such as Rogers, J. (2008) The codification of attempts and the case of 'preparation'. Crim LR 937.

■ You should refer to the Law Commission (2007a) Consultation Paper, *Conspiracy and Attempts* (No. 183), in which the Law Commission recommend the abolition of the CAA 1981 and an approach to attempts based on the last act principle as well as a further offence of criminal preparation.

■ Cite relevant authorities to support your arguments and consider key passages from judgments.

■ You could also incorporate a discussion on the rationale behind the criminalisation of attempts into your answer. Refer to Wilson, W. (2002) Criminal attempts, in *Central Issues in Criminal Theory*. Oxford: Hart Publishing.; Ashworth, A. and Horder, J. (2013) Inchoate offences, in *Principles of Criminal Law*, 7th edn., Oxford: Oxford University Press.

! **Don't be tempted to . . .**

■ Merely recite the facts of the cases on attempts as these are ancillary to the question.

■ Explore the mens rea element of an attempt or the issue of impossibility. You should instead focus on the actus reus of an attempt as the question requires you to.

📝 Question 4

'[The common law offence of incitement] was a simple offence that generated very few appeals. Unfortunately, it has been swept away with one of the most complex pieces of criminal legislation to have been drafted in recent times' (Ormerod and Laird (2015) *Smith and Hogan's Criminal Law*, 14th edn, 527).

Critically evaluate the reforms to the law on incitement brought in by the Serious Crime Act 2007.

Answer plan

➡ Address the quote in the question directly.

➡ Consider the rationale for the reforms under the Serious Crime Act 2007.

➡ Critically evaluate the framework and scope of the new offences under sections 44–46, SCA 2007.

➡ Examine academic opinions on the reforms.

Diagram plan

Address the quote in the question ⟩ What was the rationale for the reforms under the Serious Crime Act 2007? ⟩ Critically evaluate the offences under ss. 44–46, SCA 2007 ⟩ Examine academic opinions on the reforms ⟩

A printable version of this diagram plan is available from **www.pearsoned.co.uk/lawexpressqa**

Answer

[1] Address the quote in the question in the first paragraph. You must ensure you address the question rather than state everything you know about the law.

[2] Make brief mention of the reasons for the reform at the start but be sure to address this more fully later in your answer.

The Serious Crime Act 2007 (SCA 2007) abolished the old common law offence of incitement and replaced it with three offences of encouraging or assisting crime. However, as the authors in the quote above point out, whereas the old common law was relatively straightforward, Part 2 of the Serious Crime Act 2007 is wrought with complexity.[1] Part 2 of the SCA 2007 was enacted in order to plug a loophole which existed under the old law;[2] however, many academics have questioned whether such 'complex and convoluted' provisions were really necessary in order to achieve this seemingly simple objective (see Fortson, R. (2014) Case comment *R* v *Sadique (Omar)*. Crim LR 61, p. 66). The merits of the reforms under the SCA 2007 and the criticisms levelled at these provisions by the authors and other commentators will be considered.

[3] When discussing reforms of the law, ensure that you address the Law Commission recommendations which preceded the reforms as these usually provide the rationale for the reforms.

[4] Do not forget to discuss the loophole that the reforms were intended to address.

The relevant provisions of the SCA 2007 came into force on 1 October 2008. Section 59 abolished the common law offence of incitement and sections 44–46 created three new offences of encouraging or assisting an offence. The reforms made by the SCA 2007 were the result of recommendations made by the Law Commission (2006) Report, *Inchoate Liability for Assisting and Encouraging Crime* (No. 300).[3] The Law Commission was concerned that the old law left a loophole in the law under which defendants who have assisted an offence which did not actually take place would escape liability (Law Commission (2006) at Para. 3.2).[4] The reforms under the SCA 2007 were intended to cover this loophole.

As the authors of the quote point out, the old common law of incitement was relatively settled and uncontentious. The offence was defined in **Race Relations Board v Applin** [1973] 1 QB 815 as 'to urge or spur on by advice, encouragement, and persuasion', but incitement also included threatening or bringing pressure to bear on a person. Incitement could be expressed or implied (see *Invicta Plastics Ltd v Clare* [1976] RTR 251) and could be addressed to the world at large (as in *Most* (1881) 7 QBD 244). However, the incitement had to be communicated to the incitee (*Ransford* (1874) 13 Cox CC 9) and the act incited had to amount to a criminal offence if performed by the incitee (*Whitehouse* [1977] 3 All ER 737). The mens rea of the common law offence of incitement required that the defendant intended that the offence be committed by the incitee and that the defendant knew or believed that the incitee would act with the mens rea for the offence incited (*DPP v Armstrong* [2000] Crim LR 379). The old common law has been described as 'the simple and well-established common law offence of incitement' (Ormerod, D. and Fortson, R. (2009) Serious Crime Act 2007: the Part 2 offences. Crim LR 389). The old law presented no great problems to the courts and the only real criticism levelled at it was the loophole which the SCA 2007 aimed to plug. Thus, the extent to which such extensive reforms were really necessary is rightly questioned.

Turning now to the three offences of encouraging or assisting crime under the SCA 2007, the most serious of the three offences is found under section 44 and is the offence of intentionally encouraging or assisting an offence. The offence under section 45 requires a lesser form of mens rea as no intention is needed, rather a defendant may be convicted of an offence of encouraging or assisting an offence if he believes that it will be committed. Finally, the offences under section 46 are encouraging or assisting offences, believing one or more of those offences will be committed (but the defendant has no belief as to which).

[5] This sentence sets out a key criticism of the new offences. The offences under Part 2 of the SCA 2007 are widely drafted and unnecessarily enlarge scope of liability beyond that under the common law and beyond that required to close the loophole.[5] The actus reus of the offences under sections 44–46 is broader, due to the inclusion of liability for assisting the commission of a substantive offence which does not then occur. The wide mens rea of the offences has also widened the scope of liability. Section 47(5) deals with the mens rea that must be proved where the offence encouraged or assisted has a fault element or requires proof of circumstances or consequences. This complicated provision further enlarges the scope of liability. Liability is extended to a defendant who is reckless as to the fault requirement of the offence encouraged or assisted,

or as to the requirement of particular circumstances or consequences of that offence. Under the SCA 2007, even if a defendant believes that the person encouraged or assisted to commit an offence does not have the mens rea for that offence, he is guilty under the SCA 2007 if he himself had the mens rea for the offence that he encouraged or assisted. This would appear to offend principles of fairness and proportionality. The mens rea provisions are also highly complicated[6] and leave the mental element of encouraging or assisting crime unnecessarily unclear.

Academics have questioned whether such extensive reforms were necessary in order to plug such a small loophole. As Ormerod and Fortson argue, 'Even if it were to be accepted that a new facilitation offence was desirable, if not necessary, we suggest that this might have been achieved with a simple provision comprising no more than a few lines of statute' (Ormerod, D. and Fortson, R. (2009), p. 397).[7] In terms of practical application, the creation of a new offence of facilitation of an inchoate offence will not only have an extensive impact on the area of inchoate liability, but will also impact upon accessorial liability. The offences under the SCA 2007 now overlap significantly with accessorial liability[8] because the SCA 2007 does not insist upon the offence assisted or encouraged being an inchoate offence, but it also encompasses encouraging or assisting an offence which is committed. At the time of enactment, the Law Commission also considered secondary liability, and its recommendations were published in Law Commission (2007b) Report, *Participating in Crime* (No. 305). It is surprising that Parliament enacted the SCA 2007 dealing with such a narrow loophole without also considering the wider issue of secondary liability. Parliament's failure to consider both inchoate and secondary liability together has led to a significant overlap, and consequentially, a lack of clarity in the criminal law. Thus, commentators have criticised the provisions, arguing that they are 'not fit for purpose' (Virgo, G. (2013) Part 2 of the Serious Crime Act 2007 – Enough is Enough. 3 *Archbold News*, April 2013) and that they need to be revised in order to ensure 'fairness, proportionality, clarity of expression, and practical application' (Fortson, R. (2014) Case comment *R* v *Sadique (Omar)*. Crim LR 61, p. 66).

It is not clear why the over-complicated reforms under Part 2, SCA 2007 were necessary, especially since the old common law offence of incitement was well settled.[9] The loophole which the SCA 2007 provisions were designed to plug could easily have been addressed by a much simpler amending provision.

[6] Try to address the key words from the quote at various points in your answer.

[7] Cite academic opinion in support of your argument and to demonstrate that you have read widely around the topic.

[8] This sentence sets out a further criticism of the reforms under the SCA 2007 which you could develop further to demonstrate a wider knowledge of other areas of criminal law and how they fit together.

[9] Use the conclusion to address the question again, drawing your arguments together in support of your view.

✓ Make your answer stand out

- You should refer to academic opinion, such as Ormerod, D. and Fortson, R. (2009) Serious Crime Act 2007: the Part 2 offences. Crim LR 389; Virgo, G. (2013) *R* v *Sadique*: making sense of section 46 of the Serious Crime Act 2007. *7 Archbold News* 4–6; and Fortson, R. (2008) *Blackstone's Guide to the Serious Crime Act 2007*. Oxford: Oxford University Press.

- You could make greater reference to the Law Commission Reports: Law Commission (2006) Report, *Inchoate Liability for Assisting and Encouraging Crime* (No. 300); and Law Commission (2007b) Report, *Participating in Crime* (No. 305).

- You could address the recommendations for reform made in respect of accessorial liability.

- Demonstrate your level of knowledge and ability to think critically by providing your own opinion of the SCA 2007. You must ensure that you support your opinion with critical evaluation of the addition of these inchoate offences.

! Don't be tempted to . . .

- Merely set out everything you know about the reforms under the SCA 2007 or the old common law offence of incitement. This question requires a critical evaluation of the reforms and, as such, you need to address whether the reforms were necessary and/or over-complicated.

- Recite the statutory provisions of the SCA 2007 verbatim. It is much more important to demonstrate to the examiner that you understand the provisions of the Act, rather than showing that you are able to memorise them.

@ Try it yourself

Now take a look at the question below and attempt to answer it. You can check your response against the answer guidance available on the companion website (**www.pearsoned.co.uk/lawexpressqa**).

> Evaluate the rationale for criminalising inchoate offences. To what extent is the law on inchoate liability clear and accessible?

www.pearsoned.co.uk/lawexpressqa

 Go online to access more revision support including additional essay and problem questions with diagram plans, You be the marker questions, and download all diagrams from the book.

12

Accessorial liability

How this topic may come up in exams

Accessorial liability is commonly examined by problem questions. A problem question might test your knowledge of the liability of secondary parties under the Accessories and Abettors Act 1861 and the Serious Crime Act 2007. Problem questions lend themselves easily to simultaneous examination of inchoate liability; you may find questions involve a conspiracy as well. Problem questions will require you to have knowledge of other offences, such as burglary, theft, and offences against the person. Essay questions might require you to critically evaluate the scope of accessorial liability, the recent decision in *R* v *Jogee* [2016] UKSC 8, or the overlap between accessorial liability and inchoate liability.

■ Before you begin

It's a good idea to consider the following key themes of accessorial liability before tackling a question on this topic.

A printable version of this diagram is available from **www.pearsoned.co.uk/lawexpressqa**

❓ Question 1

Hugh is the leader of a radical political party which is calling for the restriction of immigration to the United Kingdom and the arrest of all asylum seekers. Tony, a civil rights activist, decides in the interest of safeguarding civil rights and the prevention of racism, to kill Hugh. Tony discusses his intentions with Valerie, a fellow civil rights activist, and she encourages Tony's decision, telling Tony that it is important to make a stand for civil liberties, even if that means sacrificing one's own liberty in the process.

Albert, Tony's brother, has connections with convicted criminals. Tony tells Albert that he needs a knife and asks Albert if he can get one for him. Albert suspects that Tony is up to something and that he might use the knife for 'something illegal'. Nevertheless, Albert manages to obtain a knife and gives it to Tony. Tony decides to carry out his attack at the next meeting of Hugh's political party. He turns up at the meeting in disguise and manages to get in. While Hugh is mingling with party members, Tony sneaks up behind him and stabs him in the back. Mark is a member of Hugh's political party, but has recently been having serious doubts about the party's policies. Upon seeing Tony stab Hugh, Mark is secretly pleased. Mark does not rush to Hugh's aid but instead in his mind he wills Tony to kill Hugh. Tony stabs Hugh again, killing him.

Discuss the criminal liability of the parties.

Diagram plan

Liability of Tony	Liability of Valerie	Liability of Albert	Liability of Mark
• Principal offender • Common law offence of murder	• Secondary party • Counselling murder under s. 8, AAA 1861 • Intentionally encouraging murder under s. 44, SCA 2007	• Is Albert a secondary party? • Aiding murder? Sufficient MR? *Bainbridge* (1960) • Assisting crime under ss. 45–46, SCA 2007. Does he have sufficient MR?	• Not a secondary party • Present at the scene • But no encouragement so not abetting: *Allan and others* (1965)

A printable version of this diagram plan is available from **www.pearsoned.co.uk/lawexpressqa**

Answer plan

➔ Consider Tony's liability for murder.

➔ Examine Valerie's liability as a secondary party under section 8, Accessories and Abettors Act (AAA) 1861 and the Serious Crime Act (SCA) 2007.

➔ Examine Albert's liability as a secondary party under section 8 of the AAA 1861 and the SCA 2007 and whether his suspicions constitute sufficient mens rea.

➔ Consider whether Mark is liable as a secondary party for his secret encouragement and failure to help Hugh.

Answer

[1] Always begin by dealing with the liability of the principal offender before exploring the potential liability of secondary parties.

[2] This demonstrates your understanding of the terminology surrounding accessorial liability, in particular that of a principal offender.

[3] This shows that you are aware of procedural matters, such as matters relating to the drafting of the indictment.

Tony will be criminally liable as a principal offender in respect of the death of Hugh.[1] As Tony has killed Hugh with the knife, he will be charged with the common law offence of murder. In order to secure a conviction, the prosecution will need to prove that Tony unlawfully caused the death of Hugh and that he intended to kill or cause grievous bodily harm (*Vickers* [1957] 2 QB 664). Tony will be the principal offender here as he is the most direct cause of the actus reus with the appropriate mens rea.[2]

Valerie might also be charged as a secondary party to the GBH since she participates in the crime by encouraging it (*R v Jogee* [2016] UKSC 8 at [88] and [89]). She could be charged with aiding, abetting, counselling or procuring the commission of the offence of GBH under section 8, Accessories and Abettors Act (AAA) 1861. According to Lord Widgery CJ in *Attorney General's Reference (No. 1 of 1975)* [1975] QB 773, these words should be given their ordinary meaning. There is a great deal of overlap between these words and the prosecution will charge Albert with 'aiding, abetting, counselling or procuring' in accordance with the Court of Appeal decision in *Bryce* [2004] EWCA Crim 1231.[3] The actus reus of this offence would be satisfied by proof that Valerie counselled, i.e. encouraged, the offence of murder. Counselling occurs before the commission of the offence (*Giannetto* (1997) 1 Cr App R 1). She counsels the commission of the offence by encouraging Tony to kill Hugh before the offence.

The prosecution would also need to prove that the mens rea of the offence was satisfied. The first element of mens rea is intention to do the acts of assistance (this was confirmed in *National Coal Board* v **Gamble** [1959] 1 QB 11). This will clearly be established because Valerie did intend to encourage Tony to kill Hugh here. The second element of mens rea is that Valerie knew of the circumstances which constituted the offence (this element was confirmed in **Johnson v Youden** [1950] 1 KB 544 and recently reaffirmed by the Supreme Court in **R v Jogee** [2016] UKSC 8 at [9]. This is unlikely to be a problem here as Tony discussed his plan with Valerie, thus Valerie does know that Tony intends to kill Hugh.

⁴ The SCA 2007 obviously now overlaps heavily with the AAA 1861, thus you will need to discuss both pieces of legislation wherever a defendant has assisted (aided) or encouraged (abetted or counselled) an offence.

⁵ Do not forget to deal with the complicated mens rea provisions under the SCA 2007.

Valerie might alternatively be charged under the SCA 2007, with intentionally assisting the commission of an offence under section 44 of the Act.⁴ The actus reus here is clearly made out as Valerie expressly encourages the offence. The mens rea requires that Valerie intends to assist the commission of an offence: section 44(1)(b) and section 47(2) – this is clearly present here. The requirement under section 47(5)(a) is also likely to be met because Valerie believes or is at least reckless as to whether Tony intends to kill or cause GBH. Similarly, under section 47(5)(b), Valerie believes or is at least reckless as to the consequences which result (i.e. that Tony will kill Hugh).⁵

Albert assists Tony by supplying him with a knife. As such, Albert could be liable as a secondary party. Albert could be charged with aiding, abetting, counselling or procuring the commission of GBH under section 8 of the AAA 1861. The actus reus of this offence would be satisfied by proof that Albert aided (i.e. assisted the offence of murder), namely by supplying the knife. Aiding occurs before or during the commission of the offence. The prosecution would need to prove that the mens rea of the offence was also satisfied. The first element of intention to do the acts of assistance will clearly be established because Albert did intend to supply Tony with the knife. The second element, namely that Albert knew of the circumstances which constituted the offence is more problematic because Albert might argue in his defence that he has no knowledge of the circumstances which constitute the offence. This element requires Albert to have knowledge of the elements which amount to the actus reus of the offence as well as the elements of the mens rea of the offence committed by Tony. Albert does not know specifically that Tony is going to the meeting to kill Hugh, but he is suspicious that Tony wants the knife for something illegal. According to Lord Parker CJ in **Bainbridge** [1960] 1 QB 129, 'there must not be merely suspicion but knowledge that a crime of the type in question was intended'.[6] If Albert knows that Tony intends to use the knife to kill or cause serious harm, then he will have the mens rea of a secondary party. He does not need to have knowledge of the precise details relating to the offence, such as who the intended victim is and where the offence will take place.

Alternatively, Albert might be charged with an offence under the SCA 2007. Albert is unlikely to be convicted of intentionally assisting the offence of GBH under section 44 because the prosecution would be unable to prove that he intended to assist in the commission of the offence. However, he may be charged with an offence under section 45 or section 46. He has the actus reus because he does an act which is capable of assisting the commission of one or more offences of violence by supplying Tony with the knife. The mens rea will be present if he believes that one or more offences will be committed and that his act will assist its commission. However, although belief does not equate to knowledge, it requires proof of more than mere suspicion (see **Moys** (1984) 79 Cr App R 72).[7] Thus, it is not clear on the facts that this will be established.

[7] Explain any unclear terms using case law and then be sure to apply the explanation to the facts of the question.

Finally, Mark will not be liable for a criminal offence as a secondary party. He witnesses the attack by Tony and does nothing to prevent it. However, he does not really participate in the offence – this does not equate to aiding, abetting, counselling or procuring the commission of an offence. He certainly does not assist any offence, neither does he encourage it. Abetting requires proof of encouragement as well as presence at the scene, and presence alone is not enough: see **Wilcox v Jeffery** [1951] 1 All ER 464. It has specifically been held that merely witnessing a fight and doing nothing to prevent it is insufficient for liability as a secondary party: see **Allan and others** [1965] 1 QB 130. This is so even despite any secret intention that Mark might have had to join in and help.[8] No criminal liability is imposed for 'evil thoughts' alone – a defendant must perform some act of encouragement or assistance in order to be liable as a secondary party.

[8] Where there is a clear authority on the point of law in question, cite it and apply the principle without setting out the facts of the case in detail.

Make your answer stand out

- Refer to judicial comment to support the arguments you put forward in your answer. You should learn several short key quotes from leading cases, along with the name of the relevant judge in order that you can use these to demonstrate an awareness of judicial opinion on this subject.
- When referring to secondary liability under section 8, AAA 1861, be sure to identify precisely which of the four actus reus elements the defendant has performed and explain why.
- You should refer to any new authorities on this developing area of common law.
- You could refer to the recommendations made by the Law Commission in Law Commission (2007) Report, *Participating in Crime* (No. 305).

! **Don't be tempted to . . .**

- Forget to address the offences under the SCA 2007. Remember that there is now a significant overlap between the offences under sections 44–46, SCA 2007 and section 8, AAA 1861, such that where a defendant is guilty of an offence under section 8, AAA 1861, he is also likely to be guilty of an offence under sections 44–46, SCA 2007.
- Fail to set out and apply both the actus reus and the mens rea of all the offences and in respect of each party. A common mistake made in exam answers to questions on secondary parties is to deal with whether the defendant has aided, abetted, counselled or procured the offence, but then to forget to cover the mens rea of this liability.

❓ Question 2

Will and Muneeba are habitual burglars who decide to break into a house. They plan to carry knives to threaten the householder with if he disturbs them, but they agree that they will not actually use their knives to cause injury. They ask their friend, Alec, to get a couple of knives for them, and Alec does so. Will has carried out burglaries previously with Muneeba and knows that she has a tendency to lose control when confronted. Armed with their knives, they break into the property. They both make their way around the house, stealing jewellery and other valuable items. After five minutes Will is confronted by the householder who shouts, 'Get out of my house'. However, Muneeba pulls out her knife and approaches the householder from behind. Will sees Muneeba with the knife and shouts, 'No, Muneeba' and he runs out of the room. However, Muneeba stabs the householder in the back, killing him.

Discuss the criminal liability of Alec, Will and Muneeba.

Answer plan

→ Consider the conspiracy to commit a burglary.

→ Explore whether Alec is liable as a secondary party under the AAA 1861 and the SCA 2007.

→ Discuss the fact that Will and Muneeba are joint principals in the burglary and apply principles of accessorial liability in respect of the burglary.

→ Consider whether Will can escape liability for the murder.

→ Examine whether Will has withdrawn his participation.

Diagram plan

A printable version of this diagram plan is available from **www.pearsoned.co.uk/lawexpressqa**

Answer

[1] When a question involves accessorial liability, it might be preceded by a conspiracy between the parties. Be sure to look out for this and deal with this in your answer, if appropriate.

This answer will consider the liability of Will and Muneeba for conspiracy to commit burglary, Alec's liability as a secondary party to the burglary and Will and Muneeba's liability in respect of the burglary and murder. The first offence that Will and Muneeba commit is conspiracy to commit burglary contrary to section 1(1) of the Criminal Law Act 1977.[1] The actus reus of a conspiracy is present as two or more people do agree to pursue a course of conduct amounting to a criminal offence. They agree to carry out a burglary of a dwelling. The mens rea of conspiracy requires firstly that the parties intend to enter into the agreement; this is clear on the facts. The second requirement is that the defendants intend that the agreement be carried out and that the burglary be committed: see *McPhillips* [1989] NI 360 and *Yip Chiu-Cheung v R* [1995] 1 AC 111. Under section 1(2) of the CLA 1977 it must also be proved that the defendants intended or knew that the circumstances constituting the actus reus of the offence exist. As the burglary does in fact take place, the mens rea elements of conspiracy are clearly satisfied. Thus, Will and Muneeba are guilty of conspiracy to commit burglary.

Alec does not actually take part in the burglary or the murder, but instead he supplies Will and Muneeba with a couple of knives which they then use in the burglary, and one of which is ultimately used in the murder. Thus, Alec is not a principal offender in respect of the burglary or the murder, but he may be convicted as a secondary party. There are three possible offences he could be charged with. One option would be to charge him with aiding, abetting, counselling or procuring the burglary, contrary to section 8, AAA 1861. By supplying the knives, he aids the offences, helping Will and Muneeba to commit the burglary and Muneeba to commit the murder. He also has the mens rea of a secondary party because he intends to do the act of assistance as he intends to supply the knives (*National Coal Board v Gamble* [1959] 1 QB 11). It is not clear whether Alec knew of the circumstances which constituted the offence (*Johnson v Youden* [1950] 1 KB 544 and *R v Jogee* [2016] UKSC 8), although if he knows that Will and Muneeba are habitual burglars, he may very well have known what they would want the knives for. An alternative option would be to charge Alec with intentionally assisting the burglary and intentionally assisting the murder under section 44, SCA 2007.[2] The actus reus here is clearly made out as Alec does an act capable of assisting the offences by supplying the knives. The mens rea requires that Alec intends to assist the commission of an offence: section 44(1)(b). If Alec knows that Will and Muneeba are burglars, then this element may also be satisfied. Additionally, under section 47(5)(a), Alec may believe that Will and Muneeba intend to commit burglary. Similarly, under section 47(5)(b), Alec may believe that the act would be done in the circumstances or with the consequences required of the

[2] Consider all options that the prosecution has available to them.

anticipated offence (burglary). If so, he could be convicted of either of these offences.

[3] Deal with the fact that the offenders are joint principals before considering accessorial liability.

Since Will and Muneeba are both the direct cause of the actus reus of burglary with the relevant mens rea, they are joint principals in respect of the burglary.[3] Thus, they will be charged as principals to burglary under section 9(1)(b) of the Theft Act 1968. The actus reus of burglary is satisfied because they both entered a building as trespassers, and once inside they both stole property.[4] They also have the requisite mens rea for burglary as their entry was intentional, they knew that they were trespassing, and they had the necessary mens rea for the theft that they commit inside the building.

[4] Ensure that you establish the liability of the principal offenders by reference to the offence committed.

[5] Explore liability for the burglary before moving on to the murder.

When Muneeba kills the householder, she becomes the principal offender in respect of murder.[5] She performs the actus reus of murder by unlawfully killing the householder and she has the mens rea of murder because she intends to kill or cause GBH to the householder (**Vickers** [1957] 2 QB 664). However, the question of whether Will can also be liable in respect of the murder as a secondary party requires further consideration. The key issues here are whether Will has participated in the murder and whether he has the necessary mens rea. He will be a participant if he assisted or encouraged the commission of the crime, and it is also necessary to prove that he 'intended to assist the intentional infliction of grievous bodily harm at least' and this 'will often . . . be answered by asking simply whether he himself intended grievous bodily harm at least' (**R v Jogee** [2016] UKSC 8 at [98]). In **R v Jogee** [2016] UKSC 8, the Supreme Court held that the previous approach of the law in equating foresight with an intention to assist as a matter of law was wrong, and that 'the correct approach is to treat [foresight] as evidence of intent' from which the jury can infer intention (at [87]).[6] Thus, Will may also be guilty of murder if he himself intended to kill or cause GBH. This is not entirely clear on the facts: they both enter the property armed with knives, which could provide evidence of an intention to inflict grievous bodily harm, but Will's reaction when he sees Muneeba pull out her knife might provide evidence that he did not have the necessary intention.

[6] You must make reference to the leading authority on accessorial liability from the Supreme Court in any answer to a question on accessorial liability.

If Will is found to have the necessary intention for murder, the final issue to consider is whether he can evade liability by arguing that he has withdrawn his participation. As Will tries to withdraw from the burglary after it has begun, he is required to do more than merely communicate to Muneeba his intention to play no further part in the events. According to Roskill LJ in **Becerra and Cooper** (1976) 62 Cr App R 212, the defendant would have to 'countermand' or 'repent'.

[7] Do not just state that he has failed to withdraw, but also explain what Will would have needed to do in order for the withdrawal to be effective.

Thus, Will would be required to do far more than merely communicate withdrawal; he would be expected to try to prevent the offence from occurring by physically intervening.[7] Consequently, Will's withdrawal is not effective.

 Make your answer stand out

- You must adopt a logical structure when dealing with questions involving accessorial liability.
- First you should deal with the principal offender and then with the liability of any secondary parties.
- You should consider and apply the recent decision of the Supreme Court in *R* v *Jogee* [2016] UKSC 8.

! Don't be tempted to . . .

- Restrict your answer to a discussion of accessorial liability. Do not forget to explore liability for conspiracy and liability under the SCA 2007.
- Misstate the test for secondary liability. It is not sufficient that the defendant merely foresaw that the principal would act as he/she did with the requisite mens rea, but the defendant must have the intention to encourage or assist the principal to commit the crime, acting with the requisite mens rea for the offence committed by the principal.
- Forget to distinguish between withdrawal of participation before the offence has begun and withdrawal once the offence has started, as different rules apply to each.

📝 Question 3

'Those who are concerned with criminal justice, including members of the public, are entitled to expect from this court a clear statement of the relevant principles. We consider that the proper course for this court is to re-state, as nearly and clearly as we may, the principles which had been established over many years before the law took a wrong turn. The error was to equate foresight with intent to assist, as a matter of law; the correct approach is to treat it as evidence of intent' (Lord Hughes and Lord Toulson in *R* v *Jogee* [2016] UKSC 8 at [87]).

Critically evaluate the development of the law on accessorial liability.

Diagram plan

Consider secondary liability under s. 8, AAA 1861

Explain the doctrine of joint enterprise

Where did the law take a 'wrong turn' according to the Supreme Court in *R v Jogee* [2016] UKSC 8?

Is the law clearer now?

A printable version of this diagram plan is available from **www.pearsoned.co.uk/lawexpressqa**

Answer plan

→ Consider secondary liability under s. 8, AAA 1861.

→ Explain the doctrine of joint enterprise.

→ Offer a critique of the position under the old law, prior to the decision of the Supreme Court in *R v Jogee* [2016] UKSC 8.

→ Explain where the law took a 'wrong turn' according to the Supreme Court in *R v Jogee* [2016] UKSC 8.

→ Consider the extent to which *R v Jogee* [2016] UKSC 8 has clarified the law on accessorial liability.

Answer

[1] Address the question in your introduction.

The law on accessorial liability has recently been revisited and restated by the Supreme Court in the landmark case of *R v Jogee* [2016] UKSC 8.[1] Prior to this decision, the law was confusing and ill-defined. The law relating to accessorial liability has always been plagued by complications. In recent years, a string of appeals to the Court of Appeal have sought clarification on the status doctrine of joint enterprise and the extent to which the doctrine overlapped with ordinary principles of secondary liability. In **R v Jogee** [2016] UKSC 8, the Supreme Court stated that the law took a wrong turn 30 years ago in relation to the mens rea required for accessorial liability.[2] The law prior to **R v Jogee** and the decision in **R v Jogee** will be considered in this answer.

[2] Highlight the key issue in this leading decision early on in your answer to demonstrate your understanding of the case.

The traditional form of liability for a secondary party requires that the defendant aided, abetted, counselled or procured the commission of the substantive offence by the principal offender. The procedure and punishment for such liability is set down in section 8 of the Accessories and Abettors Act 1861 (AAA 1861). This provision provides for punishment of the secondary party as if he were a principal offender. This form of liability requires proof that the defendant did some act of assistance or encouraged the commission of the substantive offence by the principal. There must also be proof that the defendant intended to do the acts of assistance or encouragement (**National Coal Board v Gamble** [1959] 1 QB 11) and that he has knowledge of the circumstances that constitute the offence (**Johnson v Youden** [1950] 1 KB 544, which was reaffirmed by the Supreme Court in **R v Jogee** [2016] UKSC 8). Thus, although the secondary party may have done acts which were of a different and significantly lesser level of culpability than those performed by the principal, the secondary party is punished as if he were as culpable as the principal.[3] For instance, where the principal offender commits murder by shooting the victim, the secondary party who merely aided the murder by supplying the principal with the gun will be punished as if he had himself shot the victim, provided that the requisite mens rea element is satisfied. Under the AAA 1861, this is true even where the secondary party was not present at the scene of the shooting. Thus, the secondary party is punished for his participation in the offence even though the elements of the substantive offence could not be established in respect of the secondary party. Wilson explains that the system 'operate[s] on the basis that those who help or encourage the commission of a criminal offence should be punished along with the perpetrator for that offence (which they have not committed) rather than for the wrong they have committed – helping or encouraging a person to commit a crime'. (Wilson, W. (2008a) A rational scheme of liability for participating in crime. Crim LR 3).[4]

[3] Be sure to explain how the principle of secondary liability works.

[4] Try to incorporate some academic literature into your answer where appropriate.

This form of secondary liability overlapped significantly with the doctrine of joint enterprise. In **Mendez and another** [2011] 3 WLR 1, the Court of Appeal held that joint enterprise liability did not differ doctrinally from the ordinary principles of secondary liability, but that joint enterprise liability was instead an aspect of secondary liability. The doctrine of joint enterprise imposed liability upon any party who was part of the joint venture for the acts done by the principal offender in pursuance of a common purpose. This included imposing liability upon a party for the foreseeable acts of the principal offender which were not part of the common purpose. Unusually, under this doctrine, a defendant need do no more than merely be present at the scene of the offence sharing the common purpose of the principal and he was held liable for the acts of the principal committed in pursuance of that joint enterprise: *Anderson and Morris* [1966] 2 QB 110.[5] His continued participation in the common purpose along with the requisite foresight that the principal might commit the offence with the necessary intention[6] was enough to impose liability upon the accessory for the offence committed by the principal: *Powell and Daniels; English* [1997] 4 All ER 545.

[5] This demonstrates your understanding of the doctrine of joint enterprise. Cite *Anderson and Morris* as a key authority for the application of the doctrine.

[6] Ensure that you correctly state the degree of foresight formerly required to be liable under the doctrine of joint enterprise.

However, this doctrine came under fire in the recent Supreme Court decision in *R v Jogee* [2016] UKSC 8. The Court held that the law relating to joint enterprise had been wrongly stated in *Chan Wing-Siu* [1985] AC 168 and applied in later decisions, including by the House of Lords in *R v Powell and Daniels; R v English* [1999] 1 AC 1. The Court reversed a legal principle which had been applied for the past 30 years, restating the mens rea required in order to be convicted under the 'doctrine of joint enterprise'. It was held that the Privy Council in *Chan Wing-Siu* [1985] AC 168 had made a mistake by equating foresight with an intention to assist, as a matter of law.[7] Instead, foresight should only amount to evidence from which the jury can infer intention (at [87]). So, the mens rea required to convict a defendant as a secondary party to murder is '[intention] to assist the intentional infliction of grievous bodily harm at least' and this 'will often . . . be answered by asking simply whether he himself intended grievous bodily harm at least' (at [98]). The Court criticised the previous legal position under *Chan Wing-Siu* [1985] AC 168 for extending the mens rea threshold for murder in the case of accessories (at [82]) and requiring a lower mental threshold of liability for accessories than for principals (at [83]).

[7] Identify the 'wrong turn' that the Supreme Court say that the law took as this is directly referred to in the quote in the question.

The Court expressed dissatisfaction with the term 'joint enterprise' and stated that there was no separate form of secondary liability as formulated in **Chan Wing-Siu**, rather the ordinary principles of secondary liability are of general application (at [76]). Restating the principles of accessorial liability, the Court held that it is not necessary for the prosecution to prove that the defendant was a principal offender or an accessory, but it is 'sufficient to be able to prove that he participated in the crime in one way or another' (at [88]). A defendant participates if he assists or encourages the commission of the crime (at [89]). As stated above, the requisite mens rea is that the defendant 'intended to encourage or assist D1 to commit the crime, acting with whatever mental element the offence requires of D1 . . . If the crime requires a particular intent, D2 must intend . . . to assist D1 to act with such intent' (at [90]).

[8] Consider some academic critique of the case. You should explore this in a bit more detail if you have time.

The Supreme Court intended the decision in **R v Jogee** [2016] UKSC 8 to provide clarity to the law. However, academic commentary has '[doubted] the extent to which the Supreme Court has conclusively resolved the problems that bedeviled this area of the law' (Ormerod, D. and Laird, K. (2016) *Jogee*: not the end of a legal saga but the start of one? Crim LR 539 at 539).[8] The authors argue that the case raises some questions, such as how an intention to assist or encourage the offence to be committed with intent is to be reconciled with knowledge of the circumstances that constitute the offence, the meaning of intention in which context, and how, if at all, the mens rea for an accessory to murder differs from that of the principal. Whether this decision will soon become the subject of further clarification remains to be seen.

✓ Make your answer stand out

- Explore the arguments in Ormerod, D. and Laird, K. (2016) *Jogee*: not the end of a legal saga but the start of one? Crim LR 539 at 539 in more detail.
- Discuss further academic opinion on the Supreme Court decision in **R v Jogee** [2016] UKSC 8.
- Consider the rationale underlying accessorial liability and how this fits in with the decision in **R v Jogee** [2016] UKSC 8.
- Consider the Law Commission proposals for reform in Law Commission (2006) Report, *Inchoate Liability for Assisting and Encouraging Crime* (No. 300) and the reasons underlying these recommendations.

! Don't be tempted to . . .

- Provide a purely descriptive narrative of the case law on secondary liability and the doctrine of joint enterprise.
- Forget to discuss the new Supreme Court decision in *R v Jogee* [2016] UKSC 8.
- Misstate the mens rea requirement as now stated by the Supreme Court in *R v Jogee* [2016] UKSC 8.

@ Try it yourself

Now take a look at the question below and attempt to answer it. You can check your response against the answer guidance available on the companion website (**www.pearsoned.co.uk/lawexpressqa**).

Lee decides to beat up a former friend called Harold. Lee consults his friend and semi-professional boxer, Max, about technique. Max offers to give Lee some boxing training. Lee decides to go round to Harold's house to confront him. Lee asks his girlfriend, Janet, to drive him to Harold's house. Janet knows that Lee really doesn't like Harold and she suspects that Lee might become aggressive with Harold, but she agrees to drive Lee to Harold's house anyway. She drops Lee off and waits in the car outside Harold's house. When Harold opens his front door, Lee pushes his way into Harold's house and punches Harold in the face, causing him serious harm. Joanne, Harold's girlfriend, witnesses the attack and does nothing to prevent it. In fact, she has suffered physical violence from Harold for years and she secretly nurses an intention to join in and help Lee if needed.

Discuss the criminal liability of the parties.

www.pearsoned.co.uk/lawexpressqa

 Go online to access more revision support including additional essay and problem questions with diagram plans, You be the marker questions, and download all diagrams from the book.

Mixed questions

How this topic may come up in exams

This chapter provides examples of **mixed** problem questions. Although you could be examined on any mixture of offences and defences, there are certain topics which are inevitably examined together, largely due to the fact that they are inherently linked to one another. This chapter will provide examples of such questions, although you should be ready to deal with any mixture of offences and defences. While mixed problem questions may cover several topics, you are expected to deal with these in less detail than you would for a question which focuses on one or two key areas of criminal law.

Before you begin

It's a good idea to consider the following key themes before tackling a mixed problem question.

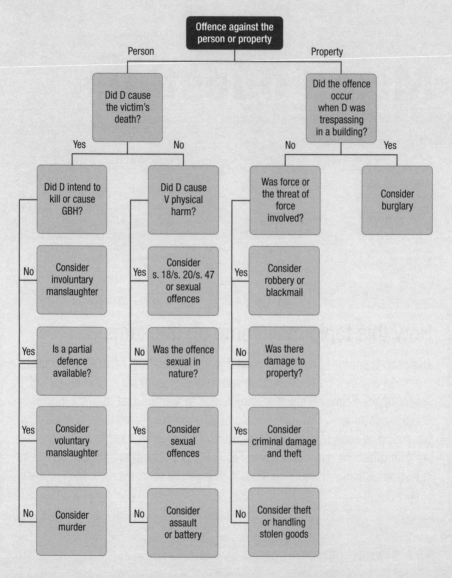

A printable version of this diagram is available from **www.pearsoned.co.uk/lawexpressqa**

❓ Question 1

Jasmine and Vas have been in a volatile relationship for two years. Vas is suspicious that Jasmine has been having an affair with a colleague at work, so he drives to her place of work and waits outside after office hours. Shortly after 5.30pm, Vas sees Jasmine leave her workplace hand in hand with her colleague, Neville. Vas then observes Jasmine and Neville enjoying a passionate kiss. When Jasmine gets home from work, Vas confronts her and accuses her of having an affair. When Jasmine tells Vas she is leaving him for Neville, Vas snaps and grabs Jasmine by the throat. He strangles Jasmine until she dies.

Determined to avenge Jasmine's death, Neville follows Vas when he leaves his home late one night. When they reach a secluded location, Neville approaches Vas, pulls Vas's glasses off his face and throws them to the floor, stamping on them to break them. Vas is unable to see very clearly and he feels disorientated. At this point, Neville produces a knife and stabs Vas in the thigh. He then forces Vas to the ground and has sexual intercourse with him.

Discuss the criminal liability of the parties.

Diagram plan

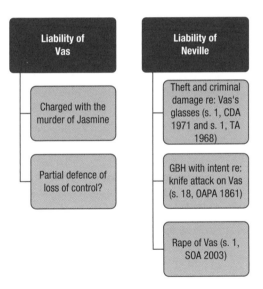

A printable version of this diagram plan is available from **www.pearsoned.co.uk/lawexpressqa**

Answer plan

→ Evaluate Vas's liability in respect of killing Jasmine and whether he has a partial defence of loss of control.

→ Consider whether Neville is guilty of theft and criminal damage of Vas's glasses.

→ Consider whether Neville is guilty of a non-fatal offence against the person in respect of the knife attack.

→ Address Neville's liability for the rape of Vas.

Answer

[1] As this question involves many different issues, you should state the definition simply. There is no need to make reference to Coke's classic definition here.

[2] As causation is clearly satisfied here, you should deal with causation in a sentence. There is no need to go into any more detail.

Vas will be charged with murder in respect of killing Jasmine. Murder is a common law offence defined as unlawfully causing the death of a person within the Queen's peace and with the intention to kill or cause GBH:[1] *Vickers* [1957] 2 QB 664. Vas is clearly the factual cause (applying the 'but for' test: *White* [1910] 2 KB 124) and the legal cause of Jasmine's death (applying the 'significant contribution' test: *Cheshire* [1991] 3 All ER 670).[2] The mens rea of murder is present as Vas does intend to kill Jasmine by strangling her to death. Vas might have a partial defence to murder available to him which would reduce his liability to manslaughter.

Vas might rely on loss of control under section 54(1) of the Coroners and Justice Act 2009. There are three main elements of the defence: (a) at the time of the killing, Vas must have suffered a loss of self-control; (b) there must have been a qualifying trigger under section 55; and (c) someone of the same age and sex as Vas, with a normal degree of tolerance and self-restraint and in the circumstances of Vas, might have reacted in the same or a similar way. Whether Vas suffered a loss of self-control is subjectively assessed. Under section 54(2), it does not matter whether the loss of control was sudden or not. On the facts, there is likely to be sufficient evidence to prove that Vas did suffer a loss of control. The next question is whether there is a qualifying trigger under section 55. Vas will not

[3] Be clear from the start that this will not constitute a qualifying trigger due to the exclusion of sexual infidelity under section 55(6)(c).

be able to rely on the anger trigger under section 55(4)[3] because Jasmine's affair with Neville constitutes sexual infidelity, which must be disregarded under section 55(6)(c), although it may be considered as part of the contextual background to a case where there is another potential qualifying trigger (*Clinton* [2012] EWCA Crim 2). There is no

[4] Do not spend time explaining the fear trigger if there is no evidence of this trigger on the facts.

[5] This demonstrates to the examiner that you have a good understanding of the law and are thinking widely. Do not forget that the actus reus of theft is so widely construed that damage to property could constitute appropriation.

[6] In order to save time, you should state and apply the *Ghosh* test in one sentence.

evidence that the fear trigger applies,[4] thus Vas may not rely on loss of control as a partial defence and will be guilty of murder.

Neville will be guilty of both theft and criminal damage of Vas's glasses. He may be charged with criminal damage under section 1(1) of the Criminal Damage Act 1971. He intentionally damages property belonging to another (Vas). This could also constitute theft under section 1 of the Theft Act 1968.[5] The actus reus of theft is widely construed and appropriation involves assuming the rights of the owner (s. 3). By taking and then damaging Vas's glasses, Neville assumes the rights of the owner over them. Only one single right of the owner need be assumed (*Morris* [1983] 3 All ER 288), and this is clearly satisfied here. Neville assumes two rights here – the right of possession and the right to destroy or damage the glasses. The glasses are tangible property under section 4 and they belong to Vas (s. 5). Thus, the actus reus elements of theft are satisfied. Neville would have the mens rea of theft if it can be proved that the honest and reasonable person would regard what he did as dishonest and that he realises this[6] (*Ghosh* [1982] 1 All ER 491). However, although the reasonable person might regard this as wrong, Neville might not consider it dishonest in light of Neville's purpose of avenging Jasmine's death. This is a question of fact for the jury to determine. There is no defence under section 2(1). It can also be argued that Neville intends to permanently deprive Vas of the glasses because he intends to destroy them. He intends to dispose of the property by treating the glasses as his own to deal with as he likes (see *DPP* v *Lavender* [1994] Crim LR 297). He does not intend to return the glasses, but even on a stricter interpretation of intention to permanently deprive, Neville would intend to return the glasses in such a changed state that it could truly be said that all of their goodness and virtue has gone: *Lloyd* [1985] QB 829. This is satisfied as the glasses are likely to be damaged beyond repair.

In respect of Vas's injuries from the knife, Neville will be liable for wounding or causing grievous bodily harm with intent under section 18 of the Offences Against the Person Act 1861 (OAPA 1861). There is clearly a wound here because Neville stabs Vas in the thigh and breaks the continuity of the skin: *Moriarty* v *Brooks* (1834) 6 C & P 684. The CPS Charging Standards specify that to be charged under section 18, the injury must be 'really serious' and includes

[7] If you can refer to the CPS Charging Standards, then do so as these are what will be used in practice to determine the charge.

[8] You should correctly state the mens rea of section 18 and look for evidence of this in the facts.

[9] There is evidence of violence by Neville on Vas immediately prior to the rape, so you should apply the presumptions under section 75(1).

injuries which involve a substantial loss of blood.[7] The injury here is likely to be serious enough to warrant a charge under section 18. The mens rea of section 18 is an intention to cause grievous bodily harm. It is clear from the facts that Neville intended to cause really serious harm to Vas, so the mens rea is clearly satisfied.[8]

The next incident involves an act of sexual intercourse when Neville forces Vas to have sexual intercourse with him. Neville will be charged with an offence of rape under section 1 of the Sexual Offences Act 2003 (SOA 2003). The facts state that sexual intercourse takes place and for the purposes of section 1 of the SOA 2003, both non-consensual anal sexual intercourse and non-consensual oral sexual intercourse may constitute rape (provided that the defendant did not reasonably believe that the complainant was consenting). There is no evidence that Vas consents to sexual intercourse here. In fact, Neville has clearly used violence against Vas here and he knows that he has done so, thus it may be presumed that Vas did not consent and that Neville did not reasonably believe that Vas was consenting (s. 75(2)(a) and s. 75(1), SOA 2003).[9] Thus, there will be an evidential burden on Neville to adduce to rebut this presumption to the contrary. On the facts, there appears to be no evidence which may be adduced in rebuttal, so Neville is likely to be convicted of rape.

Make your answer stand out

- As there are quite a few offences to deal with here, you will need to ensure that you adopt a clear and logical structure. Use separate paragraphs for each major issue or offence.

- You could also use headings to distinguish between each incident and ensure you remained focused.

- Where the defendant might be charged with a number of different offences, you should opt for the most appropriate ones as you will not have time to discuss them all. For instance, there is no real point discussing liability for assault or an offence under sections 47 or 20 OAPA 1861 re the injury caused by the knife. Section 18 is much more appropriate here.

- You might also choose to provide some academic opinion on controversial provisions or cases that you have relied upon. In particular, in this question you might refer to academic critique about the defence of loss of control and the case of *Clinton*.

> **!** **Don't be tempted to . . .**
>
> ■ Waste time unnecessarily explaining principles of law which are not contentious or which do not apply on the facts. For instance, there is no need to provide a detailed discussion of causation in respect of any of the offences here as causation is not likely to be disputed.
>
> ■ Spend a disproportionate amount of time discussing one issue. This question covers a number of different offences and you should not spend all your time discussing just one offence to the detriment of the other issues in the question. You will lose valuable marks if you do not address all the key issues in the scenario.

❓ Question 2

Matt and Dan are career criminals who have made their living through deceiving and threatening people. Matt meets Deborah through an internet chat room. Deborah is married to a very wealthy and famous businessman, Simon, but they have been going through marital difficulties. Matt spends hours in an internet chat room consoling Deborah about her problems. He then suggests that they meet and while she is feeling vulnerable, Deborah embarks upon an extra-marital affair with Matt. Three months after the affair begins, Matt sends Deborah an email telling her that unless she gives him £20,000 he will expose their affair. Deborah is terrified and sends Matt the money.

When he thinks that both Deborah and Simon are away on a business trips, Matt decides to break into their house in order to steal valuable items of property. However, Simon is in the house at the time and he hears Matt break in. Concerned that his property is being stolen, Simon arms himself with a saucepan and strikes Matt round the head with it, causing serious harm. Matt escapes.

In revenge for the attack by Simon, Matt telephones a national newspaper and falsely informs the reporter that Simon's business is facing massive financial difficulties and is likely to go into administration. The reporter doesn't believe Matt and so does not print the story. Still intent on revenge, Matt tells Dan that he will break his legs unless Dan carries out a robbery on Simon. One evening, Dan waits for Simon after work and follows him home. He pushes Simon violently to the ground and steals his Rolex watch.

Discuss the criminal liability of the parties.

Answer plan

→ Examine Matt's liability for blackmail and burglary.

→ Address Simon's liability for GBH and the defence of prevention of crime.

→ Discuss Matt's liability for fraud by false representation.

→ Consider Dan's liability for robbery and/or theft and any potential defence of duress.

Diagram plan

Liability of Matt

Blackmail

Burglary s. 9(1)(a), TA 1968

Fraud by false representation

Liability of Simon

GBH under s. 18, OAPA 1861

Defence of prevention of crime (s. 3(1), CLA 1967)

Liability of Dan

Robbery/theft

Defence of duress to robbery/theft

A printable version of this diagram plan is available from **www.pearsoned.co.uk/lawexpressqa**

Answer

[1] Use the introduction to make brief reference to the offences and defences you will be discussing in your answer to show the examiner what you plan to explore.

Matt may be liable for blackmail and burglary, and Simon may be charged with GBH in respect of striking Matt with the saucepan, but he might plead the prevention of crime as a defence. Matt might also be liable for fraud; while Dan might be liable for robbery and theft, but he may plead duress.[1]

Matt might first be guilty of blackmail under section 21 of the Theft Act 1968. This offence is satisfied because Matt makes an unwarranted demand for £20,000 towards Deborah with menaces, namely that he will expose their affair if she does not give him the money. He intends to make the demand and he does so with a view to gain £20,000 from her. Thus, the offence is made out.

Matt could also be charged with burglary in respect of his entry into Deborah and Simon's home. Under section 9(1)(a) of the Theft Act 1968, a defendant commits burglary if he enters a building or part of a building as a trespasser with the intention to steal, inflict GBH or do unlawful damage (s. 9(2)). It is clear that Matt enters a building when he gains entry to the house and he does so without permission, and thus as a trespasser. Matt has the requisite mens rea in respect of the trespass because he knows that he is trespassing. He will have the mens rea of burglary under section 9(1)(a) if he enters the house with the intention to steal something. There is evidence on the facts that he has such an intention upon entry. There appears to be no offence

[2] You should rule out section 9(1)(b) in a short sentence in order to show the examiner that you have considered both offences of burglary.

[3] Be sure to show your awareness of the difference between the common law defence of self-defence and the statutory defence of the prevention of crime.

[4] Identify the most relevant of the three ways in which fraud can be committed.

of burglary under section 9(1)(b), because Matt does not actually steal anything or inflict GBH on Simon and nor does he attempt to do so.[2]

Simon might be charged with wounding or causing GBH under section 18 of the Offences Against the Person Act 1861. He clearly causes GBH to Matt and has the intention to do so. However, he may rely on the defence of the prevention of crime under section 3(1) of the Criminal Law Act 1967. This defence permits the use of reasonable force in the prevention of crime.[3] This defence is wider than the common law defence of self-defence, and section 76 of the Criminal Justice and Immigration Act 2008 now applies to both defences. The question here will be whether Simon was acting in the prevention of crime rather than out of revenge, and whether the degree of force he used was reasonable in the circumstances. If pleaded successfully, the prevention of crime will provide a complete defence to any charge of GBH and Simon will be acquitted.

Matt might be convicted of fraud in respect of the telephone call to the national newspaper. Fraud is an offence under section 1 of the Fraud Act 2006, which may be committed in one of three ways. Matt might be guilty of fraud by false representation under section 2.[4] The actus reus of this offence requires that Matt makes a false representation, which he does when he informs the reporter that Simon's business is in financial difficulties. Under section 2(3), a representation includes a representation as to fact, which this is. This is a false representation under section 2(2)(a) because Matt does not have any information as to the financial state of Simon's business and certainly has no information that it is in financial difficulties. The mens rea requires that Matt knows that the representation is or might be untrue or misleading under section 2(2)(b). Matt clearly knows that the representation is untrue because he has made it up and is making the call out of revenge. The offence of fraud also requires proof of dishonesty. The *Ghosh* test must be applied here. Applying the first objective limb of *Ghosh* [1982] 2 All ER 689, the honest and reasonable person would regard making such a false statement as dishonest. The second limb is subjective and requires consideration of whether Matt realised that the honest and reasonable person would regard this as dishonest. If he did, then he will be dishonest. The final mens rea element which needs to be established is that Matt intended to make a gain for himself or another or cause loss to another or to expose another to

[5] Do not forget to set out and apply this final element of mens rea.

[6] This sentence demonstrates your application of the law to the facts of the question.

a risk of loss (s. 2(1)(b)).[5] Under section 5(2)(a), gain and loss extend only to gain or loss of money or other property. Property includes real or personal property, things in action and other intangible property (s. 5(2)(b)). Matt intends to expose Simon's business to a risk of loss in the sense of a loss in confidence in his business by shareholders which might result in the company share price decreasing.[6] Thus, Matt will be guilty of fraud.

Dan may be convicted of robbery in respect of the Rolex watch. This is charged under section 8 of the Theft Act 1968 and requires proof that immediately before or at the time of stealing, and in order to steal, Dan used force on Simon or put or sought to put Simon in fear of being then and there subjected to force. There is evidence here that Dan did actually use force as he pushed Simon violently to the ground.[7] All the elements of robbery (and incidentally, theft under section 1 of the Theft Act 1968) are satisfied. Dan will raise the defence of duress by threats, which is a complete defence to robbery and theft if pleaded successfully. The test for duress is set out in the Court of Appeal decision in *Graham* (1982) 74 Cr App R 235 and the House of Lords authority of *Hasan* [2005] UKHL 22.[8] The test requires consideration of two questions: the first asks whether the defendant was impelled to act as he did because he reasonably feared that if he didn't, he would be subjected to death or serious personal injury? This is the subjective limb (looking at the actual defendant's belief) which contains an objective element (whether the fear felt by the defendant was reasonable). The second question asks whether a sober person of reasonable firmness, sharing the defendant's characteristics, would have responded to the defendant's belief in the same way. This is the objective limb (comparing the response of a reasonable man) which contains a subjective element (the reasonable man may share certain characteristics of the defendant: *Bowen* [1996] 2 Cr App R 157). The threat here was one of serious injury to Dan himself and the threat is immediate. Only Dan's age and sex will be taken into account in determining whether a sober person of reasonable firmness would have responded to the defendant's belief in the same way. There is no evidence of any other characteristics of the defendant which might be relevant here.[9] There is a sufficient nexus between the threat and the offence: *Cole* [1994] Crim LR 582. Thus, the defence of duress is likely to be successful here.

[7] Be sure to identify whether force has actually been used or whether it has been threatened as either is sufficient for the offence of robbery.

[8] You should really cite both of these cases in respect of the test for duress in order to show the examiner that you are aware of the importance of each one.

[9] Ensure you only apply relevant facts. Do not speculate about the existence of facts you are not given any evidence of.

Make your answer stand out

■ Ensure that you adopt a logical structure and deal with each offence chronologically. You might wish to use headings to divide up your answer and ensure that you remain focused.

■ You should also consider the offence of blackmail in more detail, making reference to case law where appropriate.

■ You should explore the defence of the prevention of crime under section 3(1), CLA 1967 in more detail. Your discussion should encompass the principles under section 76, CJIA 2008, including those relating to householders.

■ You should also explore and apply the principles of duress by threats in more detail.

! Don't be tempted to . . .

■ Consider the possibility of fraud having been committed by a failure to disclose information or fraud by abuse of position if they are not relevant to the facts in the problem question.

■ Spend too much time discussing each issue, as there are so many of them in this question. Ensure that you identify all of the relevant offences and defences and apply the main principles of law with appropriate supporting authorities.

■ Misstate the *Ghosh* test in respect of fraud and theft.

? Question 3

Raymond goes on a date with Chloe. He places a strong sedative in her drink, and when she becomes sleepy, he takes her back to his house. He then carries Chloe into the bedroom and has sex with her. Chloe is sleepy and does not resist. The following morning, Raymond tries to wake Chloe, but he is unable to do so. He telephones for an ambulance and Chloe is taken to hospital. At hospital, Chloe is seen by a doctor who is overworked and very tired. He thinks that Chloe is just drunk and sends her home with Raymond. In fact, Raymond had given Chloe an excessively strong dose of the sedative, and Chloe dies later at Raymond's house.

Consider Raymond's criminal liability.

Answer plan

→ Evaluate Raymond's liability for rape.

→ Discuss the issue of consent.

→ Consider Raymond's liability for unlawful act manslaughter.

→ Does the conduct of the doctor break the chain of causation?

Diagram plan

A printable version of this diagram plan is available from **www.pearsoned.co.uk/lawexpressqa**

Answer

[1] Identify the key issues (as well as the offences) that you will need to discuss in your opening paragraph.

Raymond will be convicted of rape in respect of Chloe, and we need to consider the issue of consent here. He might also be liable for unlawful act manslaughter in respect of the death of Chloe, although he may argue that the chain of causation was broken by the doctor in the hospital.[1]

Rape is defined under section 1(1) of the Sexual Offences Act 2003 (SOA 2003). The actus reus requires the penetration of the vagina, anus or mouth, with the defendant's penis, where the complainant does not consent. The mens rea is intentional penetration, where the defendant had no reasonable belief in consent. Raymond has sexual intercourse with Chloe and there is nothing to doubt the fact that the intercourse involved the penetration of the vagina or anus of Chloe with Raymond's penis. It is also clear that the penetration is intentional; thus, the issue here is really one of consent. In order to secure a conviction, the prosecution must establish that Chloe was not consenting and that Raymond did not reasonably believe that she was consenting.[2]

[2] Do not forget to state and apply the mens rea in respect of consent. This is often forgotten by students and your answer will be incomplete without it.

Consideration must be given to the evidential presumptions under section 75(1), SOA 2003. Section 75(1) sets out two evidential presumptions: that the complainant did not consent and that the defendant

³ Do not forget that there are
two presumptions which are
made under section 75(1) and
one relates to the mens rea of
the defendant.

did not reasonably believe that she consented. These are relevant where one of the circumstances under section 75(2) is applicable and the defendant knew this.³ These presumptions may apply as Chloe is sleepy when Raymond begins to have intercourse with her (s. 75(2)(d)). Although we are told that she is 'sleepy', it is unclear on the facts whether she is actually asleep or otherwise unconscious or not at this stage.⁴ If she is, and if Raymond is aware that Chloe is asleep, the evidential presumptions under section 75(1) are triggered, which means that she is presumed not to have consented and it is presumed that Raymond did not reasonably believe that she was consenting. These presumptions are rebuttable and Raymond may adduce evidence to the contrary; however, he is unlikely to be able to in this scenario. If she is not asleep, the prosecution will seek to rely on section 75(2) (f) because Raymond administered, without Chloe's consent, a drug which he placed in her drink, which was a substance capable of causing or enabling Chloe to be stupefied or overpowered at the time, and he was aware of these circumstances. Thus, the presumptions under section 75(1) will be triggered.⁵ There is also an alternative line of argument, that under section 74 Chloe did not consent because due to her intoxication by virtue of the sedative, she did not agree to sex by choice, with the capacity and freedom to make that choice. According to **Bree** [2007] EWCA Crim 804, the complainant will not consent to sexual intercourse if he/she loses his/her capacity to consent through the consumption of alcohol. However, if the complainant still has the capacity to choose to consent to sexual intercourse despite his/her intoxication, he/she may still consent to sex. It will be for the jury to determine whether Chloe had the capacity to consent in this scenario, although it looks unlikely that she did consent.

⁴ You should not assume that she is asleep, but you need to deal with the facts exactly as given to you. Do not invent or twist the facts to suit an answer which is more convenient.

⁵ Remember to provide an alternative argument which may be used by the prosecution.

Raymond might also be charged with unlawful act manslaughter in respect of the death of Chloe. It is clear that he does not have the mens rea for murder as he has no intention to kill or cause GBH⁶ (**Vickers** [1957] 2 QB 664). Raymond might be guilty of unlawful act manslaughter. This offence was defined in **Larkin** (1944) 29 Cr App R 18: there must be an intentional act, which is unlawful, objectively dangerous and which causes death (Lord Salmon, **DPP v Newbury and Jones** [1977] AC 500).

⁶ Rule out murder from the start where there is clearly no mens rea for murder. This demonstrates a logical thought process in arriving at the decision to discuss involuntary manslaughter.

The prosecution must prove that Raymond intentionally did an act. This must be a positive act: **Lowe** [1976] QB 702. His act is intentionally placing a strong sedative in Chloe's drink. The act must be unlawful in the sense that it must constitute a criminal offence: **Franklin** (1883) 15 Cox CC 163. The criminal act here is unlawfully and maliciously administering a noxious thing with intent to injure, aggrieve or annoy, contrary to section 24, Offences Against the Person Act 1861. Both the actus reus and mens rea elements of the assault must be established: **Lamb** [1967] 2 QB 981. The elements of this offence are satisfied. Raymond intentionally administers the drug to her drink without her consent, it is likely to be a poison (applying **Marcus** (1981) 73 Cr App R 49 the sedative is likely to be a poison in light of the quantity in which it was administered, although this is a question of fact and degree for the jury). By the administration, Raymond intends to injure Chloe. Applying **Hill** (1986) 83 Cr App R 386, the defendant's purpose will be considered and a malevolent purpose is more likely to provide evidence of the necessary intent.[7]

[7] Once you have identified the unlawful act, you must also show that both the actus reus and mens rea elements of that offence are satisfied.

It must also be proved that the act was objectively dangerous. The test was laid down in **Church** [1966] 1 QB 59, in which it was stated that 'the unlawful act must be such as all sober and reasonable people would inevitably recognise must subject the other person to, at least, the risk of some harm . . . albeit not serious harm'. Providing Chloe with a strong dose of a sedative is something that the reasonable person would recognise carries the risk of some harm.

Finally, the usual rules of causation apply. Applying the test for factual causation: but for Raymond's act, Chloe would not have died: **White** [1910] 2 KB 124. His act was also a more than minimal cause of death: **Cato** [1976] 1 WLR 110. However, there may be an intervening event as the doctor is negligent in treating Chloe. This may be treated as negligent medical treatment. However, negligent medical treatment will only break the chain of causation where it is so independent of the defendant's act and so potent in causing death that it renders the defendant's conduct insignificant (**Cheshire** [1991] 1 WLR 844). Negligent medical treatment is unlikely to break the chain of causation and the chain will probably not be broken here and Raymond will likely be guilty of unlawful act manslaughter.

Make your answer stand out

- You might consider the more serious offence of unlawfully and maliciously administering a noxious thing under section 23, Offences Against the Person Act 1861 in addition to the offence under section 24.
- You might elaborate on the issue of causation and refer to other cases as well as academic opinion.
- You might incorporate any relevant academic opinion.

! Don't be tempted to . . .

- Invent facts or assume that certain facts are present. For instance, the question states that the complainant was 'sleepy' but does not specifically state that she was 'asleep'.
- Confuse the issue of the potential new intervening act (the negligent medical treatment) with the issue of any potential liability of the doctor. You are only asked about the liability of Raymond here, and not that of the doctor.

? Question 4

Martin and Debbie are animal rights activists. They have heard that Hertsco, a local company, have been testing their products on animals. Martin and Debbie decide to break into the laboratories at Hertsco in order to free the animals there. Martin and Debbie go straight to the laboratories. They decide which window they are going to break in through, but as they approach the window, a light goes on inside the building. Afraid of being noticed, Martin and Debbie make a quick getaway. They decide to try again later that evening.

Later that evening, Debbie acts as lookout while Martin breaks open a window. Both of them then climb in through the window. They find a number of animals locked up and use a jemmy to free them. Debbie sees a puppy which she likes and decides to take him home with her. As she picks the puppy up, they are confronted by an employee of Hertsco who had been working late. Martin pulls out a gun and points it at the employee. Debbie shouts, 'You never mentioned guns! Don't shoot!' and escapes from the building. Martin shoots and kills the employee.

Advise Martin and Debbie as to their criminal liability, if any.

Diagram plan

A printable version of this diagram plan is available from **www.pearsoned.co.uk/lawexpressqa**

Answer plan

→ Discuss the conspiracies to commit criminal damage and burglary.

→ Assess whether Martin and Debbie are liable for attempted burglary.

→ Consider Martin's liability for burglary and criminal damage and Debbie's corresponding liability as a secondary party.

→ Evaluate Debbie's liability for theft and burglary.

→ Consider whether Debbie is liable for the murder of the employee as a secondary party.

Answer

The first offences to arise in the scenario are the conspiracies to commit criminal damage and/or burglary.[1] Conspiracy is charged contrary to section 1(1) of the Criminal Law Act 1977. There may be an agreement here between two people (Martin and Debbie) to pursue a course of conduct which amounts to an offence. It must be asked whether Martin and Debbie agree to commit criminal damage in the process of breaking into the property or once inside the building. If they do, the actus reus of a conspiracy to commit criminal damage is certainly present. If they agree to enter in order to commit criminal damage, they may be guilty of a conspiracy to commit burglary. The requisite mens rea of conspiracy is an intention to carry out the agreement. According to *Siracusa* (1990) 90 Cr App R 340, to 'play some part' in the offence means no more than that the defendant must continue to concur with the activity of another or to fail to stop the offence from being committed. This means that participation can be passive. This can be contrasted against the decision of the House of Lords in *Anderson* [1986] AC 27, which appears to require active participation. Either way, the mens rea of a conspiracy is satisfied here.[2]

Martin and Debbie may also be convicted of attempted burglary when they first approach the building with a view to breaking into it. Attempted burglary would be charged contrary to section 1(1) of the Criminal Attempts Act 1981. An attempt involves taking steps which are more than merely preparatory towards the commission of an offence. Martin and Debbie both approach a window to the building, with a view to breaking in. If Martin and Debbie merely approach the window without touching it, this is unlikely to be considered enough for an attempted burglary and is more likely to amount to mere preparation. In *Campbell* (1991) 93 Cr App R 350, the defendant was not convicted of attempted robbery of a post office because although he was loitering outside the building, he never actually entered the post office.[3] However, in the case of *Tosti* [1997] Crim LR 746, examining a padlock on a door was enough to constitute an attempt to commit burglary. The necessary mens rea of an attempt is the intention to commit the full offence, so Martin and Debbie must intend to commit burglary, which on the facts they may do. It would be necessary to ascertain their intention once inside the building. Although the facts

The margin notes read:

[1] Whenever you see a question on accessorial liability there will usually be an agreement to commit an offence at the start of the question, requiring consideration of conspiracy.

[2] Where there are conflicting authorities, be sure to mention both.

[3] Cite an authority to support the conclusion that you draw and justify that conclusion with a brief explanation.

state that they intend to free the animals, it is less clear whether they will commit criminal damage in order to do so, or even whether they will take the animals away with them.

Later that evening when they return to the building, Debbie may be convicted of aiding, abetting, counselling or procuring the burglary and criminal damage by keeping lookout under section 8 of the Accessories and Abettors Act 1861. Aiding merely means assisting, which Debbie is certainly doing by keeping lookout. The mens rea for aiding an offence is: (i) an intention to do the acts of assistance (Debbie clearly intends to aid Martin here by keeping lookout); and (ii) knowledge of the circumstances which constitute the offence: *Bryce* [2004] EWCA Crim 1231 (Debbie is clearly aware of the circumstances which constitute the offence as she has been involved in the planning of the offence throughout).[4]

[4] These sentences are what the examiner is looking for to demonstrate your application of the law to the question.

Martin will be liable for criminal damage to the window under section 1(1) of the Criminal Damage Act 1971. He clearly destroys or damages property belonging to another here. He also has the requisite mens rea because he intends to break the window, or is at the very least subjectively reckless as to whether the window would be broken. Martin and Debbie will also be convicted of burglary under section 9(1)(a) of the Theft Act 1968. Both Martin and Debbie enter the building as trespassers as they have no permission to be there: *Collins* [1973] QB 100. They intend to enter the building and know that they are trespassing. Their intention on entry must be explored: if they intend to commit criminal damage or steal or inflict GBH inside, they will be guilty of burglary under section 9(1)(a). They probably at least enter with intent to commit criminal damage or to steal the animals (even merely setting the animals free could constitute theft as it amounts to appropriation, provided of course that the necessary intention to permanently deprive can be proved).[5]

[5] This sentence also demonstrates application of the law to the specific facts of the question.

Debbie will also be guilty of burglary under section 9(1)(b) of the Theft Act 1968 because having entered the building as a trespasser, knowing that she was trespassing, Debbie does steal the puppy. The elements of theft need to be established here. Under section 1(1) of the Theft Act 1968, theft is defined as the dishonest appropriation of property belonging to another with intent to permanently deprive. Debbie appropriates the dog as she assumes a single right of the owner over the dog (under section 3 and *Morris* [1984] AC 320),

⁶You should be able to set out the principles of law on appropriation and apply them in one sentence.

that of possession.⁶ The dog is certainly property under section 4 and it belongs to another (presumably Hertsco). Thus, the actus reus elements of theft are satisfied. Section 2(1) does not apply here, and *Ghosh* [1982] QB 1053 only need be applied where dishonesty needs further explanation to the jury. This is unlikely to be the case here as it would be difficult to argue that she lacked dishonesty. Debbie will intend to permanently deprive the owner of the dog if she intends to treat the dog as her own to dispose of regardless of the other's rights. It must be asked what she plans to do with the dog.

Martin will also be guilty of burglary under section 9(1)(b) if he participated in this offence and intended to assist or encourage Debbie to commit the burglary with the requisite intention. When Martin pulls out a gun and kills the employee, he will be guilty of murder as the principal offender because he unlawfully causes the death of the employee with the intention to kill or cause GBH (*Vickers* [1957] 2 QB 664).⁷ The next key issue is then whether Debbie may be convicted of murder as an accessory. This requires both participation by Debbie and the relevant mens rea. Applying *Jogee* [2016] UKSC 8, Debbie must intend to assist or encourage Martin to act with an intention to kill or cause GBH.⁸ The final issue to consider is whether, if she did have the necessary intention, Debbie successfully withdraws her participation and evades liability for the murder. Once the offence is being committed, nothing less than physical intervention will do in order to withdraw: *Becerra and Cooper* (1976) 62 Cr App R 212. On the facts, Debbie merely shouts out then runs away, and this would not be enough for a withdrawal.

⁷Be sure to establish the liability of the principal before looking at that of the accessory as the accessory's liability is derived from that of the principal.

⁸This sentence succinctly highlights the main issue here and states the key principle with the appropriate leading authority.

✓ Make your answer stand out

- Although this is obviously a question involving inchoate and accessorial liability, you should not cover the inchoate offences and accessorial liability in great detail to the exclusion of other key offences.
- This question requires some exploration of various property offences, such as criminal damage, burglary and theft, which play a significant part in the question.
- You must demonstrate that you are able to distinguish accurately between the offences of burglary under sections 9(1)(a) and (b) of the Theft Act 1968.
- Ensure that you provide a balanced answer that gives appropriate attention to the important issues in the question.

Don't be tempted to . . .

- Spend too much time exploring one issue or offence to the detriment of others.
- Misstate the tests for the mens rea of a secondary party under *Jogee* [2016] UKSC 8.
- Misstate the test for withdrawal of participation at the scene of the crime once the offence has begun.

@ Try it yourself

Now take a look at the question below and attempt to answer it. You can check your response against the answer guidance available on the companion website (**www.pearsoned.co.uk/lawexpressqa**).

> David is a member of a criminal gang. He puts an advert in a newspaper offering his car for sale. He states that the car has only done 40,000 miles. In fact, the car has done 140,000 miles and David has tampered with the tachometer. Peter sees the car advertised and buys the car from David, paying £3,000. However, after taking the car to his local mechanic, Peter realises that the true mileage of the car is closer to 140,000 miles. Peter drives to David's house in order to confront him. He shouts at David, 'I want my money back with interest. If you don't give me £20,000 by the end of the day, I will kill you'. Fearing for his life, David carries out a raid on a post office. He uses an imitation firearm to threaten the post office master. The post office master hands David £20,000.
>
> Discuss the criminal liability of the parties.

---

www.pearsoned.co.uk/lawexpressqa

 Go online to access more revision support including additional essay and problem questions with diagram plans, You be the marker questions, and download all diagrams from the book.

Bibliography

Allen, M. J. (2013) *Textbook on Criminal Law*, 12th edn. Oxford: Oxford University Press.
Allgrove, B. and Sellers, S. (2009) The Fraud Act 2006: is breach of confidence now a crime? 4 JIPLP 278.
Ashworth, A. (1989) The scope of criminal liability for omissions. LQR 424.
Ashworth, A. (1993) Taking the consequences, in S. Shute, J. Gardner and J. Horder (eds), *Action and Value in Criminal Law*. Oxford: Clarendon Press.
Ashworth, A. (2007) Principles, pragmatism and the Law Commission's recommendations on homicide law reform. Crim LR 333.
Ashworth, A. (2009) *Principles of Criminal Law*, 6th edn. Oxford: Oxford University Press.
Ashworth, A. and Horder, J. (2013) Inchoate offences, in *Principles of Criminal Law*, 7th edn. Oxford: Oxford University Press.

Bamforth, N. (1994) Sado-masochism and consent. Crim LR 661.
Bantekas, I. (2008) Can touching always be sexual when there is no sexual intent? 73 *Journal of Criminal Law* 251.
Bingham, Lord (2007) The Rule of Law. CLJ 67.

Campbell, K. (1994) The test of dishonesty in *Ghosh*. 43 CLJ 349.
Clarkson, C. M. V. (2000) Context and culpability in involuntary manslaughter, in A. Ashworth (ed.), *Rethinking English Homicide Law*. Oxford: Oxford University Press.
Coke, Sir E. 3 Inst. 47 *Institutes of the Lawes of England* 47.
Criminal Law Revision Committee (1980) 14th Report, *Offences Against the Person*. London: The Stationery Office.
Crosby, C. (2008) Recklessness – the continuing search for a definition. 72 JCL 313.
Crown Prosecution Service, Offences Against the Person, incorporating the Charging Standards. http://www.cps.gov.uk/legal/l_to_o/offences_against_the_person/. Accessed 25 March 2017.

Dennis, I. H. (1982) The Criminal Attempts Act 1981. Crim LR 5.
Dennis, I. (2006) Reviewing the law of homicide. Crim LR 187.
Dennis, I. (2008) A pointless exercise. Crim LR 507.

Edwards, I. (2009) Banksy's Graffiti: a not-so-simple case of criminal damage? 73 JCL 345.
Elliott, D. W. (1982) Dishonesty in theft: a dispensable concept. Crim LR 395.

Farrell, S., Yeo, N. and Landenberg, G. (2007) *Blackstone's Guide to the Fraud Act 2006.* Oxford: Oxford University Press.
Fortson, R. (2008) *Blackstone's Guide to the Serious Crime Act 2007.* Oxford: Oxford University Press.
Fortson, R. (2014) Case comment *R* v *Sadique (Omar).* Crim LR 61.

Gardner, J. (1994) Rationality and the rule of law in offences against the person. 53 CLJ 502.
Gardner, J. (2007) Complicity and causality. 1 *Criminal Law and Philosophy* 127.
Gardner, S. (1996) Appreciating *Olugboja.* 16 *Legal Studies* 275.
Gobert, J. (2008) The Corporate Manslaughter and Corporate Homicide Act. 71(3) MLR 413.
Gough, S. (2000) Surviving without *Majewski.* Crim LR 719.
Greaves, C. (1862) *The Criminal Law Consolidation and Amendment Acts,* 2nd edn. London: Stevens, Sons and Haynes, Sweet & Maxwell.
Griew, E. J. (1985) Dishonesty: the objections to *Feely* and *Ghosh.* Crim LR 341.
Griew, E. (1986) *The Theft Acts 1968 and 1978.* London: Sweet & Maxwell.
Griffin, S. and Moran, J. (2010) Accountability for deaths attributable to the gross negligent act or omission of a police force: the impact of the Corporate Manslaughter and Corporate Homicide Act 2007. 74 JCL 358.
Gunn, M. and Ormerod, D. (1995) The legality of boxing. 15 *Legal Studies* 181.

Halpin, A. (2004) *Definition in the Criminal Law.* Oxford: Hart.
Hart, H. L. A. and Honoré, A. M. (1985) *Causation in the Law,* 2nd edn. Oxford: Oxford University Press.
Heaton, R. (2003) Dealing in death. Crim LR 497.
Hogan, B. (1987) Omissions and the duty myth, in P. Smith (ed.), *Criminal Law: Essays in Honour of J C Smith.* London: Butterworths.
Home Office (2002) Protecting the Public, Cm 5668, p. 9.
Home Office (2003) Government Reply to the Fifth Report from the Home Affairs Committee Session 2002–2003, Cm 5986, pp. 1–2.
Home Office/DHSS (1975) Report of the Committee on Mentally Abnormal Offenders (The Butler Report), Cmnd. 6244, London: HMSO.
Horder, J. (2002) Strict liability, statutory construction, and the spirit of liberty. LQR 458.
Hyman Gross, A. (1979) *A Theory of Criminal Justice.* Oxford: Oxford University Press.

Jefferson, M. (2011) *Criminal Law.* London: Pearson Longman.

Lacey, Wells and Quick (2003) *Reconstructing Criminal Law Text and Materials,* 3rd edn. Cambridge: Cambridge University Press.

Law Commission (1980) Report, *Attempt: The Impossibility in Relation to Attempt, Conspiracy and Incitement* (No. 102).

Law Commission (1989) Report, *Draft Criminal Code* (No. 177).

Law Commission (1994a) Consultation Paper, *Consent and Offences Against the Person* (No. 134).

Law Commission (1994b) Consultation Paper, *Criminal Law: Involuntary Manslaughter* (No. 135).

Law Commission (1996) Report, *Legislating the Criminal Code: Involuntary Manslaughter* (No. 237).

Law Commission (1999) Consultation Paper, *Legislating the Criminal Code: Fraud and Deception* (No. 155).

Law Commission (2002) Report, *Fraud* (No. 276).

Law Commission (2005) Consultation Paper, *A New Homicide Act for England and Wales?* (No. 177).

Law Commission (2006) Report, *Inchoate Liability for Assisting and Encouraging Crime* (No. 300).

Law Commission (2007a) Consultation Paper, *Conspiracy and Attempts* (No. 183).

Law Commission (2007b) Report, *Participating in Crime* (No. 305).

Law Commission (2009) Report, *Intoxication and Criminal Liability* (No. 314).

Law Commission (2010) Consultation Paper, *Unfitness to Plead and the Insanity Defence*. www.lawcom.gov.uk/insanity. Accessed 25 March 2017.

Law Commission (2013) Discussion Paper, *Insanity and Automatism*. http://www.lawcom .gov.uk/wp-content/uploads/2015/06/insanity_discussion.pdf. Accessed 25 March 2017.

Law Commission (2015) Report, *Reform of Offences Against the Person*, (No. 361).

Law Society (2013) Parliamentary Brief, Crime and Courts Bill, HC Second Reading, Monday 14 January 2013 at Paras. 14–17.

Leigh, L. (2009) Duty of care and manslaughter. 173 JPN 296.

Leigh, L. (2010) Two new partial defences to murder. 174 JPN 53.

Mackay, R. D. (1990) Fact and fiction about the insanity defence. Crim LR 247.

Mackay, R. D. (1998) *Mental Condition Defences in Criminal Law*. Oxford: Oxford University Press.

Mackay, R. D. and Kearns, G. (1999) More fact(s) about the insanity defence. Crim LR 714.

Mackay, R. D. and Reuber, M. (2007) Epilepsy and the defence of insanity – time for a change. Crim LR 782.

Mackay, R. D., Mitchell, B. and Howe, L. (2006) Yet more facts about the insanity defence. Crim LR 399.

BIBLIOGRAPHY

Malcolm, T. (2012) How far is too far? The extent to which consent is a defence to non-fatal offences against the person, in N. Geach and C. Monaghan (eds), *Dissenting Judgments in the Law*. London: Wildy, Simmonds and Hill.

Marston, G. (1970) Contemporaneity of act and intention in crimes. 86 LQR 208.

Mitchell, B. (2008) Minding the gap in unlawful and dangerous act manslaughter: a moral defence of one-punch killers. 72 JCL 537.

Monaghan, C. (2010) To prosecute or not to prosecute? A reconsideration of the overzealous prosecution of parents under the Fraud Act 2006. 74 *Journal of Criminal Law* 259.

Monaghan, N. (2016) *Criminal Law Directions*, 4th edn. Oxford: Oxford University Press.

Norrie, A. (1999) After *Woollin*. Crim LR 532.

Norrie, A. (2010) The Coroners and Justice Act – partial defences to murder (1) Loss of control. Crim LR 275.

O'Doherty, S. (2008) The Corporate Manslaughter and Corporate Homicide Act 2007. 172 JPN 244.

Ormerod, D. (2007) The Fraud Act 2006 – criminalising lying? Crim LR 193.

Ormerod, D. (2008) *Smith and Hogan Criminal Law*, 12th edn. Oxford: Oxford University Press.

Ormerod, D. (2009a) Case comment *R* v *Drane (Paul)*: self-defence: summing up – subjective element. Crim LR 202.

Ormerod, D. (2009b) Cheating the public revenue. Crim LR 202.

Ormerod, D. (2011) *Smith and Hogan's Criminal Law*, 13th edn. Oxford: Oxford University Press.

Ormerod, D. and Fortson, R. (2009) Serious Crime Act 2007: the Part 2 offences. Crim LR 389.

Ormerod, D. and Laird, K. (2015) *Smith and Hogan's Criminal Law*, 14th edn. Oxford: Oxford University Press.

Ormerod, D. and Laird, K. (2016) *Jogee*: not the end of a legal saga but the start of one? Crim LR 539.

Ormerod, D. and Taylor, R. (2008) The Corporate Manslaughter and Corporate Homicide Act 2007. Crim LR 589.

Ormerod, D. and Williams, D. (2007) *Smith's Law of Theft*, 9th edn. Oxford: Oxford University Press.

Padfield, N. (2008) The Criminal Justice and Immigration Act 2008. *Archbold News* 5.

Raz, J. (1977) The Rule of Law and its virtue. 93 LQR 195.

Rogers, J. (2006) The Law Commission's proposed restructuring of homicide. 70(3) JCL 223.

Rogers, J. (2008) The codification of attempts and the case of 'preparation'. Crim LR 937.

Ryan, S. (2006) Reckless transmission of HIV: knowledge and culpability. Crim LR 981.

Shute, S. (2002) Appropriation and the law of theft. Crim LR 445.

Simester, A. (2006) *Appraising Strict Liability*. Oxford: Oxford University Press.

Simester, A. (2009) Intoxication is never a defence. Crim LR 3.

Simester, A. and Sullivan, R. (2007) *Criminal Law: Theory and Doctrine*. Oxford: Hart.

Simester, A., Sullivan, G. R., Spencer, J. and Virgo, G. (2010) *Simester and Sullivan's Criminal Law: Theory and Doctrine*. Oxford: Hart. p. 701.

Smith, A. T. H. (2001) Theft and sharp practice: who cares now? CLJ 21.

Smith, J. C. (1982) Commentary, *R* v *Ghosh*. Crim LR 608.

Smith, J. C. (1991) Proximity in attempt. Crim LR 576.

Smith, J. C. (1993) Case Commentary, *R* v *Gomez*. Crim LR 304.

Spencer, J. R. (1982) Dishonesty: what the jury thinks the defendant thought the jury would have thought. CLJ 222.

Stephen, J. F. (1883) *A History of the Criminal Law of England*. London: Macmillan.

Stephen, J. F. (1887) *A Digest of the Criminal Law*. London: Macmillan.

Sullivan, G. R. (1993) Cause and the contemporaneity of actus reus and mens rea. CLJ 487.

Sullivan, G. R. (2008) Participating in crime. Crim LR 19.

Tadros, V. (2002) Recklessness and the duty to take care, in S. Shute and A. Simester (eds), *Criminal Law Theory*. Oxford: Oxford University Press.

Taylor, R. (2008) Procuring, causation, innocent agency and the Law Commission. Crim LR 32.

Temkin, J. (2002) *Rape and the Legal Process*. Oxford: Oxford University Press.

Temkin, J. and Ashworth, A. (2004) Rape, sexual assaults and the problem of consent. Crim LR 328.

Virgo, G. (2013) *R* v *Sadique*: making sense of section 46 of the Serious Crime Act 2007. 7 *Archbold News* 4–6.

Virgo, G. (2013) Part 2 of the Serious Crime Act 2007 – Enough is Enough. 3 *Archbold News*, April 2013.

Weait, M. (2005) Knowledge, autonomy and consent: *R* v *Konzani*. Crim LR 763.

Wells, C. (1982) Swatting the subjectivist bug. Crim LR 209.

Wells, C. (1996) The Law Commission Report on Involuntary Manslaughter. Crim LR 545.

Williams, B. (1991) Criminal omissions: the conventional view. LQR 86.

Williams, G. (1976) Case commentary. CJL 15.

Williams, G. (1983) *Textbook of Criminal Law*. London: Stevens & Sons.

Williams, G. (1987) Oblique intention. CLJ 417.

Williams, G. (1989) The mens rea for murder: leave it alone. 105 LQR 387.

Williams, G. (1991) Wrong turning on the law of attempt. Crim LR 416.

Wilson, W. (2002a) *Central Issues in Criminal Theory*. Oxford: Hart.

Wilson, W. (2002b) Criminal attempts, in *Central Issues in Criminal Theory*. Oxford: Hart.

BIBLIOGRAPHY

Wilson, W. (2006) The structure of criminal homicide. Crim LR 471.
Wilson, W. (2008a) A rational scheme of liability for participating in crime. Crim LR 3.
Wilson, W. (2008b) *Criminal Law: Doctrine and Theory*, 3rd edn. London: Longman.
Wilson, W. (2014) *Criminal Law*, 5th edn. London: Longman.
Withey, C. (2007) The Fraud Act 2006 – some early observations and comparisons with the former law. 71 JCL 220.

Index